Birding from a Tractor Seat

Birding from a Tractor Seat

by

CHARLES T. FLUGUM

Illustrations by Dr. Walter J. Breckinridge

Thomas Y. Crowell Company
New York / Established 1834

Manufactured in the United States of America

2 3 4 5 6 7 8 9 10

Library of Congress Cataloging in Publication Data

Flugum, Charles T. 1905-
 Birding from a tractor seat.

 Includes index.
 1. Bird watching. I. Breckenridge, Walter John, 1903-   II. Title.
QL676.F65 1975 598.2'08   75-11534
ISBN 0-690-00971-2

To Mother, who enjoyed birds and maintained that their virtues far outweighed any of their misdeeds and who understood her birdwatching son's need for answers to unending questions.

Author's Acknowledgments

I am deeply grateful to all who have helped me along the way.

To Faye Hamilton, my high school freshman English teacher, for suggesting that I might enjoy reading the eight bird books in the Albert Lea High School library.

To Ethel B. Green, my high school sophomore English teacher, who worked mightily to instruct me in syntax and rhetoric.

To the Newspaper Institute of America, for their correspondence course in newspaper writing.

To my wife, Martha, who carefully checks everything I write for errors in spelling.

To Dr. F. W. Calhoun and Ed Ahern, who first encouraged me to write my monthly column.

To *Community Magazine* editor Maclay Lyon, without whose understanding and patient help the column, "Watching the Birds," might never have been written.

To the people at the Andersen Typesetting Company and the North Central Publishing Company, whose advice on the technical matters involved in publishing a book is greatlyh appreciated.

To the many naturalists I have met, as their schedules brought them to Albert Lea for Audubon Wildlife Film lectures, for the knowledge that I could not help absorbing as I visited with them when they were overnight guests at our house.

Among them: Dr. Arthur A. Allen, William A. Anderson, Walter H. Berlet, Dick Bird, Roy E. Coy, Ernest P. Edwards, Cleveland and Ruth Grant, Tom and Arlene Hadley, Robert C. Hermes, Edgar T. Jones, Chester P. Lyons (who made helpful suggestions for improving my writing), Eben McMillan, Howard L. Orians, Lucie Palmer (who read from my scrapbook every word of every column that I had written up to the time she lectured here, commenting on the expressions she especially liked), Dr. Olin Sewall Pettingill, Jr. (who told me about the Pierce Book Company of Winthrop, Iowa, from which have come most of the bird books I own), Emerson Scott, Patricia Bailey Witherspoon and Albert J. Wool.

My grateful thanks also to Betty Carnes, a very active member of the American Ornithologists Union, who subscribed to the *Community Magazine* from her home in New Jersey and often wrote to me, urging me to bring my articles to a larger audience. Betty, who now lives in Arizona, is the lady referred to on page 215 who used a most novel technique in capturing and banding a peregrine falcon.

I wish to express my gratitude to Mrs. Kenneth Woodmen, whose patient and understanding participation in typing successive revisions of the manuscript brought it finally to completion.

I am most deeply indebted to my son Merlin, for his interest and steadfast belief that these articles could be successfully brought out in book form. We have had many sessions on editing. But he has undertaken the big job of checking and exploring the many problems involved in book publishing.

The illustrations appearing throughout the book have been reprinted by permission of the artist, Dr. Walter J. Breckenridge, and Burgess Publishing Company, Minneapolis, Minnesota, from *A Laboratory and Field Manual of Ornithology*, 4th Ed., 1970, by Olin Sewall Pettingill, Jr.

I am forever grateful to Dr. Roger Tory Peterson, for his excellent *Field Guide to the Birds* which, by the way, is now badly worn from the constant use to which I have subjected it in identifying the many species of warblers and other small birds I have come to know.

I feel honored to have the foreword to *Birding from a Tractor Seat* written by the respected and popular naturalist Howard H. Cleaves of Staten Island, New York. Howard Cleaves has the ability to relive his birding experiences verbally so well that all who come in contact with him have a deeper enjoyment and appreciation of birds than they might have had had they never met this man. I remember especially the way he brought our children to wide-eyed attention by recounting his many experiences in filming wildlife after dark.

Also, I would like to acknowledge the Thomas Y. Crowell Company for their assistance in the publication of this book.

Foreword

During my long career as photo-naturalist and lecturer it has been my pleasant experience to meet many personalities who have distinguished themselves as friends of the earth, either through their writings or by direct action on behalf of what we have come to call the ENVIRONMENT. Being now (1973) in my 86th year, my memory goes far back. It was in April about 1909 that I was invited to attend a birthday party for John Burroughs, held in a private studio in Carnegie Hall, New York, and arranged by the late Dwight Franklin and his mother. I recall giving Mr. Burroughs an enlarged photograph of a chipmunk which I had taken. Burroughs had contributed an article on the chipmunk to the magazine *Country Life in America* a short time previous.

It would take a lot of space to list all of the celebrities whose paths have crossed my own, but a partial roster contains these names: Rachel Carson, Enos A. Mills, Ernest Harold Baynes, Sigurd Olson, Edwin Way Teale, Dr. Frank M. Chapman, Dr. Roger Tory Peterson, Richard H. Pough, William T. Davis, Alexander Sprunt, Elizabeth Barlow, Louis Bromfield.

In the more recent years, while giving illustrated programs on wild life in schools all over the state of Minnesota under the auspices of the University of Minnesota, I had the good fortune to meet an authentic dirt farmer who well qualifies to be added to the above listing. His name is Charles Flugum, a son of Norway who has spent most of his days in Iowa and Minnesota. Although a man of the soil, unlike most farmers Mr. Flugum has made himself sharply aware of all contained in his surroundings. Particularly he took note of bird life and the habits of birds. For many years he recorded in a journal-diary his observations and reactions. Now Mr. Flugum's son Merlin, with much diligence, has edited his father's notes for printing. The resulting book will attract a well-deserved readership.

HOWARD H. CLEAVES

Written at Staten Island, N.Y., March 30, 1973

Author's Preface

This is a book of personal essays originally written as a monthly column for the *Community Magazine*, published by the Trades Publishing Company of Albert Lea, Minnesota. It concerns many of my experiences with birds, spanning a period from earliest recollections to adulthood.

Those early years were filled with delight in discovering new species and wide-eyed wonder at the many strange sounds made by birds, some of which remained mysterious for years. For a lad with a burning curiosity about birds, that prairie farm home near Thompson, Iowa, was a wonderful place to spend boyhood. Windbreak trees, the dredge ditch and the nearby cattail and bulrush sloughs attracted birds in abundance and variety. In a haphazard sort of way I learned to know many of them and their winsome ways.

As I grew older I retained my avid interest in birds. By the time I began farming on my own, most field work was being done with tractor power, and I discovered that, as a vantage point from which to see birds at close range, a tractor seat is ideal. Birds that could not be approached within several rods by birdwatchers on foot would remain perched or walk confidently within a few feet of my noisy tractor. Apparently birds consider the driver to be a part of the machine and do not associate the tractor with danger. Because he is in the fields day after day a farmer is in a good position to see, not only the birds of the field, but also the migrating birds that fly overhead and occasionally stop to feed or rest while enroute to more northerly or southerly climates.

When the Albert Lea Audubon Society was organized in 1948 I began meeting other bird enthusiasts. It was my privilege to serve that organization for two years as Vice-President, three years as President and eleven years as Audubon Wildlife Film Chairman. My hobby was now expanded by the acquisition of binoculars, bird guides and, eventually, a three foot shelf of reference books. It was during this period that I began to write my column, "Watching the Birds." Membership in the Minnesota Ornithologists Union led to statewide field trips with members of other bird organizations and annual meetings of the Wilson Ornithological Society and the American Ornithologists Union, where amateur birdwatchers could hobnob with professional ornithologists.

Listening to the presentation of technical papers at these meetings is as highbrow as one can get in bird study. However, there were times between sessions when one could meet and visit with both professionals and laymen from various parts of the United States and other parts of the world. I particularly enjoyed visiting with Dr. Alexander Wetmore, Research

Associate and former Secretary of the Smithsonian Institute, past President of the American Ornithologists Union and Trustee of the National Geographic Society. With similar boyhood backgrounds—he in Wisconsin and I in Iowa—we talked like a couple of farm boys about such things as climbing box elder trees to look into grackle and robin nests and otherwise prying into the secrets of those active, abundant and gaily vocal fellow creatures called birds. We also spoke about birds in their relation to man and the need to guard against the extinction of species by the lack of understanding—and even the greedy disregard—of mankind.

I have often been encouraged by my family and many of my fellow birders to publish in book form the 137 monthly columns I wrote for the *Community Magazine*. So here finally is the book so long in the making. I hope it reflects some of the joy I have found along the way in the sight, sound and activity of birds. I hope also that it reflects concern, lest we lose some feathered species through ignorance, apathy or plain disregard. Birds have their place in the order of things. Watch them. Listen to them. And enjoy their winsome ways.

June, 1973   Charles T. Flugum
                                               Rural Route No. 1
                                               Albert Lea, Minnesota

Contents

List of Illustrations

Birding from a Tractor Seat

... *Great horned owl,*
screech owl

January, 1952

With sun-dogs, crunchy snow and frosty breath to remind us that winter is here in earnest it may seem early to look for nesting birds. But the great horned owl sometimes starts nesting in January.

I remember well my first encounter with this tiger of the air. One day, during my mud-pie age, a duty had been neglected until dusk. At our house twilight was not accepted as an excuse for shirking a duty, so I resolved to do this job as quickly as possible by taking a shortcut through the Scotch pine portion of our windbreak. After ducking under the heavily needled canopy of the outer branches I straightened up and stopped short, for I was face to face with a great horned owl about three feet from my nose. Retreating with more haste than dignity, I remember being painfully short of breath while trying to describe the terrible creature I had seen. Perhaps it's just as well that the owl didn't at that moment sound forth its low-pitched, blood-curdling "Hoo-hoo hoo-hoo-hoo."

The great horned owl inhabits most of wooded North America. Only when driven by food scarcity will it migrate. With a wingspread of up to 4½ feet (and in flight larger than our largest hawks) this great bird of the deep woods is the largest, most savage and formidable looking of our owls. Usually an old hawk or crow nest is remodeled by adding twigs, grass and pieces of bark. Male and female take turns incubating the two or three dull white eggs, which hatch in about thirty days. The slow maturing owlets remain in the nest about six weeks and are very poor flyers, even then.

BRECKENRIDGE

Contrary to general opinion, it can see perfectly in daylight, though most of its hunting is done at twilight and on moonlit nights for security reasons. Keen hearing, remarkable eyesight, silent flight, and powerful talons combine with aggressiveness to make this owl a very successful hunter. Although rabbits and rats constitute its principal food, its diet is varied. If you hear a flock of crows making a great commotion in the woods they are quite likely mobbing a great horned owl. They have no love for the bird because they are a favorite item on its bill of fare. Included also are such items as insects, fish, mice, weasels, smaller owls, hawks, game and other birds. If hungry, it will also make raids on domestic chickens, ducks, geese and turkeys. I have lost no poultry from owl raids even though they have nested on my farm for years. While they do get into trouble often enough to keep them off the state's list of protected birds, the worst that can be said of great horned owls as a species is that they are neutral in effect, taking both desirable and undesirable species.

I once came upon a young owl on the ground. Though almost grown, it made no attempt to fly. When I came near, it assumed a threatening pose by fluffing out its feathers and wings in cluck hen fashion. When it started snapping its beak both parent birds suddenly appeared and began diving at me and swerving off. I marveled at the speed and skill with which these great birds flew among the tree branches and at the dead silence of their flight. One can hear a sparrow's flutter from half a block and the whistle of a duck's wings at several hundred feet but — even though these owls came quite close to me — the only sound I heard was the snapping of their beaks. Their flight was made silent by the soft velvety edges of their wing feathers. This is a good example of how nature equips her creatures for the role they are to play in the wildlife equilibrium.

By far the most numerous and frequently encountered owl in this locality is the screech owl, a ten inch miniature "spittin' image" of its great horned relative, ear tufts and all. There are two color phases — gray and reddish. The screech owl's call — a soft tremulous wail heard only at night — is a familiar sound about farms and in the city, especially during the nesting season from late March through June.

Screech owls are great insect eaters. They also eat mice, lizards and other birds. During the winter, when insect life is dormant and mice, having sought shelter from the cold, are hard to find, these little owls often live on English sparrows, of which there are plenty.

One summer, as a youngster, I aroused the ire of a screech owl family by imitating their calls. What my whistled mocking meant in owl language I do not know, but it must have been very annoying because the parent owls flew at me and dashed into my straw hat.

The other evening one entered my lighted henhouse through a broken window pane. Apparently unable to find its way out again, it flew around as confused as the hens. Light and as fluffy as a handful of cotton, it made no attempt to escape as I carried it to the house for my family to see. When released, it sat for a moment on my hand while its eyes became accustomed to the change in light. Then, with a little spring, it flew into the darkness as silent as a shadow.

Screech owls are very beneficial birds deserving every protection. Although the United States Department of Agriculture has stated that owls are the most beneficial of all birds, they are perhaps the least appreciated.

. . . Red-tailed hawk

About this time of year one can begin looking for the return of the red-tailed hawk. Widely distributed, and in this territory the most common of our woodland nesting hawks, the red-tailed belongs to the group called buteos, or buzzard hawks. This group is characterized by chunky bodies, broad wings, broad rounded tails and leisurely flight. Although there is much variation in the color pattern of different individuals in this species, a reliable identification mark of adults is the rusty red upper surface of the tail.

These hawks mate for life and return year after year to the same nest of coarse sticks, dead leaves, grass and bark strips built high in an oak tree. The young are blind and very helpless when hatched and mature slowly. Their voracious appetites keep the parent birds busy hunting rodents.

Some years ago it was my good fortune to have a pair of these hawks make their home in the ten acre woods on my farm. How long they had nested in this woods before I came here I do not know, but for fourteen years the pair worked for their living here and reared a brood of young every year, which gave me ample opportunity to observe their family life. Although their defended territory probably included several sections of land, my farm, being nearest their home, was no doubt the most thoroughly hunted.

The male bird and I became friends in a way. I liked having the majestic mouser about and he seemed to enjoy working in the same field with me, trusting me enough when I was on the tractor to come within five or six rods to catch mice. However, one day when he plummeted from the sky to snatch a mouse scarcely two rods ahead of my tractor, I got the impression from

the look in his eye that he owned the place and that I was merely being tolerated.

When I took to the fields in the spring, "old red-tail" was in his glory. Of all my implements, he preferred the disc. It took a wide swath and penetrated deeply enough to dislodge mice from their hideouts. With his spouse on nesting duty he would perch on a dead limb at the edge of the woods or atop a post beside the field and watch my work intently. When a mouse was routed, "old red-tail" left his perch. Gliding gracefully to where the mouse was busily looking for a new hiding place, he would simply drop one foot and grasp the victim in his talons. The capture seemed easy when compared to a cat's vicious pounce.

For sport, I sometimes pointed at the mice I saw and "old red-tail" came after them so faithfully that one might have thought he was acting under my direction. One day I counted 32 mice, one rat and three young jack rabbits captured by my vigilant friend while I disced a thirty acre field of cornstalks. The hunting was not always as good. Another day he watched patiently from his perch for about three hours before a mouse was disturbed near the opposite end of the field. Immediately, the keen-eyed mouser was on the wing, having seen his prey from a distance of over eighty rods.

One spring day back in the lean years, a high pressure salesman was at my place extolling his wares. Seeing my attention wander, he looked skyward to see my two hawks circling in courtship flight, their red tails flashing in the sunlight.

"We should have had a good rifle," he suggested.

A moment before he had commented that one of my cats looked like a good mouser. Although this is the popular attitude, it has always seemed strange to me that folks so ready to credit cats with good mousing should be so loath to extend a like regard to hawks for the same virtue.

Early settlers in this country unfortunately applied the name "hawk" to all day-flying birds of prey, thereby burdening many valuable birds with the bad reputation associated with the word "hawk." The birds responsible for this prejudice are the true hawks, or accipiters, such as the Cooper's hawk, the goshawk and the sharp-shinned hawk, which are characterized by slender bodies, small heads, short rounded wings, long narrow tails and swift darting flight. Even with these hawks the chicken-taking reputation is exaggerated, though the habit is much more pronounced than with other hawks. With their elusive and sneaky ways, they usually manage to escape and let innocent hawks pay for their crimes.

It is true that an occasional red-tailed hawk will develop the poultry eating habit, and with such individuals I have no sympathy. Like the sheep-killing dog, they deserve a charge of shot. However, it is unjust to condemn the whole species for the acts of the Capones and the Dillingers. In all probability, not more than one buteo hawk in a hundred actually takes chickens.

The role of hawks in the balance of nature is to counteract the dangerously rapid reproductive rate of mice and other rodents. It is sound conservation practice to protect all our hawks, except those individuals actually caught in the act of taking poultry. There has been some improvement in the attitude toward our birds of prey in recent years, especially in securing legislation for their protection.

We have a long way to go, however, before an enlightened and aroused public will give these laws the support they need to make them really effective.

... *Brewer's blackbird*

April, 1952

As a vantage point from which to see field birds and their activities at close range, a tractor seat is ideal. Birds lose much of their fear of man when approached in any way other than on foot. Some species develop remarkable confidence and actually follow tillage implements across the fields to devour the insects which the implement exposes.

Among the most confiding is the Brewer's blackbird. Several of these birds are usually found following every farmer's plow or cultivator. While searching for insect larvae they walk on the loose and freshly turned dirt with long hurried purposeful strides, their wings slightly drooped in readiness should a rolling lump underfoot throw them off balance. They frequently take flight to catch up as if fearful that some of their quarry will have time to get back into hiding. So eager are they in their search that often they seem in danger of being crushed by the wheels or getting plowed under.

By the time the fields are ready for tillage in the spring, Brewer's blackbirds have paired. One can see them coming from a quarter of a mile away — two of them — one a little larger than the other. As they set their wings and glide in for a landing from a few rods away one can see that the larger one is shiny black, with a purplish iridescence on the head which blends into a greenish color on the shoulders and back. It also has conspicuous milky white eyes. The smaller one — the female — is brownish-gray with dark eyes. If one of the pair flies to get closer to the implement, the other immediately follows. When one has found a beakful of worms and flies nestward the other does likewise, even though it may not have found any.

It has been my observation that the female is usually the better hunter. Not only does she find the most worms, but she usually makes the decision of when to fly. Perhaps this is because the male takes time out occasionally to fluff out his feathers and utter a wheezy "que-ee" to tell his wife he still loves her. She pays no noticeable attention, although she no doubt appreciates the gesture.

After watching the industrious Brewer's blackbird one can have little doubt, either, about the economic value of the Brewer's blackbird as a destroyer of crop pests. White grubs (a serious pest of corn) and wire worms (the larva of click beetles) cause damage by feeding on the roots of the young plant. Cutworms (the larva of owlet moths or millers) cause damage by eating off the corn sprout at the ground surface during the night, then hide underground or in trash in daylight. These pests are exposed in great numbers by tillage implements and taken as food by these vigilant birds. Dependent as we are in this area on the success of the corn crop, it is fortunate that these and other insect pests are the natural food of birds and fortunate also that the Brewer's blackbird has adapted itself to harvest them in the wake of our tillage implements. They are faithful servants charging no other wages than a place in a meadow or fence row to build a nest, some waste grain and perhaps some milky tip kernels of corn in the fall when they flock with the redwings before journeying southward.

The Brewer's blackbird, a typical farm country blackbird, is a very common blackbird of the west that has been moving eastward in recent years. Lately, it has even bred in Ontario. Although sometimes called a small grackle, it can be distingushed from the grackle when both are seen together — especially by its shorter tail, which is spread flat and fanwise in flight. The grackle's center tailfeathers are longer than the outer ones and, when spread in flight, the tail is held in a distinct V or keel shape. The nest of the Brewer's blackbird, found on the ground or in a shrub, is built of twigs and coarse grass and lined with finer grass. The four to seven eggs are dull white, much blotched with brown and black.

While listening to my phonograph recordings of bird songs a friend was inspired to tell about the last bird he ever killed. As a young lad, cultivating corn with a team of horses and a single row cultivator, he was waiting for his dad, who had come to the field to caution him about driving the horses too hard in the sweltering heat. Seeing a blackbird walking near the cultivator, he reached for the willow stick he used for a horse prod and held it in readiness. At just the right moment he brought the stick down, striking the bird a fatal blow on the head.

"I got him," he yelled in jubilation at his marksmanship.

"Yes, so I see," replied his father. "But why did you do that? The bird was picking worms, which are just as bad for the corn as the weeds you are destroying with the cultivator."

"I never thought of that," said the boy, as he watched the last convulsive kicks of the unfortunate bird, "and now it's too late."

Timely advice and a wildlife conservation lesson well learned at the cost of just one Brewer's blackbird and perhaps a nestful of young.

... *The killdeer*

May, 1952

The killdeer is a bird that has adapted itself to a cultivated field habitat. When nesting in a cornfield, as it often does, it places its nest close to a hill of corn. Whether by ingenuity or by accident, this works well for the bird's survival, since the incubation period is long — about 28 days. When cultivating corn, the farmer, in sparing the hill of corn, will also spare the killdeer's nest. The eggs may get covered with dirt, but the killdeer — a practical bird — digs them up and sets on them again as if nothing had happened. Only when corn planting is delayed does the bird get into trouble, for then the disc, the spike tooth harrow and the corn planter all have to go over the field and, unless special care is taken, the nest will be destroyed. The bird's feigned injury, plaintive pleading and its attempt to lead the intruder away when its nest is threatened is enough to arouse sympathy in all but the most calloused. Its loud call can be heard above the noise of any tractor. The killdeer has probably won the hearts of more farmers than has any other bird. In addition to being a valuable destroyer of insect pests, its many charming ways appeal to everyone. In true plover fashion, it never walks. When on the ground it either stands still or runs. When running, it holds its body rigid. Only its legs are a whir of motion. When standing, it often teeters or bobs, lifting the fore part of its body impressively upward and down again. Whether on the ground or in the air this handsome shore bird is very noisy, uttering its frequent loud cry of "killdeer," or "killdee." Its Latin name—*vociferus*—is very fitting.

When hatched, the killdeer chick, though covered with down, is a striking image of its parent. Being precocial, they find all their own food from the start. The parents, however, are very solicitous of their welfare. They are good at knowing the whereabouts of each of their offspring. I once caught a young killdeer at dinnertime and put it in my shirt pocket to take home to show the children. There was no lack of interest. The young plover's abrupt starts and stops weren't meant for linoleum floors. I had intended to take it back to the field after dinner but the parent birds hovered about the farmstead, so I released the chick in the cowyard where they met it and escorted it back to its family circle.

While discing a field for silage corn one June, I pulled the tractor clutch as a killdeer scream pierced my ears. A few feet ahead I found the nest, if it can be called a nest. It was made of a few broken pieces of last year's stubble and held four pointed eggs, which were buff-white with blackish-chocolate markings, especially towards the larger end. Swinging the disc aside, I left a little patch around the nest unpulverized. When using the spike tooth harrow — a wide implement — I straddled the nest with the tractor wheels and pulled ahead until the drag was near the nest. Then I moved the eggs and nesting material back of the implement and went on. When I returned, the bird was not sitting on the eggs but on the spot where the eggs had been. I moved the eggs back to their original location and was glad to see when I returned that madam killdeer was on the eggs and all was well. It was more difficult to miss the nest with the four row corn planter without making a noticeable kink in the rows, but I made it. One more harrowing and the disturbance was over.

The killdeer is easily recognized by its distinct color pattern — olive brown above and pure white below. It has a white ring extending around the neck and two black bands across the breast. Its buffy-yellowish rump shows plainly in flight. One might think that a bird as conspicuously colored as this would be easily seen but, strangely enough, it is harder to see when standing still than a sparrow. It achieves its camouflage by a breaking up of its outline.

It is almost entirely insectivorous. It feeds on flies,

grasshoppers, beetles, mosquitoes, cutworms, wireworms, weevils, billbugs, etc. It is one of the most useful of farm birds. Although it is frequently seen near water, it spends much of its time in cultivated fields and pastures, especially during the nesting season.

Even though its flesh is inferior and inedible, this bird was almost driven to extinction during the market hunting days of the 80's and 90's. It is now protected by law in Canada, the United States and Mexico. We hope their numbers will increase.

. . . *Dickcissel, bobolink*

June, 1952

The call of the dickcissel is a simple, easily heard little ditty, repeated often and persistently throughout the hot summer weather of June, July and August. This song (from which the bird gets it name) is often represented as "Dickciss-ciss-ciss." To me, it sounds more like "trick-three-three-three" — the last three notes uttered with a sort of lisp.

It is about the size of an English sparrow, with which the female bird is sometimes confused by amateurs. The dickcissel is strictly a tall-grass bird, with a special preference for alfalfa fields, which are sure to harbor grasshoppers and a host of other insects. It is sometimes called the little meadow lark because the male's yellow breast and black bib remind one of this larger bird. The male bird is the singer, characteristically rendering his serenade from the top of a tall weed, a fence post, a wire or a telephone line.

For me, the song of the dickcissel will always be associated with the smell of new mown hay and the hard work and sweaty shirts of haying and harvest time. It also brings back to memory the two weary miles we children trudged to and from parochial school in June, years ago.

For some reason, as yet unexplained, the number of these birds varies greatly from year to year, especially at the edges of its range, where it may in some years be entirely absent and in other years be quite numerous. This year dickcissels are numerous. If we drove from Albert Lea to St. Louis or Kansas City, we would very likely see and hear from one to several of these birds on every mile of the way.

The dickcissel used to be common even in the Atlantic states, but for some reason its range has now become more limited. It is typically a midwestern bird, but breeds throughout the interior United States. Its food includes weed and grass seeds and some waste grain. But, while in its nesting territory, its diet runs heavily to insects, with grasshoppers being a favorite item.

Far from spectacular in either plumage or song, the dickcissel is just a plain good neighbor, with a personality all its own, lending cheer to a season when most bird songs have quieted down. It is also an interesting fellow creature because of the mysterious uncertainty of its presence from season to season.

Quite unlike its comely plain spoken neighbor, the bobolink (another hayland bird) is a show-off in plumage and song alike. In flashy springtime get-up, the male bird reverses birddom tradition, wearing his suit upside down, with black below and white above. It is this gaudy spring dressed male that is more widely recognized than the female and young, who dress in plainer garb. His song—a bubbling burst of glee poured forth with explosive rapture, often while on the wing — has endeared the bird to all who know it on its northern range. Inspired by it, William Cullen Bryant penned that classic poem, "Robert of Lincoln."

The bobolink's menu while on its nesting range consists almost entirely of insect food, including such pests as grasshoppers, cutworms and cankerworms. After nesting time bobolinks flock and change their diet to weed seeds, which they eat in enormous quantities. The male replaces his flashy plumage with a plain one similar to that of the female and the young and stops his delightful song.

Bobolinks winter in South America, going as far south as Argentina, migrating principally via Dixie and the Bahamas. In the South (where it is called "reed bird") it is as bitterly hated as it is admired in the North, and for good reason. The migrating flocks descend on the rice fields, where they eat enough of this grain to run the loss to individual planters into thousands of dollars. The solution seems to be to move the rice fields out of the bobolinks' migration path. In the Bahamas — fat, plump and fresh from our southern rice fields — the bobolinks (now called "butter birds") are much prized as food and are taken in great numbers. Because of this treatment, and the limitation of its northern tall grass nesting habitat, is it any wonder that bobolink numbers are decreasing, even though now protected by law in the United States?

. . . *The cowbird*

July, 1952

It isn't necessary to go to distant places to find birds with strange habits. The cowbird, a common summer resident in this territory, is one of the rare birds which is a total parasite. As parents, most birds perform their duties well. Traditionally, the female builds the nest, broods the eggs and feeds the young. In most cases, the male not only assists in building the nest and feeding the young but takes his turn brooding the eggs as well. In some cases, the male assumes responsibility for all domestic duties except, of course, laying the eggs.

In the case of the cowbird, however, both parents manage to escape all family cares. They carry the baby sitting idea to the extent that they never build a nest of their own and never brood any eggs or feed any young. The entire burden is shifted to other, and usually much smaller, birds. They don't even pair, preferring instead to mate promiscuously.

The male bird may be easily identified. It is the only blackbird with a chocolate brown head. The female is evenly gray. The young also are uniformly gray, but are a little lighter colored than mature females.

Early in the nesting season the female cowbird searches fields, fencerows, shrubbery and woods until she locates the nests of several small birds. When she is ready to lay an egg she goes to one of the nests while the rightful owner is away, or waits until it leaves. Then she slips onto the nest, lays her egg and flies her carefree way, without another thought of her progeny.

Since most perching birds do not start brooding their eggs until the full clutch is laid, the cowbird has little trouble finding a nest with the owner absent. This scheme does not always work.

Sometimes the prospective victims do not leave their nest in time and she has to lay her egg on the ground. Native sparrows, warblers, vireos, wrens and bluebirds are those most often parasitized by the cowbird.

When the yellow warbler finds the strange egg with its own it builds another story to its nest, which covers up the intruding egg and its own. Then she lays another clutch of eggs to brood. Wrens meet the situation by puncturing the strange egg so it will not hatch. Some birds even desert their nest. However, most parasitized birds, although they may resent the presence of the foreign egg, are unable to get rid of it, and proceed to brood it along with their own.

The cowbird egg is designed by nature to hatch in a shorter period of time than the eggs of even smaller birds, meaning the intruding nestling gets a head start. Being larger and more robust, it demands and gets most of the attention, with the result that the rightful young either starve to death or are crowded out of the nest. The parent birds then find themselves feeding only their adopted young.

My first experience with this parasitism was in the spring of 1920 when I found a bluebird's nest in a cavity in an old fence post. The nest contained four blue eggs and one much larger speckled one. I always think of this incident when I see cowbirds near our bluebird houses. Whether the defeated look about these birds is imaginary or real, the defeat is real, since the 1½-inch entrance to these houses is intentionally made too small for the cowbirds to enter.

While cutting weeds some years ago, I heard what I thought was a young blackbird clamoring for food. Looking up, I saw a young cowbird in the top of a dead cherry tree. But, strangely, there was no parent bird about. Just then, a tiny northern yellowthroat flew to a small branch just above the youngster and stretched down to feed it, half disappearing into its throat. The contrast in size seemed ridiculous when the young cowbird, like most young birds about to be fed, fluffed out its feathers in such a way as to appear twice its normal size.

This spring I saw a young cowbird flying about a field. It

was being followed and faithfully fed by a vesper sparrow. Loathsome as this labor saving system may seem, it certainly works, as evidenced by the number of cowbirds to be seen.

When it is able to find its own food the young cowbird leaves its foster parents and flocks with others of its own kind. How it is able to recognize its own kin after having been given care only by foster parents is one of the riddles of nature.

This bird can usually be seen wherever cows are grazing. It gets its name from its habit of following cows to eat insects which the animals disturb. Sometimes it gathers insects from their backs. Judged on the basis of food habits the cowbird is a valuable bird. But it is hard to overlook the fact that each individual bird of this species represents the sacrifice of an entire family of smaller and more valuable birds.

How did the cowbird acquire this strange habit? Did it at first use abandoned nests, as several other species do? Did it then find them too scarce and begin using any handy nest from which the owners were absent, only to be driven away when they returned? Did it, when driven from nest to nest, finally adopt its present system? This question is another puzzle of nature.

The cowbird's mischievous days are over for this season. They will soon be flocking with the blackbirds in preparation for their southward journey. Next spring they will be back, whether welcome or not.

. . . Goldfinch, indigo bunting

August, 1952

Most people know the goldfinch and few tire of seeing this small, friendly, delightful bird. It is easily recognized by its bright golden-yellow color and roller coaster flight. The goldfinch is commonly called "wild canary" because the color of its plumage resembles that of the domesticated cage bird. While some goldfinches are with us the year around, they are seen in their greatest numbers during July, August and September when they congregate among thistles and feast on the tiny seeds. With surprising deftness, they remove and discard the hulls. Warbling in festive gaiety, they pay little attention to humans, who may sometimes approach to within a few feet without disturbing them. Even when molested into flight they utter no discordant or scolding note, only a cheerful "per-chic-o-ree" with every dip in their undulating flight.

Goldfinches nest late. Nests are common in August, September and even later, when other birds have finished nesting. Thus they avoid being parasitized by the cowbird, and also find plenty of choice nesting material. The neat cup-shaped nests, constructed of grass, bark strips and various plant fibers interwoven and lined with thistledown, may be found anywhere from a thistle stalk to thirty feet up in a tree. Most nests, however, are not over five feet above the ground.

Goldfinches are almost exclusively seed eaters. Even the young, which have no other access to water than that which is brought to them in their food, are fed seeds from the very start. The parents feed them soft seeds by regurgitation. By no means limited to a diet of thistle seeds, the goldfinch eats a great variety, changing its menu with the seasons. Seeds of dandelion, catnip, asters, goldenrod, evening primrose, burdock, mullein and sunflower are favorites, as are fruits of alder, elm, birch, hemlock, spruce, etc. I have also seen them eating lilac seeds in January.

Goldfinches may cause some damage to the crops of commercial garden seed growers, but are otherwise entirely beneficial birds. Being quite numerous and fairly tame, with a conspicuous plumage visible at a considerable distance, the goldfinch is commonly known and welcomed. I have been asked about the goldfinch more often than about any other bird.

Another equally colorful bird, the indigo bunting, is with us from late April until October, yet most people never see it. It is not as numerous as the goldfinch and, here in its nesting territory, it is never seen in groups, although there are nesting pairs in every rural neighborhood.

The male bird's entire plumage, as the name indicates, is blue — a color which is not visible from as great a distance as the goldfinch's yellow. Furthermore, its color — which is the result of reflected light from its peculiar feather structure — is of a quality that changes with the background. When seen against the sky, the male indigo bunting appears entirely black. In the shady isles of the woods its color is dark blue. The full tropical splendor of its peacock blue is best revealed when seen — as I first saw it — in bright sunlight, at close range and against a background of lush green vegetation. Indigo buntings nest in low bushes. Field edges, brushy fence rows and patches of hardwood are favorite habitats.

Although not as confiding as the goldfinch, it is not an especially shy bird. It may stop singing momentarily when it notices it is being spied upon but it cannot remain quiet for very long, and a brief search will reveal its whereabouts. Aside from accidental discovery, however, the charms of the indigo bunting are reserved for those who know its call. The male bird is an inveterate singer all through the two-brood nesting season. Its song, which consists of a series of notes uttered in pairs and which to me sounds like "cheep cheep, cheer cheer, chew chew, sweet sweet," is repeated every few seconds for a half-hour or more at a time. Changing its perch, the bird then repeats the performance. It does not sing at night, but finds enough time during daylight hours to repeat its call several thousand times. It is a good call to know. The sight of a male indigo bunting lends spice to any field trip. The brilliant plumage never fails to bring out the "ohs" and "ahs" from any group.

. . . American egret

September, 1952

A few days back, a large white bird flew low over the windbreak not far from our house. With a slow measured wingbeat and a snow white plumage against a background of blue sky, it was beauty one would travel far to see. For this writer the moment was one of jubilation because the American egret is more than a creature of beauty. It is a living symbol of the long, discouraging but successful struggle to save a fellow species from extinction. Without the effort of the National Association of Audubon Societies, the American egret would long since have joined the forty or more species of birds that have been completely exterminated by the hand of man.

The American egret story is one of waste, greed and shame. It is the story of the noble effort of conservation-minded people, in spite of long odds and ridicule, and of the indignation of an aroused public against cruelty toward a fellow creature, and of final success, as evidenced by the presence of American egrets today, even in Freeborn County.

During the mating and nesting season both sexes of these beautiful herons wear a train of 40 or 50 plumes, which develop on their backs and extend a foot or more beyond the tail. These plumes were eagerly sought by milliners as adornment for women's hats.

Egrets are gun shy to the extent that whole colonies will desert their nests and eggs if molested. After the eggs have hatched, however, the parents will not forsake their young. Taking advantage of this characteristic, plume hunters waited until the young appeared, then shot the parent birds as they brought home food. The young were left to a slow death by starvation.

No species could long survive such persecution. They once

numbered into the hundreds of thousands in our southern states. From a distance, roosting American egrets made trees look like snowdrifts. From this abundance, the species steadily declined until, by 1900, there were only an estimated 25 pairs left in secluded swamps in Georgia and Florida. As the birds became scarce, the price of plumes skyrocketed.

At this desperate stage the National Association of Audubon Societies was organized because of the atrocities of the feather trade. Wardens were hired to protect remaining colonies. Turning to education as a weapon, the new organization spread the true story of the plight of the American egret. Resentment grew. Public opinion began to change. Women thought about the starving young American egrets and refused to wear hats with egret plumes. Laws were enacted. The feather trade was outlawed. Sanctuaries were established. Yet only after fifteen years of effort were there glimpses of hope for the survival of the species. In recent years the National Audubon Society has greatly expanded its sanctuaries, and these beautiful birds have come back in great numbers to virtually all their former range.

The migration habit of the American egret is peculiar. After the young are able to find their own food, they fan out or spread northward in search of feeding grounds and remain until cold weather drives them back south. Some years they go further north than in other years.

American egrets feed singly or in groups, and at sunset gather in large communal roosts with a great hubbub of hoarse croaks that are not especially pleasing to human ears. Beauty of song is not an American egret virtue.

In 1946, about one hundred of these birds fed in the shallow waters of Upper Twin Lake and roosted in a clump of willows on the west shore of Mud Lake, a mile or so to the north. At sundown I could see them from my farm. I had often thought of going to Florida for sights like this but had not expected to have the experience at home. There was also a larger roost numbering about 700 birds in the willows on the west shore of Pickerel Lake near my farm that same year.

This is another American egret year and, although they are

not as numerous as in 1946, they may be seen in the shallows of almost any lake or stream. As I watched thirteen of these birds from the Juglan Bridge, an interested angler came over and we talked of American egrets for a while. While we talked, one of the birds flew closer to us, its graceful flight mirrored in the stream as it alit with its short tail spread fanwise and its long black legs reaching into the water. It seemed impossible that such a broad expanse of wing could fold into a form so trim and slender. My friend surprised me with the question, "What are they good for?" Why should this question be asked about the American egret any more than about any of the other parts of the habitat — the water, the fish and other aquatic plant and animal life, the trees and grass on shore, the cows grazing nearby, or the fishermen and observers themselves?

American egrets render us valuable service by consuming many small fish, so that those remaining may grow to greater size, just as a gardener thins out vegetables to permit room for growth. Rice farmers value the birds highly as destroyers of crayfish, which are detrimental to that crop.

On the aesthetic side, we should be thankful that the Creator has chosen to give us a heron as beautiful as the American egret, and that man has at long last seen fit to put forth enough effort to spare this fellow species from extinction.

... *Ring-necked pheasant*

October, 1952

The bird we know as the ring-necked pheasant is a hybrid, resulting from the mingling of four introduced races. Although the number actually introduced was small, this well known game bird has found suitable environment in the northern half of the United States, where it has increased in numbers rapidly, particularly in the heavy grain producing areas of the Upper Midwest. The greatest concentration is found in Minnesota, Iowa and South Dakota.

The birds are not as numerous as they were twenty years ago, when their popultion became greater than they apparently were able to maintain. It is firmly established on our farmlands in this territory, however, and is now the only upland game bird which, under present circumstances, is able to produce a harvestable surplus.

Its success as a species has been achieved partly because of its pugnacious aggressiveness in crowding out native species such as the prairie chicken and quail. For a time the prairie chicken and quail increased greatly in numbers as farming spread westward. But when native grassland became limited, prairie chicken numbers began to dwindle. As ungrazed woodland and brier patches disappeared, the quail also decreased in numbers. The quail had the additional disadvantage of being a southern bird which had been able to extend its range northward only by developing a hardy strain. Excessive hunting killed off most of these hardy birds, and the hardiness of the remaining few was destroyed by crossing with less hardy southern stock which was brought in and released in an attempt to increase the number of northern birds.

The ring-necked pheasant, in some measure at least, replaces these two highly desirable native game birds. We shall miss the booming courtship call of the prairie chicken roosters and the loud, clear, cheerful whistle of the bobwhite and have to accept as a poor substitute the rasping clatter of the male pheasant.

The ring-necked pheasant has other faults too. Its habit of concentrating in large flocks during the winter in places where food is available — often causing heavy crop losses, and even interfering with traffic safety — is certainly an undesirable charcteristic. It has also acquired many enemies by destroying newly planted corn in areas where the birds are too numerous.

Despite its faults, the ring-necked pheasant is a good game bird. Like other species of the chicken kind it is polygamous and only one male is needed for every 5 to 15 females to produce a full crop of chicks. The other males can thus be considered shootable surplus. The bird has a good lease on the future, also. Besides being more versatile in selecting nesting sites, it can also be reared in captivity yet be wild when released. It can be thought of as a sort of semi-domesticated chicken or as a very manageable game bird.

The male ring-necked pheasant is a grand bird as he struts in stately dignity. But how quickly his bearing changes when the hunting season opens! How well he knows the first law of nature — self preservation. His bag of tricks often enables him to elude the craftiest of hunters, and even their trained and trusted dogs. His feats of cunning are always a lively topic for discussion at this season. Some male pheasants drop to the ground like a bag of sand when a gun is discharged, yet aren't to be found when the man or dog reaches the spot where they fell. Some strut and squawk, conspicuously drawing attention to one spot, then crouch and run like a streak of lightning to repeat the performance in another place. Wise cocks learn that flight is not the best method for escape. Often they remain in cover even when hunters and dogs are near at hand. Letting chivalry go hang, they stay put while law-protected hens draw attention by bursting into flight. I have even seen them follow my corn wagon across the field while hunters, with a sense of guilt for not having asked my permission to hunt, stayed at a safe distance. Cock pheasants are always more numerous about my farmstead during hunting season. Perhaps this is also from a sense of protection.

The pheasant's remarkable skill at hiding wears down the hunter's zeal so successfully that there isn't much hunting after the first few days, even though the season may extend for a considerable period. In other words, the ring-necked pheasant is a bird that can stand the hunting pressure we have, and thus serves the purpose for which it was introduced.

In the spring the great winter flocks spread out. The cocks establish crowing territories to attract a number of females. There are many spirited fights between males in establishing the boundaries of these territories. Dense marsh borders are good nesting places, as are ungrazed woodlands, weedy fence rows, roadsides and waste corners. Pheasants, unfortunately, often choose to nest in alfalfa and clover fields, with the result that mowing often kills or fatally injures the hen and destroys the eggs. I accidentally destroyed thirteen nests in this way in 1930, but lately the number has dropped to two or three in a season because my mowing has been delayed.

Heavy spring rains kill many pheasant chicks. They can be protected by the mother bird against a reasonable shower, but a deluge will drown or chill them beyond endurance. Wandering cats, weasels, skunks, foxes and birds of prey take their toll also. All of these factors, in addition to shooting, are involved in the pheasant's ability to maintain itself as a species.

One can always get into an argument as to whether foxes do or do not take pheasants, and data may be quoted to substantiate both claims. I have had both foxes and pheasants live on my farm long enough to know that foxes do take pheasants, and also leghorn chickens — leaving feathers at their dens as mute evidence. Last spring a mother red fox made a determined attempt to capture a mature hen pheasant less than ten rods from where I was cleaning off my plow at dusk. While I was putting my pullets into the laying house this fall a fox attempted to take one that had flown from a tree onto the ground. I ran to the scene of the commotion and rescued the crippled bird. Many feathers were missing from her side and four wounds showed plainly where the fox's canine teeth had pierced her body. I hesitate to pardon the theft of my leghorns but, as for the pheasants, let the birds beware. Foxes will never exterminate pheasants but they are a factor in holding their number in check. I like to have pheasants about and I also like to see an occasional fox. I don't condemn the fox for taking pheasants as food. Don't we do the same thing?

. . . *Golden plover*

While plowing soybean ground on October 27th — a cold blustery day — I was pleasantly surprised to find that I had rare visitors from the Arctic region. Thousands of miles off their regular migration course, en route from the far northern tundra to the even more distant pampas of Argentina, seven golden plovers spent the afternoon feasting on angleworms and other choice morsels gleaned from my freshly turned furrows. I first became aware of the presence of the strange birds when I heard their call — a loud, harsh "Quee-del-eee" reminiscent of the clatter of guinea hens and easily heard above the noise of the tractor.

A check with Peterson's *Bird Guide* verified my guess that my plump, stocky globe-trotting guests were golden plovers. There is always an element of surprise in seeing a bird for the first time. Although the form and coloration may be familiar from photographs and portraits, the actual size and behavior pattern can only be observed by seeing the bird itself. In autumn plumage, as these birds were, golden plovers are plain brownish birds with dark enough upper parts to be rather inconspicuous on plowed land if they remain motionless. In flight, their evenly greyish underparts show up plainly. The seven birds stayed in a concentrated group, flew in close formation and lit on the plowing, all facing the same direction. They had the habit of bobbing their heads quite often. They did not follow my plow, as some species do, but stayed on a low part of the field and flew off a short distance as the tractor approached.

The American golden plover is one of the most interesting species in all bird lore, particularly because of its long and unusual migration route. From their nesting grounds on the tundra they gather in flocks during August and fly eastward over Hudson Bay to Labrador, where they leisurely feed and fatten on snails and other aquatic life as they work southward along the coast to the peninsula of Nova Scotia. From there they take off southward over the Atlantic Ocean for 3,000 miles to the northeast coast of South America from Venezuela to Brazil, where they often arrive thin and emaciated from their long, continuous over-water journey.

Migrating inland, they winter from Bolivia to eastern Argentina. Their northward journey, beginning in February, takes them westward over the Andes Mountains to the Pacific coast in Peru, where they again feast on sea life washed ashore. Leisurely following the coast northward, they cross the Isthmus of Panama, then fly across the Gulf of Mexico and arrive in the United States along the coast of Louisiana and Texas.

Now in striking spring plumage, the birds have coal black underparts from beak to tail. Upper parts are brown with yellow or gold spots. A broad white line extends from the forehead over the eyes and down the sides of the neck. This seemingly conspicuous marking breaks up the birds' outline and thus actually aids their camouflage.

Following the Mississippi Valley, the plovers leisurely accompany the spring northward to Arkansas, then veer westward, missing our locality and passing thru the Dakotas in May. June finds them again on their nesting grounds.

From Point Barrow on the Arctic coast of Alaska eastward and southward to Churchill on Hudson Bay, the plovers build their nests — mere depressions in the reindeer moss of the open tundra. The brown and gold mottled back of the bird blends perfectly with the surrounding reindeer moss, effectively concealing the sitting bird from prying enemy eyes.

A few golden plovers migrate over the Pacific to winter in the Hawaiian Islands. Some reach South America by migrating down the Pacific coast. A few find their way southward through the Mississippi Valley, and it was to seven of these that I was host the other day.

The history of the golden plover as a species follows the same pattern as that of many of our other birds. Formerly abundant, it suffered greatly and was almost exterminated during the market hunting era, especially after the passenger pigeon became scarce. Strong east winds during the fall migration often drove the birds in great concentration to the Atlantic coast from New England southward, where gunners, taking advantage of the birds' plight, wrought great slaughter.

A similar fate awaited the plovers when they arrived plump and fat on our southern coast in spring. The birds' habit of flying in concentrated flocks and their characteristic of being easily decoyed combined to make them easy prey for hunters. Under belated protection its numbers are increasing, although its progress is slow and by no means certain. Being an intercontinental bird, its protection is not complete, since we have so far been unsuccessful in obtaining the cooperation of South American countries in this matter.

. . . *English sparrow*

December, 1952

If a trophy were in order for the wild bird most closely and successfully associated with man, the English sparrow would certainly merit that award. I doubt, however, if any such tribute will be forthcoming, because the aggressive little alien, at first considered beneficial as a weed-seed eater and destroyer of harmful insects, has proved itself to be a pesky nuisance, to say the least.

Some folks defend the English sparrow and make it welcome at their homes. They have come to like the plucky little bird and, of course, there is no law against this. Whether we like it or not, however, we will have to put up with it because the saucy little chirper has come to stay. All attempts to control its numbers by trapping or by other methods have been ineffective.

This native of Europe was introduced more than one hundred years ago. In its new home the English sparrow (or house sparrow, as it is sometimes called) multiplied and, with man's help, spread rapidly. It is now firmly established almost everywhere that man lives in any numbers. It is an all-season resident and it clusters about human habitations in both city and country, occupying much the same position among birds as the rat does among mammals. Its hardiness, indiscriminate food habits, fecundity, relative freedom from natural enemies and mistaken encouragement by man have combined to make this bird a tremendously successful species.

As a lad, I was gathering sparrow eggs one day, and was successful in finding almost a gallon of them. Our strawstack was always perforated with roosting and nesting holes made by sparrows. It was great winter sport to catch sparrows in the strawstack at dusk by covering these holes with our hands before the roosting birds had a chance to fly. My attempts to shoot sparrows with the air rifle weren't very successful, because by the time that weapon had come down as far as to my place in the family — seventh in line — it had seen its best days and was barely able to boost a BB to the peak of the barn roof where it would bounce off a sparrow's breast and come rolling down the roof again.

Since 1915, English sparrow numbers have decreased considerably. Some folks attribute this reversal in sparrow population to Henry Ford, whose idea of placing an automobile in every American home heralded the age of mechanized power and started the decline of the horse as a beast of burden. There is food for thought in this theory for those who have seen swarms of these birds feeding on undigested oats around hitching posts and livery barns. What is more likely, however, is that the introduced bird, having temporarily reached a greater population level than it can maintain, has made, or is making, a downward adjustment to a level it can maintain in competition with all adverse factors in its environment.

The old proverb, "Familiarity breeds contempt," applies well to the English sparrow. Undoubtedly, more faults have been found with this bird than with any other. Hovering about our homes like so many belligerent watchdogs, they keep milder-mannered native song birds at a distance. By taking over nesting houses, bossing bird feeders, birdbaths and even monopolizing roosting quarters, they have become a bird-watcher's headache. Any native bird nesting near our homes does so at the risk of being harassed or driven away by having their nest, eggs or young destroyed by a gang of the ruffians. A friend told me recently about a downy woodpecker that excavated a nesting cavity in a poplar tree close enough to his house to be easily observed from a window. However, the little carpenter had to leave before actually nesting because English sparrows moved in.

Their winter habit of gathering in large flocks to roost, defiling buildings in city and country alike, is disgusting. Being winter residents, their feed bill runs high. Other birds eat grain also, but most of these glean what would otherwise be waste. English sparrows help themselves wherever crops are stored, often wasting more than they eat.

Their slovenly nesting habits win them no friends. Every available cranny on or near buildings is stuffed with straw or trash and chicken feathers. Even lighted cigarette butts are sometimes used, with disastrous results. Eave spouts, ventilator shafts, awning folds, light fixtures and grain spouts are favorite nesting sites.

Of all the sins of the English sparrow, however, there is none so exasperating to a farmer as its persistence in building nests in the hay carrier. A hay carrier is a wonderful invention designed to lift heavy loads of hay and distribute them wherever desired in the hay loft by means of a track under the peak of the barn roof. A sparrow nest in the carrier anchors the carrier securely wherever it comes to rest on the track. If it is in the center of the barn, and one has no better facilities for reaching it, the only remedy is to shinny up the barn wall like a human fly and climb like a sloth under the carrier track to where the carrier is. With both heels and one hand hanging onto the track, one hand is free to pull out the nest, bit by bit, while chaff, feathers and sparrow litter fall into one's face. The longer one hangs, the heavier one seems to get, and it's twenty feet down to the haymow floor. Finally, the nest is all out and one can crawl back feet first with aching arms and clumsy feet to the barn wall and down along the studdings. Safely down again, one is ready for a hard day's work in the hayfield, while the undaunted sparrow is free to build another nest in the carrier.

I'm sure those who introduced the English sparrow weren't thinking of hay carriers when they brought over the first English sparrows, but perhaps we can take an object lesson from this bird and ponder deeply before advocating the introduction of other foreign species.

... *Tufted titmouse*

January, 1953

In this latitude nature usually sets a scanty table for its feathered folk in January. This is especially true in a year like this when, in this territory at least, the ground has been covered with snow and ice since mid-November. An ever-increasing number of people in both city and country are thoughtfully coming to the birds' assistance by providing food of some kind where their guests may be observed while feeding. Besides having the satisfaction of being true wildlife conservationists, these people are rewarded with a ringside seat at a winter-bird pageant. In addition to the regular visitors, such as the ever-present English sparrows, which sometimes eat most of the food, unusual birds sometimes seek the supplementary handout. One of these rarities, which several Albert Lea people have reported seeing at their bird feeders this winter, is the tufted titmouse.

This close relative of the familiar black-capped chickadee is popular with bird watchers because of its sprightly appearance and interesting habits. A small, extremely active, mouse-colored bird, with lighter under parts and rusty flanks, it is easily recognized by its high crest, which it raises and lowers according to its mood. Its characteristic clear whistled call, "Peter Peter Peter" or "here, here, here," is easily remembered. Like the chickadee, it usually nests in a natural tree cavity or a deserted woodpecker hole. But it has been known to enter a house through a broken windowpane and nest indoors under the curious scrutiny of the human occupants.

It does not migrate in search of a milder climate as so many birds do, but gets about considerably in search of food, which it sometimes has the habit of storing. It takes a great deal of food to satisfy the appetite of such an active bird, especially during cold weather. Considering the amount of feed, housing and care required to keep our domestic stock healthy at this season, one cannot help but marvel at the hardiness and the survival ability of this tiny mite of the bird world. We are fortunate to have a representative of the titmouse family as a winter resident, because it is at this season that they render their most valuable service.

The winter job of titmice in keeping nature's house in order is to find and devour the countless tiny insects, insect pupae and eggs which are hidden on the small branches and twigs of trees and shrubs. Woodpeckers, nuthatches and brown creepers diligently search the trunks and larger branches but are ill suited for getting about the finer parts of trees, and there is much there that needs attention. The titmice take over the job where the larger birds leave off and find much that has been overlooked. Here we have another example of different species of birds doing essentially the same job but in a different area. The nathatches, active acrobats that they are, demand a firm object for their grasp, while titmice cling to swinging, swaying branches while searching twigs to their very tips, often hanging upside down in the process.

The sense of sight is highly developed in most birds. Titmice are gifted with microscopic eyesight, as evidenced by the fact that they consume great quantities of aphid eggs, many of which are too small to be seen by the human eye without the aid of a magnifying glass. It takes a lot of these eggs to make a square meal!

Aphids (or plant lice) cause much damage by sucking sap from tender growing parts of plants. There are a great many different species of aphids, each of which prefers its own species of host plant. These tiny insects typically spend the winter in the egg stage. The destruction of a single winter egg means the elimination of a great number of potential plant lice. What a lousy plant world we would have if it were not for the good work of the various species of titmice during the winter months.

Another titmouse winter food specialty is scale insects, or

bark lice. These peculiar insects, under a protective waxlike scale, attach themselves permanently to the bark of most fruit-producing plants and suck their food from the host plant. When numerous, these pests are highly destructive and are one of the headaches of the orchardist and nurseryman. I once examined a hedge which looked especially unhealthy and found the bark of the shrubs so crowded with scale insects that there was hardly room for another scale. Titmice, with their small sharp beaks and barbed tongues, are able to detach and eat these scale insects.

In addition to their winter insect diet, titmice relish such plant food as acorns, nuts and small fruits. These hardy little birds are opportunists, and are always ready to accept easily obtained food. When they see a squirrel munching a nut, they search for particles that fall to the ground. Start splitting wood and notice how soon chickadees gather to search for exposed wood borers. They are particularly appreciative of suet, which they will industriously carry away to store for future use. During the warmer months their diet consists largely of insects and insect eggs, of which there are then a great plenty.

There can be no doubt that titmice are highly beneficial to man's interests. The species prevalent in this territory is the black-capped chickadee. We can watch its activities and hope that occasionally we may see and hear its gay relative, the tufted titmouse.

. . . Horned lark

February, 1953

Have you ever wondered which is the most numerous bird in the world? Is it the English sparrow? Or the robin, so common in everyone's dooryard? Or the red-winged blackbird that is sometimes seen in such great concentration? It will no doubt surprise many to learn that some ornithologists believe this distinction should go to the horned lark, a bird that most people do not even know, although it lives right in our midst. Seldom seen in any great concentration, the horned lark is quite generally distributed throughout a far-flung territory, including virtually all of North America and areas of the same latitude around the world. A glance at a globe will show that this includes a lot of land. Besides being spread over a vast territory the horned lark can be found in a great variety of habitats as well. It is a ground-loving bird of the open spaces, where it seldom crosses the path of most people. It can often be found on the seashore. It is sometimes called shore lark. But this name is misleading, since it is also found inland across the prairies, tundra, desert, foothills, and even on bare mountaintops.

On January 10th we motored to Owatonna where we saw Bert Harwell's Screen Tour film *Canada North.* This splendid motion picture showed horned larks nesting on the tundra near the Arctic Ocean. The same species nests in the fields on my farm every year and as far south as Missouri. This is the only species of lark native to the Western Hemisphere. Ornithologists list as many as sixteen races or subspecies. But the differences are of minor importance. If you know one you will recognize them all. The various races nest in their own particular locality. But during the winter they concentrate mainly in the southern

United States, where several of the races may be seen in the same area.

Experienced bird watchers will recognize the horned lark at a distance by its habit of always perching on the ground and walking or running nimbly rather than hopping, as a sparrow always does. Others will probably meet it first along a road in February or early March. The little birds, often in small flocks, that take flight so suddenly from bare spots along highway shoulders as your car approaches are not English sparrows but horned larks. They like to gather on these spots that are free from snow because they find perching there more convenient, and also because they may find grain or feed spilled from passing trucks. If your eyes are good you can see the black tail feathers that the birds show plainly in flight. At close range you might even see the black collar, or band, under the yellowish throat, the black cheek patches and the twin black tufts that show conspicuously on the bird's head, especially when it is startled. It is from these tufts, or horns, that the bird gets its name. In common with other larks, the claws on the hind toes are very long, presumably to aid the bird in walking on grass.

Although some have been known to winter as far north as Newfoundland, northern races of horned larks usually migrate southward for the winter, but return early, arriving in this latitude in February or early March. I have seen them as early as January, perched on a frozen clod and twittering contentedly during a howling blizzard. They are hardy birds and may build nests here as early as March while snow still covers the ground. By the time farmers get into their fields for spring work the young larks of the first brood are already old enough to keep out of the path of tillage implements.

The cup-shaped nests of loosely placed grass are always on the ground, usually in a little depression, and at least partially hidden by a tuft of grass. Three to five eggs are laid and two or three broods per season are the rule.

The song of the horned lark is a high-pitched, irregular musical twitter. During the breeding season this song is often prolonged and is uttered from high in the air. One Sunday morning in May 1951, when the Albert Lea Audubon Society was to meet early at a local physician's farm near Spring Valley, I arose very early to do my chores. One of the first bird songs I heard was that of a horned lark high overhead in the darkness. The uninterrupted song continued for so long that I could not wait for the last of it lest the delay cause me to be late in getting to our scheduled field trip. While listening to this bird sing, I wondered if the European skylark is really a better singer, as claimed, and if its fame is not partially attributable to Shelley's poetic skill.

These modest, inconspicuous little birds can be seen every day in every farmer's fields during the entire field work season, often in family groups. Your bird feeders will not attract any of these ground-loving field birds. When farm implements get too close the horned larks take flight, twittering as they go, as though they were headed for parts unknown, but they invariably circle back to alight in almost the same spot from which they started. The next trip across the field will find the same birds repeating their flight.

The food of horned larks is about three-fourths vegetable matter, consisting mostly of weed seeds and waste grain. The remainder of their diet is made up of various insects such as caterpillars and grasshoppers, with cutworms also being a great favorite. The young are fed largely on insects until they are able to forage for themselves. Weed- and insect-conscious farmers should welcome the news that these little, highly useful and cheerful field companions are probably the most numerous birds in the world.

... *Bluebird*

Our birds are on the move again. With that age-old urge for elbow room and other optimums in rearing young, they come from nearby and distant winter homes to swell the roll call daily. Some reach their destination here, while others merely pause en route to nesting grounds at various latitudes to the north. Although the crest of migration here will not be reached until the latter part of May when most of our warblers arrive, the early birds are here already and, if they do not always "get the worm" this early, they will be here to get it when it does arrive.

The males usually come first, all decked out in their springtime best. In the bird world the boys put on the glamour while the girls are content with less bewitching garb. A few days before the arrival of the gentler sex they take possession of territories large enough in their opinion to yield food for their prospective families. Within these areas they will not tolerate the presence of another male of the same species. Proclaiming his rights by song, each adds his own refrain to nature's symphony. The song of birds is as much a part of spring as bursting buds and thunder showers.

Robins, meadow larks, killdeer and song sparrows have all been hailed as harbingers of spring. For some folks there is nothing like the soft friendly contented warble of bluebirds to drive away the last thought of winter. Other birds also have held this distinction in the days before their calls were silenced by extinction.

One spring day in the distant past I was accompanying my dad on an errand out to the fields when he suddenly stopped to listen and search the sky.

"Crane," he said, pointing to where I could faintly see a formation of birds. "I seldom hear them anymore. They used to alight in the field just over that hill each spring — big gray birds, as tall as a man." I have not yet had a good look at a sandhill crane, but hope to eventually, since a remnant of the species still exists.

Local folks less than thirty years old have probably never seen, or even heard, prairie chickens. To those of us who are a little older, and have been awakened on early spring mornings by the booming calls of prairie chicken roosters, it seems cruel to think that we will never hear them again. The area which is now a commercial truck farm south of my farm used to be a favorite spring rendezvous for these birds, which gathered in such concentration as to make the place roar with their courtship calls. A covey of ten birds flushed from a stubble field on our Minnesota farm in the fall of 1920 is the last I have seen of this species. Unable to survive under conditions of intense agricultural development and hunting pressure, they are definitely on the way to complete extinction, although they may still be found in Kansas, Nebraska and, perhaps, even in western Minnesota. With their passing, spring has lost some of its charm.

It is always discouraging for a bird enthusiast to witness the disappearance of one after another of our native species of birds and have to stand by, realizing that there is not much of anything specific one can do to help in a very effective way. It is heartening, under these circumstances, to find a species which will respond to our efforts at rehabilitation. The bluebird is such a species. Most people will agree that the bluebird is a desirable fellow to have around. For his enchanting song, for his beauty and as an economic asset, the bluebird is tops. Although this area is normal bluebird nesting territory these birds have almost been completely driven out by a limitation of nesting sites, brought about by the removal of dead and rotting trees and by competition from introduced species such as English sparrows and starlings. The good book says to cut down and cast into the fire every tree that doesn't bear good fruit. It doesn't say dead trees, however, and I maintain that any tree which harbors a family of birds, even though it be dead, is bearing good fruit.

The Albert Lea Audubon Society constructed and put up more than one hundred bluebird houses in the spring of 1949. The bluebird response has been good and we have many feet of film to prove that they have made themselves at home.

Of these nesting boxes, I have complete data on only the 41 on my own bluebird trail. Eighteen of the 41 were occupied by bluebirds in 1949. Twenty-six were occupied by bluebirds in 1950. That year I saw bluebirds every day from April until late in November. On my way to town, on my way to the fields, everywhere, I could see the flash of sky blue wings. One even perched trustingly on a fuel can out in my hayfield.

In 1951, only two of my houses were occupied. The story of bluebirds in 1951 was much the same everywhere and authorities attributed the disastrous drop in number to the winter weather. The species was not wiped out, however. That isn't nature's way. They will come back and, if we want them as neighbors, all we need do is put up nesting boxes. It's as simple as that.

Building bluebird homes is a rewarding activity for school children with an aptitude for carpentry. The bluebird isn't hard to please, so don't worry if the job isn't perfect. Most of the nesting boxes put up by the members of the Albert Lea Audubon Society were made from scrap pieces of lumber from my old house, and in a grand assortment of colors. Some were made from apple boxes and peach crates. Many were put up unpainted. The bluebirds nested in the drab and gaudy ones alike.

The dimensions for a bluebird house are, roughly, a 4" x 4" inside floor measurement and an 8" or 9" depth, with the roof slanted enough to shed rain. The entrance hole should be 1½" in diameter and 6" above the floor. A perch is not desirable, since they are often used by English sparrows to harass occupants. Some provision should be made for opening the houses for cleaning each spring. To discourage English sparrows, place houses low — about shoulder high. To discourage wrens, place houses in the open, away from trees or shrubbery. Wrens are about as sassy as they come, but they choose to do their sassing from a place where they can quickly dart to safety. If tree swallows or chickadees claim some houses, welcome them and provide a few more houses.

. . . *Sparrow hawk*

April, 1953

One of the early bird arrivals this spring was the sparrow hawk. I saw one on March 25th. At this season, particularly, this bird is often seen perching on telephone poles or electric power lines. Easily recognized by its small size and reddish brown back and tail, this species, being only a little larger than a robin, is the smallest and tamest of our hawks. More properly called American kestrel, it is actually not a hawk at all but belongs to the family of raptores called falcons, which are characterized by large heads, long, pointed, swallow-like wings and long tails. Sparrow hawks were trained and used by many people in the ancient art of falconry, or hawk hunting, although not as extensively as their larger, swifter, fiercer relative, the peregrine falcon, or duck hawk.

Of all the falcons, the sparrow hawk is the most beneficial to man's interests. Although sparrows and other small birds are sometimes taken, the principal food of the sparrow hawk is insects, including grasshoppers, crickets, beetles, caterpillars, flies, ants, etc. During the season when insects are available the sparrow hawk eats little else, although lizards, small snakes and mice are also on its bill of fare. With the keen eyesight common to all raptores, it watches for its prey from a lookout perch on a tall dead tree, telephone pole or electric power line. It also scans open fields for prey by hovering above the ground. Because of this habit it is sometimes called "windhover."

From my tractor seat I once saw three species of hawks catch mice in the same field on the same day. The big buteo, Swainson's hawk, sailed close to the ground and merely reached down with one foot to grasp its victim. The marsh hawk, or harrier, flew slowly a few feet over the ground. When it spotted a mouse, it hovered a moment before lifting its wings up over its back and pouncing down with both feet outstretched to catch the mouse, along with a little grass. It is a capable hunter, but is not as graceful as the buteo. The little kestrel hovered in one spot about 40 feet in the air for several minutes. Then, with falcon grace and speed, it plunged down and picked a fight with the large meadow mouse it had found. Striking with both feet and beak, it finally killed the mouse, which at times fought back by raising itself up and clawing after the little hawk. I got the impression that a meadow mouse is about as big game as a sparrow hawk can handle.

During the summers of 1948 and 1949 a pair of sparrow hawks nested in a dead poplar tree only a few rods west of my house. There was a cavity in the dead tree, about twenty feet above the ground. I often saw the hawks fly into a willow tree nearby and, after a little watching from the tractor seat, I discovered their home. While they nested here they were a familiar sight about our farmstead as one or the other or both perched in a tree on our lawn, on the high line or the telephone wire. Every day, they hunted in my fields and seemed quite unafraid. The male bird (easily recognized by the bluish upper wing surface) was the first to arrive in the spring. It appeared lonesome and quiet for a few days as it perched about the farmstead. When the rusty-backed female came, the male bird found its voice. Its courtship display was spectacular and, since it occurred right on our farmstead, I had plenty of opportunity to observe it. It consisted of a series of high speed perpendicular dives, after which the bird would glide expertly to where its mate was perched. Hearing the rapidly-repeated, high-pitched "Klee klee klee klee," I could easily locate the little hawk about 150 feet in the air. After plunging to within a few feet of the ground with a speed that might dash it to death, it turned and sped upward to its original height, only to half close its wings in another falcon power dive. Six or seven of these dives — each punctuated with the loud, clear, staccato cries — would take the bird across my yard — a horizontal distance of about 30 rods.

The destructive windstorm in the early spring of 1950 blew down the dead poplar in which the sparrow hawks had nested. Expecting the birds to return and find their home gone, I made a nesting box of sparrow hawk size. While this birdhouse was being prepared for exhibit at the Audubon Society booth at our local hobby show the sparrow hawks returned. For a while they considered nesting in a hollow branch of an oak tree on our lawn about one hundred feet from our house. This branch was broken off about ten feet out from the trunk. The center was rotted out, leaving a hole large enough for a squirrel to get into. With amazing speed and accuracy, the sparrow hawks flew and disappeared into this small opening. The branch was small and the little hawks must have gone far into it before they could find room to turn around. They seemed quite excited about their new location for a while, but finally decided not to nest there. They had no way of knowing that they had an intended new home on which the hobby show had a priority, so they left. I put the bird house in our basement and considered the venture a failure. In 1951 the hawks returned. But their home was again promised to the hobby show booth. In the spring of 1952 I saw a male sparrow hawk perched on the telephone wire one day, so I hurried to put up the house, but the bird never returned to see it, and a pair of sassy starlings immediately set up housekeeping there. I am still hoping for sparrow hawk tenants and am wondering what the starlings will do if this happens. I miss my hawks. Sparrow hawks make excellent pets. But a license is needed to keep one in captivity since they are protected by law in many states, including Minnesota.

Captive hawks are not serving the purpose for which they were intended in the balance of nature. When, in complete freedom, they come to live near enough to us so we can observe them in their daily activities, they are the most enjoyable.

... *Hazards faced by field-nesting birds*

May, 1953

As a farmer goes about his seasonal field work, most of the implements he uses constitute a hazard for field-nesting birds. With the exception of the pasture, all fields are thoroughly gone over by at least one — and usually several — farm machines. If these field operations come at a time when ground-nesting birds are hatching eggs or rearing helpless young, the nest and its contents — and sometimes the parent bird — are usually unavoidably destroyed. Any attempt by the farmer to spare the nest usually results in merely making its location so conspicuous that it quickly falls prey to any predator that happens along.

The mower takes a heavy toll of field-nesting birds because it must be used during the hatching season. The rapidly moving sickle travels close to the ground and under dense hay growth, where it cannot be seen. It covers every square inch of the field, so it is hard to imagine any bird nest escaping destruction.

Several species of birds nest in a tall grass habitat. In my experience these have included: grasshopper sparrows, dick-cissels, bobolinks, mallard ducks, ring-necked pheasants and marsh hawks. Of these, the ring-necked pheasant is perhaps the most frequent victim — certainly the most publicized one. Hen pheasants often make their nests in alfalfa and clover fields, which are ready to cut for hay before the pheasant eggs hatch. To make matters worse, the setting bird will not flush until the sickle actually strikes her, with the result that she is either killed on the spot or flies away minus one or, more often, both legs. Hence, not only the nest, but also the bird, is lost. Fortunately, pheasants nest in many other locations, such as fencerows, roadsides, woods, and even within a few rods of my house, where the mower does not harm them.

Less well known is the fate of young bobolinks. Leaving their nests before they are able to fly, they flutter about and cling to the standing hay, where they may be seen, where the parent birds feed them and where they learn to find food for themselves. Since they shun cut hay like a fish does dry land, they move inward in the field as the mowing progresses and concentrate in the last swaths of hay to be cut. With no more standing hay to escape into, they seek refuge on the ground, where they are right in the path of the sickle. If I have destroyed any nests of dickcissels or grasshopper sparrows, it has gone unnoticed. Apparently, the young are mature enough by mowing time to escape destruction. One mallard duck nest was ruined by my mower, but the duck flew long before the mower sickle destroyed the nest.

In 1948, a pair of marsh hawks nested in my alfalfa field and, of all places, on the highest hill. Because I was very busy with building a new house that summer, I hired my neighbor to cut my hay with his tractor mower. The mother hawk flushed in time to escape the sickle, which was quickly lifted to leave about 8" of stubble where the nest was located, thus sparing the lives of the four young hawks. Here, I thought, would be an interesting study. Would the parent hawks succeed in rearing their brood in the changed habitat? When I raked hay two days later I found the nest empty and thought some predator had taken the young hawks. The parent birds flew over the area several times a day at first and continued returning for about two weeks. Then one day I learned that my neighbor's hired man, upon hearing about the young hawks, had kidnapped them and put them in a rabbit hutch, where they were fed bacon rinds and pieces of pork and beef trimmings. They all died. At this late hour I was asked what food young hawks must have to survive. With indignation, I replied, "Do what the parent hawks would have done. Feed them their own weight in freshly killed mice every day." Perhaps I upped their ration some, but I hope the lesson sank in. Man is, indeed, the greatest predator.

Fortunately, most plowing is done either in the fall, when no birds are nesting, or early in the spring, before nesting has started. Quite often, however, some field or portion of a field is left to plow late in the spring, either because it is too wet to plow early or because other work has been more pressing. Many birds are lost by late spring plowing. Meadow larks, killdeer, vesper sparrows, Brewer's blackbirds, pheasants, blue-winged teal and upland plovers have all been in the path of my plow. With considerable effort, I once spared the nest of a blue-winged teal, only to find the next morning that some predator had devoured, not only the eleven eggs, but the duck as well. All meadow lark nests I have spared have met a similar fate.

The upland plovers nesting in my rye field in 1948 fared better. The eggs hatched five days after I had plowed the field around the nest, and the young left before I was ready to plant the field to soybeans. I have several still pictures and about 50 feet of film to record this event.

The grain binder also finds birds in its path. Occasionally, a red-winged blackbird will fasten its nest to a tall strong weed in a grain field, or a goldfinch will nest in a thistle patch. Hen pheasants with little chicks are often found along the edge of standing grain, where they can choose between ducking into the grain, out of sight, or coming into the stubble, where they can see better. Very small chicks seem confused by the noise and are endangered by the wheels of the binder and the tractor. A little care will give them a chance to get out of the way. They are not hard to see, as stubble is not much cover when viewed from overhead. On one occasion, a chick was making satisfactory progress toward the grain when, in a flash, it darted under the oncoming tractor tire, which mashed it before I could pull the clutch.

The corn cultivator finds the killdeer and its neighbor, the vesper sparrow, nesting in its path. If the corn has emerged before nesting time, however, both these birds will build their nest close to a hill of corn so that, in sparing the corn hill, the bird nest will also be spared. In late planted corn the killdeer gets into trouble, for then the disc, the spike tooth harrow, the corn planter and again the harrow must all go over the field before there is a respite. Fortunately, the killdeer's behavior makes the location of its nest easy. Its screams of distress are loud enough to be heard above the noise of any tractor.

It is good farm practice to delay the harrowing a few days after the corn is planted to give the weed seeds a chance to sprout. The harrowing then serves as a thorough cultivation. The killdeer often builds a nest in the field during this weed-sprouting intermission. Last year my wife was harrowing a cornfield while I was preparing a nearby field for soybeans. When she stopped the tractor and went back to the harrow I hurried over to see what the trouble was. She was trying to get past a killdeer's nest without breaking any eggs. The killdeer is a valuable farm bird. Sparing its nest is often a successful venture, and well worth the time and trouble it may involve.

One wouldn't expect the corn picker to endanger any nesting birds, but I have seen this happen too. The heavy snow on the first of December in 1950 caught me with twenty acres of corn yet unhusked. This corn was not picked until late May the following spring. By this time there was considerable weed growth, and pheasants, killdeer, Brewer's blackbirds and red-winged blackbirds were all nesting there. The wide wheels of the corn picker, the tractor and the corn wagons did a thorough job of mashing the nests and, since the field was later plowed, the destruction was complete. Once, I stopped to fix a broken chain and almost put my knee in the nest of a Brewer's blackbird. A colony of red-winged blackbirds nested in another part of the field. They fastened their nests to the corn stalks where the corn ear was attached. This is the only time I have seen red-winged blackbird nests, still containing the blue eggs, going up the elevator of a corn picker.

Husking corn with a machine in May is pleasant but, for the sake of the birds, I wouldn't recommend it.

... The swallows

June, 1953

Most people recognize a swallow when they see one, even though they may not know its particular species. All of our swallows have enough features in common to set them apart distinctly from any other group of songbirds. They all have short flat, triangular bills, wide flattened heads, large froglike mouths, very short legs and tiny feet. Their wings are proportionately so large that, when folded, the tips cross and extend to, or beyond, the tip of the tail. The plumage of swallows usually has luster, especially in the upper parts. Who hasn't seen the dark glossy teal-blue of the barn swallow and the iridescent, metallic greenish-blue of the tree swallow? Perhaps the most colorful of them all is the violet-green swallow of the west. Swallows are birds of the air. Their food is almost exclusively insects, which they capture and eat while in flight. When insects are numerous, swallows fly almost continuously during daylight, eating flies, mosquitoes, midges, gnats and moths until their stomachs and gullets are crammed full. If continuous cold rains keep flying insects down, many swallows and young starve to death. If the food is not in the air the swallows do not get it. They even drink while in flight by skimming close to the water surface and dipping down to scoop up mouthfuls to drink. While thus engaged, they are in danger from large fish, which sometimes leap from the water to take them. As nature turns the tables, we have fish eating birds rather than birds eating fish.

Most birds migrate at high speed during the night and stop to feed during the day. Swallows migrate leisurely during the day and gather in large concentrations to roost in marshes or trees at night.

Most swallows nest in colonies, with the cliff swallow being the most communal and the tree swallow the least. Although the various species of swallows are similar in general appearance and food habits, they certainly differ in nesting habits. Of the six species common in this territory, two of them — the barn swallow and the cliff swallow — build nests of mud. Two others — the purple martin and the tree swallow — nest in tree cavities or man-made bird boxes. The remaining two — the bank swallow and the rough-winged swallow — excavate horizontal burrows in sand or clay banks. I have never chanced to see the nesting site of rough-winged swallows but have seen several places where bank swallows nested. Sand pits are often used. Even the pile of sand which the Highway Department had at the junction of Highways 16 and 69 west of Albert Lea was used by a colony of bank swallows one summer.

Rough-winged swallows and bank swallows look very much alike, both being brown above and white below. The throat of the rough-winged is brownish, shading gradually into the white of the belly, while the bank swallow has a distinct brown band across its breast, separating the clear white throat from the white belly. The rough-winged gets its name from a series of stiff bristles along the outer wing feathers. These can easily be felt when handling the bird.

The cliff swallow is easily distinguished from other swallows by its buff colored rump. Cliff swallows tend to concentrate in occasional large colonies, leaving large areas where they are not seen. Near Madison, Wisconsin, lives a farmer who is host each summer to such a colony of cliff swallows. The birds started nesting under the eaves of his barn many years ago, and he has encouraged their increase by fastening onto the outside of his barn wall an ever-increasing number of cleats to which the swallows can conveniently attach their gourd-shaped mud nests. The colony has grown to the immense size of thousands of birds. The presence of so many swallows flying about a single farmstead like bees around a hive is an amazing sight and people from all over the country come to see them. When Howard Cleaves, wildlife photographer and recently our screen tour film speaker, visited the place, a lady in the visiting group asked the farmer if his swallows stayed all winter. In astonishment, the farmer replied, "Lady! These are bug birds!"

Anyone who has ever lived on an American farm is familiar with the barn swallow. No other bird has so completely accepted the advantages of living with civilized man. Originally, it built its nest in natural caves or under protruding cliff ledges. But now it builds under bridges, in barns or in any building where it can fly in and out freely. This is perhaps the most abundant, and certainly the most evenly distributed, of our swallows. Living as it does on farmsteads, it is particularly valuable as a destroyer of flies, mosquitoes, moths and other insect pests of man and livestock. Swift and graceful in flight, it displays its deeply forked tail when making quick turns in catching insects or dive bombing the cats.

One of the first big problems with which the National Audubon Society had to deal was putting a stop to the shooting of barn swallows to be used as adornment for women's hats.

The purple martin is the largest of our swallows, measuring about 8 inches as compared with 5½ inches for the bank swallow and the rough-winged and 7 inches for the barn swallow, including its long fancy tail. The martin is as much a city bird as the barn swallow is a country bird because more city people have put up nesting houses for it. Albert Lea has many martin houses, near which the birds announce their arrival with loud friendly chatter. The practice of putting up martin houses is not new. American Indians, and later southern Negroes, used to hang hollowed gourds to trees or poles to attract these birds. The modern practice is to put up houses with several compartments. Some of these are elaborate affairs. However, a simple house containing a dozen or more compartments is all that is necessary. It should be placed on a pole about 16 feet high. A colony of martins adds life to any home.

The tree swallow, sometimes called white-bellied swallow, is the hardiest of our swallows. It is the first to arrive in the spring and the last to leave us in the fall. It is not as totally dependent on an insect diet as are other swallows. It can, if necessary, subsist on berries and weed seeds. It is the only one of our swallows that spends the winter within the United States. Many winter further south. But great numbers winter along the Gulf coast, where they concentrate to roost in marshes at night and scatter for feeding during the day.

Tree swallows are easily attracted by putting up nesting boxes. They have become much more numerous locally since members of the Albert Lea Audubon Society put up bluebird houses. In fact, our bluebird trails are rapidly becoming tree swallow trails. Of all our swallows, the tree swallow is the most belligerent — especially at nesting time. The other day I heard tree swallows chattering excitedly, then saw two of them harassing a Cooper's hawk, which darted into my woods for shelter from his pursuers.

Tree swallows rank next to barn swallows in usefulness. Skimming low over the fields catching insects all day, they render the farmer valuable service. As a group, swallows enjoy a good reputation.

While birding on a farm near Bear Lake on May 24th, members of the Albert Lea Audubon Society saw, among the 63 species listed, all six species of swallows. The martins flew over the tree tops while all the other species flew over the water and along the shore. The bank swallows, and especially the rough-wings, sometimes startled us as they shot past, two or three feet from our faces.

... *House wren*

The first house wren I ever saw was perched momentarily on the hog lot fence near our stock watering tank one day back in my pre-school years, when Mother and I were at the well after a pail of water. Mother was interested in birds and, although she had nothing as fancy as a bird bath, she accomplished the same purpose by insisting that a piece of board be kept floating in the cow tank so that, whether the water was high or low, the birds could perch on this board to get a drink or take a bath without the danger of falling into the water and drowning. Although this board was used mainly by English sparrows, of which nuisance we had thousands, at various times most of the twenty or more species of birds nesting in our windbreak or about our farmstead could be seen there. I remember my keen disappointment in noting that the wren's tail was not pointing upward. When I first saw it, its tail pointed almost straight downward. When I voiced my disappointment, Mother had a good laugh because she knew I was thinking of the bed-time story about the contest between the birds to see which could fly the highest. The wren was victorious but, in achieving the honor, the little bird overexerted itself, became dizzy and tumbled earthward, striking the ground tail first. And that, according to the story, is why the wren's tail always sticks straight up.

Having made the acquaintance of the house wren, I naturally wanted to make him welcome, so he would stay. I wanted to build a house and put him into it.

"You needn't put him into it," prompted Mother. "Just put up a house, and it need not be fancy. An old shoe will do, and he will find it no matter how well you hide it." A discarded shoe was found and, with the help of an older brother, nailed up in a box elder tree. It was the home of a family of wrens that summer and, at that tender age, I was confident that the head of that household was the same wren that I had seen on the hog lot fence.

Since that distant day I have been well aware of the presence of wrens in our dooryard every summer. One can hardly help noticing them. The house wren has largely left his former woodland habitat to nest near our homes. Despite its small size and drab plumage, the wren is just as well known as the robin, for what it lacks in size and color it more than makes up for in voice and activity. Its rapid-fire, melodious chatter rivals the springtime song of the celebrated bobolink. No bird can scold more emphatically than the little spitfire we call "Jenny wren."

In defense of its territory the wren is bold and belligerent, often driving away other and larger species by harassing them, and sometimes even puncturing their eggs. The bluebird house in my yard was, of course, taken over promptly by English sparrows. They were well established when a pair of wrens decided to take over. And take over they did! Both of these species are aggressive and energetic, so the battle was worth watching. Courtship and war went on at the same time. For a time, both sparrows and wrens entered and left the house. In went a wren and out came a sparrow. Perched in the entrance, the wren poured out his lingo. Then both wrens chased the sparrows into a roll of woven wire nearby. With tails cocked forward over their backs they scolded the sparrows soundly, then went back to courting again. Whenever a sparrow saw a chance it flew back to the nesting box and the battle was on again. When the sparrows finally gave up their claim the wrens went to work in earnest. Out came feathers and straw and in went sticks, amid much chatter and fidgeting. Two broods were successfully reared.

Wrens are enthusiastic nest builders. They are well known for the many odd locations they place their nests. I have found them in the twine box of the binder, in a nail pail on a shelf, in an old roll of corn planter wire hanging in the shed, in the pocket of a discarded coat, in the clothes pin bag, in a tubular steel post and in an endless variety of other cozy nooks. When he arrives in late April, in advance of his mate, the male wren builds a number of cock nests. When his spouse arrives and decides on one of these locations she throws out all the sticks and together they build a new nest to her satisfaction.

Since the advent of bird banding for identification it has been found that the home life of some house wrens is scandalous, as judged by our moral standards. The male wren is somewhat of a philanderer, taking up with any female that catches his eye. The female, not to be left with the whole job of rearing her brood, proceeds to induce another male to help her with the job, and another female is left a grass widow.

On the whole, the wren is usually a good citizen and is diligent in his search for insects to satisfy his own hunger and that of his numerous youngsters. The food consists almost entirely of insects. When brood rearing is over in late August most of the wrens leave our dooryards for the woods.

There are more than 250 species of wrens throughout the world. They are most numerous in tropical America. Within the borders of the United States there are over twenty species and subspecies, including many with interesting habits. Best known, however, is our house wren, which has eastern and western representatives.

... *Song sparrows*

August, 1953

Quite often, the first bird song I hear in the morning is the clear cheerful whistle of the male song sparrow. Ever since the first days of April two of these birds have been singing incessantly from their respective territories about our farmstead. One sings from the lilac bush just outside our door, from a post near our woodshed or from the oak tree near the cowyard. The other sings from several favorite perches about the hoglot and the bordering roadside. The songs of these two birds are not exactly alike. In fact, both have a number of tunes to choose from. But all their songs are similar enough to be recognized as coming from a song sparrow. Bird songs are not easily described in writing. Some have interpreted the song sparrow as saying, "Hip, hip, hooray, boys! Spring is here." The song sparrow is well named. Even its scientific name is *Melospiza melodia*. It sings in all kinds of weather throughout its long stay. I have even heard it sing after dark.

Because of its persistent singing (usually from a conspicuous perch) and its moderately confiding nature, this hardy little minstrel is probably the best known of our many species of native sparrows. Although beginners may confuse it with other sparrows, it can readily be identified by the heavy dark streaks on its under parts. These streaks run together in a large central spot on the breast. The song sparrow also has a characteristic habit of pumping its long tail up and down as it flies. Primarily a bird of the fence rows and open brushy countryside, it often chooses to nest near our homes and, particularly, in or near gardens. Perhaps the worms there are bigger, juicier and more numerous.

The presence of these two singing males near our home means that there are two nesting pairs. Somewhere among the shrubs and weeds there are two nests and two brooding females, each zealously guarded by the male bird, whose only lease on its territory is its song. Song sparrows build their nests on the ground, in shrubbery or in low trees. These, like so many bird nests, are hard to find when vegetation is lush. Some years ago I tried several times to locate a song sparrow's nest which I knew was near our house. After frost had dropped the leaves I found the nest fastened to a sweet clover plant scarcely ten feet from our lilac bush. The nests are built of grass and weed stalks and lined with finer material. The three to seven bluish-gray and brown spotted eggs are incubated mainly by the female and hatch in about twelve days. The young leave the nest in seven to fourteen days, depending upon the abundance of their food supply. At first, unable to fly, they make their way about crawling through the grass. As soon as they are able to fly the mother bird starts laying eggs for a second brood while the male cares for the first young. This he does faithfully until the second brood hatches. He then leaves them to their own resources while he pitches in to help his spouse feed the newly hatched brood. Thus three, sometimes four, broods are reared in one season. That's industry for you! And yet there are those who think that birds do not have to work for a living.

Song sparrows are devoted parents, defending their young valiantly, often against enemies larger than themselves. Their effort is useless against snakes or cats. But they put up a defiant stand, nevertheless. Snakes and cats take a heavy toll of ground-nesting birds. There is no tastier morsel in a snake's diet than a newly hatched bird. This may be one of the reasons that so many ground nesting birds seek nesting sites in the far north, where there are no snakes. Domestic cats each take several dozen birds a year. Fortunately, song sparrows are blessed with enough offspring to maintain their numbers, despite the heavy loss.

Although the song sparrow's diet is two-thirds vegetable matter, most of this is weed seeds, with very little, if any, grain. During the summer months the diet runs heavily to insects and insect larvae. Young birds require a lot of food for their rapid growth — up to three times their own weight every day. Nestlings have no other source of water than that contained in insects and, especially, insect larvae, which are often 90% or more water. Since insect larvae are so fond of eating the tender young growing parts of plants, the young birds are likewise assured of the required nutrients, vitamins and all.

Represented by several geographical races, the song sparrow inhabits virtually all of North America at some time during the year. The race common to our territory is the eastern song sparrow.

Last spring, in late March, I saw three sparrows perched in an oak tree in my yard. There was nothing unusual about this, except that each bird belonged to a different species. The English sparrow soon gave away his identity by flying to the hay loft door. One of the others was a tree sparrow, whistling sweetly to attract a mate preparatory to taking off for the far northern tundra. The third bird was our friend, the song sparrow, newly arrived from its winter home farther south. It presently darted into a weedy fence row near the cow yard. It may have been the same bird that has been claiming this territory all summer and has been generous enough to tolerate its neighboring pair near the hog lot.

. . . Black-billed cuckoo

September, 1953

On August 17th I had the pleasant experience of seeing my first black-billed cuckoo's nest. Taking a short cut through our windbreak on a quick errand to the hayfield, I was making my way through shoulder high goldenrods about ten rods from our house when, suddenly, a black-billed cuckoo darted from an elderberry bush which stood directly in my path. The bird flew about nervously among the lower tree branches and weeds only a few feet away and uttered a peculiar muffled call. In the elderberry bush at about eye level was the nest — a crude platform of sticks with a little finer material, and only a little more substantially built than the nest of a mourning dove. The two young occupants were bristling with pin feathers and were almost coal black. I did not see the nest again until a week later when the young had already left. So rapid is the development of young birds.

Cuckoos — so called because of their peculiar song — are slender long-tailed birds, slightly larger than a brown thrasher. They are brownish-gray above and white below, with rather long curved beaks. Two species are native to this region — the black-billed and the yellow-billed. The yellow-billed is more common locally. Both species are similar in voice and general appearance. The yellow-billed can be distinguished by its yellow lower mandible, the large white spots on the under side of its tail feathers and the reddish wing primaries.

These calm, graceful birds slip quietly and rather shyly from tree to tree, generally keeping under the protection of the leaves. While perching motionless their plumage blends well with the surrounding leaves and shadows, and the birds are seldom seen.

Most birds avoid eating hairy or spiny caterpillars because their hairs are often stiff and so sharp at the end that they pierce the lining of a bird's stomach and become fastened there. This is unfortunate because many of our most tree-destructive insects are in this group, including tent caterpillars, cankerworms, fall webworms, tussock moths, gypsy moths and a great many others. Fortunately, the Creator has provided specialized birds —the cuckoos—to help in this situation.

Caterpillar hairs and spines also pierce the lining of the cuckoo's stomach so that, in time, it becomes so felted with a mass of hair and spines that digestion is obstructed. When this happens the cuckoo sheds its entire stomach lining, having meanwhile grown a new one so that it can go merrily on eating hairy caterpillars. Cuckoos not only eat hairy caterpillars but prefer them and destroy incredible numbers of them. Often one bird will eat a whole colony of tent caterpillars at a single meal.

There has been a great influx of cuckoos in northern Minnesota and adjoining regions following the outbreak of tent caterpillar infestation there, indicating that nature is taking its course in the control of this pest. At the Audubon Nature Center of Connecticut near Greenwich, Connecticut, where it was my good fortune to spend a week this fall as a guest of the National Audubon Society, I found cuckoos quite numerous and learned that the reason for their abundance was an outbreak of gypsy moths in the New England states. Not only do cuckoos concentrate wherever caterpillar outbreaks occur, but they hatch larger broods there and stay much later in the fall than usual before migrating to their winter home in South America.

The European cuckoo is entirely parasitic. Like our cowbird it always lays its eggs in other birds' nests. Our black-billed cuckoo does so only occasionally. Sometimes the egg of a black-billed cuckoo will be found in a yellow-bill's nest and vice versa. But usually both our cuckoos are self-respecting birds who build their own nests and rear their own broods.

Several of our birds are subjects of superstitions. The cuckoo somehow has acquired the name "rain crow" because of the belief that its loud throaty guttural call, "kuk kuk kuk kuk" or "cow cow cow cow," is an indication of rain. This is purely superstition. Enhanced, no doubt, by the shy, elusive and mysterious habits of this woodland recluse.

The range of the black-billed cuckoo extends farther north in both its summer and winter homes than that of the yellow-billed relative.

In Minnesota, the cuckoos arrive in May when the trees are fully leaved and remain until late July if caterpillars are scarce or until October if caterpillars are numerous. Even so, I wonder how those two young black-bills — so helpless on August 17th — will be able to find their way and endure the long trip to South America this fall.

Even though many people may fail to see these shy birds, they may take assurance of its presence should their walnut or apple trees take on the webby adornment of tent caterpillars or fall webworms. Cuckoos are highly useful birds protected by law and should be welcomed and encouraged by a bit of brushy woods where they may nest.

. . . *The hawks*

After a ten year lapse we again have red-tailed hawk neighbors. A pair of them nested and successfully reared a brood in
our ten acre woods this summer. The new tenants are much
more wary than the pair that nested here for fourteen consecutive years prior to 1943. I have missed these aerial mousers
that watched my fields so closely while tillage implements were
in operation and habitually came to within five or six rods of the
tractor to catch mice which the machinery disturbed. The
disappearance of the old faithful pair of hawks may have been
caused by the death of one of them, but I have felt that I was to
blame because I thoughtlessly sold some dead trees for firewood,
including the hawks' favorite lookout perch.

Red-tailed hawks generally return to nest in the same locality
year after year, often using the same nest. I hope that my new
tenants will do this and that I may win their confidence. Despite
their caution, I notice that they are about their beneficial
business. From my tractor I can see them catching mice at a
distance.

As I was plowing a field of alfalfa sod last spring the plow
opened a pocket gopher's burrow. These rodents insist on a dark
runway and promptly plug any opening which permits daylight
to enter. In this way they avoid such enemies as the weasel and
live a relatively safe and sheltered existence, especially since
man has so thoroughly eliminated their worst enemy — the
badger. The next time around the field the plow opened the
runway again and the pocket gopher again plugged it. This
continued for several rounds until the gopher, apparently annoyed by the persistent disturbance, made the grave mistake of

coming to the surface to investigate. He failed to notice my keen-eyed friend keeping a close watch from his perch in the woods. "Red-tail" took off, sailed low over the field, picked up the pocket gopher and carried it to the top of a highiine pole where he enjoyed a good meal.

Those who have had any experience mowing hay have no love for the pocket gopher. These disgusting rodents delight in making runways in alfalfa and clover fields. Starting at the edge of the field they dig toward the center, pushing up a mound of loose dirt every three or four feet. These mounds do the mower sickle no good as it cuts through them. If they are moist, as they usually are at haying time, the dirt sticks between the mower guards, causing the mower bar to push the standing hay forward, flattening it to the ground without having been cut. Since these runways may be many rods long, one gopher's work may necessitate several dozen stops to clean out the mower bar. I have cleaned the mower bar countless numbers of times, so I cheered as the hawk caught the pocket gopher.

All but three species of hawks are protected by Minnesota state law. All species should be protected, because most people are unable to distinguish the various species. Many of our most valuable hawks are shot by unscrupulous gunners because of their habit of perching in a conspicuous place. The greatest slaughter of hawks occurs where they may be seen in concentrated flight.

In migration, hawks like to glide on thermals, or upward currents of air. These air currents may be brought about as the wind strikes a mountain side and is turned upward. When the wind strikes the dense cool air over a large body of water it will likewise be turned upward.

Concentrated hawk flights occur at many points throughout the United States during the migration season. Perhaps the most celebrated of these is that at Hawk Mountain in Pennsylvania. This place is not readily accessible. But from this mountain top, when the wind is just right, one may see hundreds of hawks at the same time as the great flocks of buteos circle past. The daily count of hawks may run into the thousands. Another point is at Cape May. Hawks funneling down to the southern tip of New Jersey find themselves confronted with the Atlantic Ocean and the wide expanse of Delaware Bay, so they turn back to follow the coast to where the bay narrows.

I have often longed to be at one of these places at the right time to witness a mass flight. Although I have seen most of the eastern species of hawks at various times at home, I had never seen more than fifty at one time until September. Then a letter from a member of the Minnesota Ornithologists Union informed me that I was on the policy committee of that organization and that a special meeting was being held at Duluth on the 19th, which was one of the days scheduled for a hawk count. Here was an opportunity (or shall I say an excuse) for leaving my farm work for a day to watch a mass hawk flight together with other bird watchers.

The north shore of Lake Superior slants southwestward for approximately 300 miles from Nipigon, Ontario, to Duluth. Hawks that have spent the summer in woods and on prairies to the north encounter the lake in their southward migration. Rather than cross the lake, they follow the shore, which is paralleled by the Sawtooth Mountains, and glide on the upward air currents. The greatest concentration occurs at Duluth where, at last, they reach the point of the lake and fan out again in their southward flight. With binoculars and recording sheets, we watched from the skyline boulevard near 45th Avenue East overlooking the lake. At 8 o' clock only four of us were there. By noon there were 112 people watching. The hawk count was disappointing to experienced watchers. For me, it was wonderful. We counted 597 hawks. Last year, 5,646 were counted on one day. The total of 597 included 240 sharp-shinned, 27 Cooper's, 6 red-tailed, 177 broad-winged, 74 marsh hawks, 8 ospreys, 9 sparrow hawks, 4 pigeon hawks, 1 turkey vulture, 1 goshawk, 1 duck hawk and 49 which were seen at too great a distance to positively identify. We saw one mass circular flight of about 100 broad-wings. To see these hawks glide by at close range, often not over forty feet overhead, or skirting the bluff so we could look down on their backs, was an exciting and rewarding experience. It is encouraging also to know that the slaughter of hawks which took place at Duluth until three years ago has almost completely stopped through the efforts of the Duluth Bird Club, with the cooperation of the Duluth Chamber of Commerce. A similar complete change of attitude has occurred at Pennsylvania's Hawk Mountain, which has become a hawk sanctuary through the efforts of the naturalist and author Maurice Broun.

... *Snow bunting,*
Lapland longspur

November, 1953

On November 10th, I saw two dozen snowflakes. Not the conventional kind, but very special feathered ones from the arctic. I was surprised, to say the least, at seeing snow buntings (or snowflakes, as they are sometimes called) in this pleasant weather. In this region these harbingers of winter are generally accompanied by severe winter weather, bleak fields and drifting snow. There could be no mistaking their identity, however, for no other bird of this size has so much white in its plumage. In flight, these sparrow-sized birds show large conspicuous white wing patches. When overhead, the whole bird looks almost entirely white.

The small flock wheeled about in close formation and alit among the cornstalks a few rods away, reminding me that I must finish my corn picking before the arrival of more appropriate snow bunting weather. Only once before had I seen snow buntings, and then at quite a distance. So, burning with curiosity, I walked stealthily over to get a better look at my arctic visitors. They were not too shy. I walked until it seemed I must be right among them. They were remarkably well hidden as they perched motionless on the ground. Finally, I saw one bird at close range. It quickly took refuge and peek-a-booed at me from behind a cornstalk. Its plumage was quite brown. At a glance, it might have been mistaken for a large sparrow. It seemed strange that this brownish bird was one of those that had flown overhead a moment before. When I stepped closer, the harsh alarm call, "beez" or "bzzt," was sounded, and the little flock took flight, again displaying the white underplumage.

Snow buntings nest on the arctic tundra around the world. Explorers have found them on polar islands as far north as land extends. While there, they and their young subsist on the teeming insect life which is present during the short summer in the land of the musk-ox and the blue fox. During the winter snow buntings eat the seeds of weeds and grasses that protrude above the snow. As deep snow and ice covers the ground (and their food supply) the birds migrate southward.

Many birds of this species feed along the seashore and work southward with the advance of winter. In the interior United States they feed mostly in open fields, where they are seldom seen by most people. In flocks numbering from a dozen or so to several hundred, these hardy birds spend the night on the ground in the open.

During market hunting days snow buntings were shot by countless thousands and sold to epicures. This slaughter has now largely been stopped, but the birds are slow in recovering their former abundance. They are still killed and eaten by the Eskimos. Snow buntings add life to the bleak winter landscape. They are useful birds, even when judged from the standpoint of man's selfish interests.

Mingled with the flocks of snow buntings and horned larks on the midwest plains, and often outnumbering them, one may often find birds of another arctic ground-loving species, the Lapland longspur. While plowing during the last week of October this fall it was my good fortune to see a flock of Lapland longspurs which I estimated at more than 400 birds.

They were attracted to the plowed field, where their plumage matched their background so well that I could not see any of the birds as they perched. Yet, they kept taking flight continually as the tractor approached. In true lark fashion, they kept returning to the same spot in the field, only to be routed again as the tractor made another round. As they flew overhead, I noticed the under-tail pattern of black with narrow white edges. One bird, for some reason, flew only a few feet and then perched again, thus calling my attention to his exact location. I saw, plainly, the two wing bars, the dark streaks across the upper breast and a hint of rust on the neck. Without a doubt, the birds were Lapland longspurs in winter plumage.

Like the snow bunting, the Lapland longspur nests in the arctic around the world, although its summer home does not extend as far north as that of the snow bunting. The winter home of the Lapland longspur in this country is in the Mississippi Valley, where it may congregate in flocks numbering millions of birds.

This species was the one involved in the great bird disaster which occurred in southwestern Minnesota during the night of March 13, 1904. In this tragedy, an estimated five million Lapland longspurs died within a 30 mile radius of Worthington. A vast flock of migrating longspurs flew for hours into a storm of heavy wet snow. At last, utterly exhausted, they plunged to the ground where they were found dead the next morning.

It is heartening to observe that, despite such destruction through a prank of nature, there are still great flocks of longspurs to greet us when winter is near.

... *Golden-crowned kinglet*

December, 1953

The juniper tree growing near our house is host during the course of the year to a great many different kinds of birds. Some come in search of food. The fruit of the juniper is relished by more than fifty species. Like other trees, it harbors many insect pests which provide food for additional birds. Several species have found nesting sites among its profusion of branches. The dense foliage makes the tree an ideal place for roosting, especially during cold, windy winter nights when anything from pheasants to juncos may be found there. The tree rates high also as just plain cover — a place to dart into for safety. There is nothing special about this particular evergreen tree, except that it grows near my den window, from which, at such times as I have opportunity to be there, I have a ringside seat for all that goes on in the old juniper.

As I glanced up from my newspaper the other day, I saw two of those sprightly little tiny mites of the bird world — eastern golden-crowned kinglets — giving our juniper the once over. Kinglets are smaller than any of our warblers. They are noticeably short tailed. Their length from point of beak to tip of tail varies from 3½ inches to slightly over 4 inches. Only the hummingbird is smaller than the kinglets. They are nervous, active birds as they hop about in continuous search of food. They have the habit of frequently flipping their wings, which never quite seem tightly folded. At times, they hover like hummingbirds as they inspect the tip of a branch. Their nimbleness makes even the agility of the chickadees seem clumsy.

The plumage of golden-crowned kinglets is olive-gray above

and light colored below, with two pale wing bars. The most distinctive marking, however, is the conspicuous, bright yellow crown-patch edged with black. When excited, the male shows a bright orange center stripe in his otherwise yellow crown. The species is certainly well named. Young birds acquire their golden crowns in their first winter plumage, so any kinglets seen in this area without a crown-patch undoubtedly belong to another species — the ruby-crowned kinglet. The female of this species has no crown-patch and the male shows his ruby crown only when startled or in courtship display. Ruby-crowns and golden-crowns may both be seen here during the spring migration but, since all ruby-crowns have by this time departed southward, the only kinglets to be seen in this area during the winter are the golden-crowned. Most of these migrate, but they are hardy little birds and some of them remain to spend the winter almost as far north as their nesting territory extends. They nest in the northern tier of states from Minnesota eastward and in the southern Canadian provinces, including Newfoundland.

They spend the summer in the evergreen forests where they feed mainly on small flying insects, many of which they catch on the wing. Small grasshoppers, bark beetles, leafhoppers, injurious moths, aphids, weevils, caterpillars and a host of other small tree pests are included in their summer diet. During the winter months, when food is harder to find, golden-crowned kinglets wander about in groups of their own species or in company with chickadees, nuthatches and other winter woodland birds, with which they seem always on good terms. Their food search then usually extends to deciduous trees, shrubbery, weeds and even the ground. They subsist through the frozen months largely on scale insects and the eggs hidden in the crevices of the bark on the smaller twigs of trees and shrubs. As far as is known, golden-crowned kinglets eat no vegetable food but subsist throughout the year entirely on insects, insect eggs, insect larvae and other minute animal life, which characteristic makes them very valuable creatures to have around.

Most ornithologists who have made a careful study of golden-crowned kinglets agree that these birds almost invariably select a spruce tree in which to build their nest — a tree that is located in a scattered, open or mixed stand rather than in dense woods.

Golden-crowned kinglets lay large settings of eggs. Sometimes as many as ten eggs are arranged in two layers. What a "woman who lived in a shoe" sort of melee this must be when the eggs hatch! The adult birds, however, are good parents. At first, the young are fed by regurgitating partially digested food, but soon are able to take the small insects and insect larvae which the industrious parents bring to them. At nesting time golden-crowned kinglets are shy birds and will not hesitate to abandon their nest at any time during its construction if they suspect that it has been discovered. After incubation has started, however, the birds will stick with their burden in spite of any intrusion. During the winter months these birds become very confiding. They seem too preoccupied with their task of food finding to pay heed to one's approach and can often be observed at close range. We are fortunate to have such beautiful and economically valuable birds to enliven our winter months. May their numbers increase. They are most welcome to the hospitality of our juniper tree.

... *The crow*

On my way to town one day I saw a dead crow beside the road. I seldom see one at this close range. It was not necessary to consult Peterson's *Bird Guide,* or even to stop my car, to identify this familiar bird. The common crow is probably the best known of all American birds. Its large size and coal black plumage make it very conspicuous, even at a considerable distance. Furthermore, it is a noisy bird. Who hasn't heard the loud, harsh "Ca-ah, Ca-ah, Ca-ah" of an adult crow or listened to the discordant clamor of a group of crows mobbing an owl? Represented by five subspecies with very minor differences, the crow inhabits every part of the United States as well as the southern provinces of Canada.

The crow has a bad reputation, and there are reasons for its unpopularity. Crows prefer to live near man and enjoy the luxury of his wastefulness. A normal number of crows may live in an area without getting into mischief. But an overpopulation may cause considerable damage. In satisfying their voracious appetite they are no respecters of our property rights. Sometimes they devour the eggs and young of song birds, game birds and domestic fowl. But on only one occasion have I witnessed such filching. One day, during my tot years, I saw a crow fly from the top of our strawstack carrying a chicken egg in its beak. Mother complained because the crow chose to steal eggs when none of the men were home to use the gun. Crows have an uncanny way of knowing when they are safe, and this characteristic irritates us more than any of the crow's real faults. Another charge brought against the crow is that it sometimes kills toads, which are unquestionably valuable creatures to have around. Some people hate the crow because it is black, the supposed color of evil. Isn't it strange to hold this against the **crow and not against a Poland China hog, an Aberdeen Angus** cow or a rich loam soil? Perhaps the greatest damage done by the crow, however, is caused by its habit of pulling up sprouted corn to eat the moist kernels. The loss in potential crop is great with this sort of depredation. In farming areas a sizeable portion of the crow's diet may be corn. But, fortunately, most of this is eaten during the dormant season and consists of corn that would otherwise be wasted.

With so many evils attributed to it, the crow naturally has met with much persecution by man. Despite this harassment the crow has been remarkably successful as a species. As the American countryside has been changed by settlement from a wilderness to a land of cultivated crops and cities most bird species have suffered by loss of habitat or direct persecution or both. But the versatile crow has actually been helped by most of the changes and is probably more numerous today than it was before the white man came to America. As the fur trade developed in this country crows often helped themselves to carcasses of animals caught in traps. When the great American forests were cleared for crop land the remaining scattered timber patches made ideal nesting sites for crows, while farming operations on the cleared land furnished food aplenty. When the vast prairies of the Midwest were settled, farmers planted trees, thus providing the crow with nesting sites where there had been none before. As livestock farming increased, the crow was again favored. One third of the pigs farrowed die before they reach weaning age and many of these are hauled out to the fields with manure, as are dead chickens. Crows are quick to locate and devour this waste. The use of mechanical cornpickers has greatly increased the amount of waste corn left in the fields and crows are not unmindful of it. Man's relentless persecution of our birds of prey, especially the crow's most important natural enemy, the great horned owl, again has helped the crow. The fast-moving automobile is now giving the crow another handout in the many animals killed along our highways.

Despite its grave faults, the crow has virtues that fully offset its shortcomings. As a destroyer of insects, especially the large insects, the crow renders valuable service. A bird as large as the crow, measuring up to 21 inches from tip of tail to point of beak and with a wing-spread up to 40 inches, requires a lot of food, and when it changes its entire diet to a particularly relished insect, as the crow often does in season, it acts as a very effective control of that insect's numbers. Crows often feed their nestlings almost exclusively on June bugs. During outbreaks of grasshoppers, cutworms, grubs or caterpillars, crows often gorge themselves until they have difficulty in flying. Crows are also good mousers.

Crows migrate southward in autumn, especially from the northern part of their summer range. During the winter months they gather to roost at night in flocks that sometimes number hundreds of thousands. During the day they scatter, sometimes flying as much as fifty miles to feed, then return each evening to the same roost.

If taken young, crows are easily tamed and require no cage. They make amusing but mischievous pets. I wouldn't recommend one. Its pilfering might upset the whole neighborhood.

Although crows can be scoundrels, their good usually outweighs their harm. Only when they are too numerous does their ravenous appetite lead them into evil ways. Even then, they render a service as a buffer species to shoot at, thus relieving hunting pressure on other more valuable species. It takes skill to shoot crows. The more they are hunted the more wary they become. By taking advantage of their weaknesses, however, they can be lured within gun range. A stuffed crow or an artificial crow-call may arouse their curiosity, and a stuffed owl may arouse their anger to the point that they relax their caution. Even so, many a crow hunter comes home empty handed.

. . . *Meadow lark*

March, 1954

If birds were as scarce during the crop growing season as they are here during the winter months, I shudder to think of the pest-riddled crops we would have to be satisfied with. However, the season is now at hand for our field birds to begin coming back to our northern farms. The horned lark is already here. I heard the first one on January 16th. Because this bird is small, and its song unpretentious, it is often mistaken for the English sparrow by casual observers and its arrival often goes unnoticed.

Much more familiar is the loud, clear and cheerful whistle of that outspoken prophet of spring — the meadow lark. We may now expect to hear him from the bare, frozen fields any day. Perhaps you have already heard him. Of the three subspecies (designated simply as eastern, western and southern), our own — the western meadow lark — has by far the most beautiful song. In fact, it has several songs, varying from six to ten notes. All of them are flute-like, gurgling and doublenoted. The male bird pipes his buoyant tune every half minute or so during all daylight hours from March until July. Later in the season it is heard occasionally as late as November. What rural American has not seen the characteristic pose of a meadow lark perched on a fence post, its bright lemon-yellow breast with black lower-throat crescent facing the sun and its head thrown back in full-throated song? One may judge how well this song has won for the bird the affections of the people whose pastures and grassy fields it inhabits by noting the states that have chosen the meadow lark as their state bird. These states are North Dakota, South Dakota, Nebraska, Kansas, Montana, Wyoming and Oregon; all within the range of the western meadow lark.

The meadow lark is distinctly American. Its slightly variant subspecies inhabit all of the United States, the southern provinces of Canada and the northern part of Mexico. It is not found anywhere else in the world. It has several times been advocated as a fitting national emblem in place of the bald eagle. Although not strictly migratory, the birds in the northern part of the range move leisurely southward during the coldest weather and come back early enough to be caught by the late snow.

To live in our fields at this season the meadow lark must be able to subsist on weed seeds and waste grain. Painstaking research has been carried on to prove that birds do eat weed seeds by the ton. By utilizing as food weed seeds, which are of no economic value, rather than requiring something that is of value to us, weed seed-eating birds are rendering us a service, even though it may be indirect. It must be remembered, too, that weed seed-eating birds are also good insect eaters during the season when insects are available. By being on hand early to destroy the first insects that appear, these birds give us a much more effective insect control service than they would if they delayed coming until insects were numerous. Another point not to be taken lightly is the fact that these birds are here for us to see, hear and enjoy for a much longer season than the strictly insect-eating birds.

The meadow lark's food in summer consists almost entirely of insects, most of which are injurious to the crops among which the bird feeds. It is particularly destructive to cutworms that spend their first season among grass crops, where we fail to notice them but where their elimination is more timely than it would be the next season after their ravages of cultivated crops have begun. Exclusively a ground feeder, the meadow lark walks in search of food and is able to inspect closely the area it covers. Great numbers of caterpillars, beetles, grasshoppers and other injurious insects fall victim daily to the scrutinizing meadow lark.

The nest of the meadow lark is a loosely built, partially domed structure of dead grass placed on the ground. Nest building and incubation is all done by the female. As she sits on the nest the plumage pattern of her back blends perfectly with the dead grass of the nest and surrounding area. Secure in this camouflage, she will not flush until almost stepped upon. The nest is cleverly hidden and, despite the male's conspicuous show-off attitude, he never reveals the location of the nest. I have seen a number of meadow lark nests, but have never found one by searching for it. The ground is a precarious place for any bird's nest, however, and the loss due to rainstorms and predators is very heavy. Some students of this subject claim that most of these nests are destroyed and more than half of the birds that actually hatch are killed before they reach maturity. Skunks, foxes, cats and other wandering carnivores have good noses for ferreting out the location of ground nests and, of course, devour the contents of all they find. Snakes are particularly fond of ground-nesting birds' eggs and young. The struggle for survival is, of course, the big problem of every species in the natural state. Individuals of every species serve as food for other species. This is nature's way of maintaining a balance in which each species occupies a particular niche. The likelihood of the meadow lark overrunning the countryside is as remote as it is with any other species. Enough nests are successful that, with the normal loss of adult birds during the year, there will still be enough meadow larks to restock our pastures and meadows the following spring.

By classification the meadow lark is not a lark at all. It belongs to the blackbird family and is, in reality, a starling. Its plump form, short tail and manner of flight are all starling characteristics. But its habit of living and feeding on the ground in open grassy fields and singing its courtship song while in flight remind us of the true larks, so perhaps this well known and well liked bird is, after all, well named.

... *Bluebird*

The first bluebird I ever saw was perched on a fence post beside the road one sunny spring day as I was walking home from our country school near Thompson, Iowa. I was aware there were such creatures as bluebirds because I had read about them and seen highly colored pictures of them in my reader at school. I had even asked my teacher if there were bluebirds in our part of the country and she had assured me there were, but that they were not very numerous. I was naturally disappointed not to have seen one but, having learned that this was bluebird territory, I hoped that some day I might chance to see one. On this particular evening I was greeted by a bird song I had never heard before and looked about to see where the soft, friendly, contented warble was coming from. The only bird in sight just then was a small one perched on a post several rods ahead. From this distance I could not see its color. I thought that perhaps the mysterious songster was one of the native sparrows, of which I knew there were several kinds. Since its song was so pleasing I hoped to get near enough to see some distinguishing plumage marking by which I might recognize it if I ever saw it again. Just then, the bird flew, turning its back toward me so I could see the pure, rich blue of the top of its head, back, wings and tail. There was no longer any doubt that I had seen a bluebird, the smallest and most gorgeously colored member of the thrush family, the soft-voiced harbinger of spring and the symbol of happiness. As the bird flew, it continued singing, "Turwy, — cherwee, — turalowee". Ever since this thrilling childhood experience these contralto notes have remained vivid in my bird song vocabulary.

For years I wondered why this beautiful bird was so scarce.

Did its beauty make it too conspicuous for its own good? Did it have too many natural enemies to exist in greater numbers? Was it, like so many other species, disappearing because of the activities of man? As far as I know, nobody disliked the bird or persecuted it directly. Yet I had very seldom seen or even heard one. The first demonstration of the bluebird's difficulties came in the spring of 1920, the first year we lived in Minnesota. Lured by the warbling of bluebirds, I discovered a nest in a poorly excavated cavity in a decayed post. I thought this was a strange place to find these gentle birds nesting. Posts rotten enough for bluebirds to excavate cavities in are rare, because they usually have to be replaced before they reach this stage of decay. Among the bluebird's pale blue eggs in this nest was a larger, speckled egg laid by that intruding parasite, the cowbird. In addition to having difficulty finding nesting sites, the bluebird evidently was further handicapped by having to rear the young of the cowbird at the expense of its own offspring.

As the years went by, I learned more about the bluebird story. A century ago bluebirds were about as domestic as robins, habitually nesting about farmsteads and even within our cities, in natural tree cavities or abandoned woodpecker holes, especially in old orchards. Deeply ingrained in our philosophy is the idea that a dead tree or limb is unsightly and utterly worthless, except as firewood. In tidying up our premises we have removed many potential bluebird nesting sites. To make matters worse, in 1850 we dealt bluebirds a terrific blow by introducing that boisterous ruffian, the English sparrow. Later we repeated the mistake by introducing the European starling. These aggressive, quarrelsome aliens have driven the bluebirds away from human habitations by occupying or making untenable all available nesting sites.

People who enjoy having birds about them have long tried to help the bluebird's housing shortage by putting up nesting boxes for them, but there has also been strong competition for these — especially from English sparrows. My best year was 1950 when I had bluebirds nesting in 26 of my 41 houses.

Tree swallows, also desperate for nesting places and apparently a little more belligerent than bluebirds, are increasing in numbers in bluebird housing communities, so our bluebird trails are rapidly becoming tree swallow trails. Tree swallows are welcome to the houses because they are also beautiful and very useful birds. Bluebirds apparently hesitate to use a house that has been occupied by tree swallows, who are not very neat housekeepers. The answer seems to be to keep a step ahead by putting up more houses. Wrens also like to occupy bluebird houses, but can rather effectively be thwarted by placing all houses in the open, away from any trees or shrubbery. Starlings are too large to get through the 1½-inch entrance. Cowbirds are also kept out by making the opening this small. There is a great deal of satisfaction in watching a cowbird perched near a bluebird house, obviously wishing it could get in.

... *Baltimore oriole*

May, 1954

Many of the birds that come to stay for the summer or pause in their northward migration do so quite unnoticed by most people, but the Baltimore oriole attracts attention wherever it goes, not only because of its loud, clear voice and flashy plumage, but also because of the unusual nest it builds. That voice rings out as clear as a school bell, whether it be the call note, the song proper or the sharp, rapid chatter that the bird uses to express alarm or annoyance. The Baltimore oriole does not sing from a perch as so many birds do. The song — an intermittent series of rather low-pitched, mellow, whistled notes — is given in snatches of varying length and is interspersed with brief call notes as the bird goes about his business of hunting for worms. There is enough individuality in the songs to enable us to often distinguish between the singing male in our yard and the one in our neighbor's yard. The female also calls and sings, although not as often as the male. However, she can scold just as sharply as he. The young are real crybabies. After leaving the nest, they perch among the treetops, incessantly calling their plaintive, monotonous "Tee deedee, tee deedee" as they wait for their parents to bring food.

The bright orange and sharply contrasting black plumage of the male make it very conspicuous as it moves about among the treetops in search of food. Little wonder that many people, especially children, refer to it as the "fire bird," for it does look like a bit of flame among the green leaves. Among the most beautiful of birds, the Baltimore oriole has inspired many a poetic line.

Departing from birddom tradition, Baltimore orioles make no

secret of their nest-building. Conspicuous in her olive and yellow, the female — who is the architect of the family — often sings while clinging to the nest, busily weaving. Although the male never helps with the nest-building, and seldom even brings material, he shows a lot of interest in the procedure, stays constantly about, sings loudly and otherwise deports himself conspicuously. Perhaps the orioles realize, through instinct, that birds as gaudily dressed as they could not keep their nest-building a secret if they tried and concentrate rather on making their home inaccessible.

As a nesting site the Baltimore oriole chooses a large tree somewhat separated from other trees, so we frequently find it nesting in the shade trees on our lawns in town and country alike. The nest, a deep, pendulous bag of expertly woven plant fibers securely laced to the limp, drooping tip ends of a branch high in the tree and lined at the bottom with grass and other soft plant material, is one of the safest of birdhouses. It may be very conspicuous, but is also very inaccessible. No cat, squirrel or snake could venture out on a branch as far as to the nest. Larger birds, like crows, jays and owls, would find it difficult, if not impossible, to perch on these limber branch tips. And certainly no mischievous youngster, bent on nest robbing, could get anywhere near it. One might think that the position of the oriole's nest would be precarious in a windstorm. The young orioles certainly get enough swinging about, but seem able to take it. I have seen a nest swing several feet in a high gale but have never seen a young oriole that has been tossed from its nest. Elm trees are preferred, but the birds also nest freely in other trees such as cottonwood, maple and oak. Occasionally an oriole's nest in a cottonwood tree meets with disaster because cottonwood branches are sometimes quite brittle and, with the added weight of the nest, may snap in an unusually violent windstorm, dropping the nest and its contents to the ground. This actually happened in Albert Lea some years ago at the home of a local bird enthusiast. However, his oriole pair, un-daunted by the mishap, quickly built another nest and suc-cessfully reared another brood that summer. Originally,

Baltimore orioles used as nesting material the long, tough fibers from the inner bark of milkweeds and other dead and decaying plants of the previous season — strands from the inner bark of bittersweet vines, etc. But these birds are versatile and will use any string they find lying about our dooryards or that interested people have put out for their use.

One morning, a few years ago, I noticed a female Baltimore oriole inspecting a tuft of mechanic's waste which happened to be hauled home in a load of kindling wood from a local lumber company the winter before. While I watched, she seized the end of a thread, pulled out a piece about eight inches long and flew in the direction of the large elm tree growing back of our garage. In a little while she returned for another string. A few days later, on an errand past the elm, I stopped to look for the nest and discovered it at the tip of a branch about twenty feet from the ground. The entire nest looked as white as a piece of muslin. Apparently the whole exterior of the nest was woven from material in the tuft of waste. Later in the season the nest faded to gray and looked much like any other oriole's nest.

Baltimore orioles have a very strong homing instinct and often the same pair return year after year to nest in the same yard, and often in the same tree. They build a new nest every year, even though the old nest may appear well preserved for two or three years.

As a songster, the Baltimore oriole is nothing special. As a creature of beauty, it ranks high among birds. As a nest builder, it reigns supreme. It is generally conceded that the nest of the Baltimore oriole more nearly approaches perfection than the nest of any other bird.

. . . Hermit thrush

One spring day, a few years ago, I noticed a rather plain-colored little bird hopping about on our lawn. To paraphrase Abraham Lincoln, God must have loved plain-colored little birds because He made so many of them. I have found it worthwhile to determine the species of these birds, even though at first glance their plumage may appear drab and confusing, because so many of them are unusual in other ways. As I looked at this particular bird more closely I was thrilled to have it as a guest. By its robin-like form and rusty colored tail I recognized it as a hermit thrush, which is believed by many to be North America's most accomplished singer, rivaling in vocal powers even the celebrated European nightingale. It is called the American nightingale by many. Others refer to it as the "swamp angel."

It was hard to believe this shy, elusive thrush was actually hopping about with apparent unconcern so near our house. Being a night migrant, it was spending the day resting and finding food at our farmstead. I went to call our children so they might get to see the bird. But we looked out the window in disappointment, for the thrush had meanwhile disappeared. In a little while, however, it reappeared just outside our picture window. Apparently, it had hopped all the way around our house. It was closer now and we saw plainly the spotted breast and the big dreamy eyes. We watched while it hopped around our house several times. Later in the day I surprised the thrush as I stepped out the door, unaware that the bird was at that moment just outside the porch. As it darted into the lilac bush it uttered a single note of alarm, a soft yet distinct "quoit."

Our visitor did not sing at all for us that day. Like several other members of the thrush family, it never sings during migration. Because of this, very few people have heard the song of the hermit thrush. Fewer still have heard it at its best. To hear the song at all, one must journey to the bird's nesting ground in the deep, dense, moist northwoods carpeted with ferns and mosses and scented with pine near some woodland swamp, stream or lake. To hear the song at its best, one must be there at twilight, which eliminates most people. So modest and retiring is this well named woodland recluse that it will not sing if it suspects that humans are taking notice of it. Perhaps it feels some measure of security from human intrusion in the subdued light. At any rate, its song can be heard best at this hour, when most other woodland sounds have quieted down.

The song can be described as a series of phrases of different pitches, each beginning with a long, low, flute-like note followed by several short, bell-like notes. There is much variation in the quality of the notes, even from the same individual. More important, however, than a mechanical description of the song is the effect that it has on the listener. There is something solemn, peaceful and reverent about it. It has a beautiful, unhurried, hymn-like quality that goes well with that time of day when it can be heard to the best advantage.

I once listened to the song of a hermit thrush in Nerstrand Woods, one of the few remaining natural timber areas in southern Minnesota. There are 1400 acres of woodland near Northfield, of which 270 acres make up Nerstrand Woods State Park. We entered the area from the east and parked our car near the trail that leads through the woods to the falls of Prairie Creek. Stepping out of the car, I paused to listen to the woodland birds. The sharp, insistent staccato call of the ovenbird rang through the woods like a siren. There was also that ever present, talkative and curious red-eyed vireo. In the distance I heard what I thought was the song of the hermit thrush. To get nearer the singer I started walking cautiously into the woods. But before I had taken half a dozen steps the bird signed off with that same alarm note uttered by the hermit thrush darting into the lilac bush back home. We heard no more of the hermit's song in Nerstrand Woods, although we stayed there for several hours.

The hermit thrush nests on the ground or in a low shrub very near the ground. As with other ground-nesting birds, very few of the nests are successful in harboring a brood of young birds safely to maturity. By renesting after disaster strikes, the hermit thrush is able to maintain its numbers. It is the hardiest of our northern thrushes, coming north earlier in the spring and remaining much later in the fall. It arrives in this latitude about the middle of April and stays on or near its nesting grounds until October. With the coming of frost and snow, it migrates quietly southward.

... *Great blue heron*

July, 1954

Hens often peck the hand that gathers their eggs. During the process of domestication the hen has been changed a great deal since the time of her ancestor, the jungle fowl, but she still retains this now useless and annoying habit of pecking to defend herself and her nest. Ordinarily, the peck is not hard enough to inflict injury, but sometimes it is so far from gentle that I can sympathize with the farm woman living in the neighborhood where I grew up. A bit irritable about some problem, she was gathering eggs in a hurry one day when a particularly ferocious biddy pecked the back of her hand hard enough to touch off her temper. Seizing the hen by the head, she jerked it off the nest and flung it out through the hen house door. In her fit of temper she failed to release her grip and found herself holding the hen's head in her hand while the rest of the hen went on out to the yard. After a moment of shocked surprise she began preparing an unexpected chicken dinner. In this age, when agricultural geneticists have developed strains of both crops and livestock with highly specialized characteristics, it seems strange that no one has yet produced a peckless hen.

This method of defense is not limited to hens, or even to birds of the chicken kind. In the days when sandhill cranes were numerous, many a farm dog went about with only one eye, a result of an experience with a crippled crane. Notable for their pecking ability also are various members of the heron family — particularly the great blue heron.

The great blue heron is a large bird, standing four feet tall. Next to the sandhill crane, it is the largest wading bird we have in the northern United States. Much of its height is made up by its long legs and neck, for it seldom weighs more than seven pounds. The name blue crane, often applied to this bird, is incorrect. It is a true heron and, like all herons, in flight it draws its head back to its shoulders, whereas a crane flies with its neck stretched straight forward, as a goose would. The long, broad, well-rounded wings measure six feet from tip to tip. A bald eagle, weighing more than twice as much, has a wingspread of less than seven feet. The great blue heron flies with a slow steady wingbeat. Like other herons, it seldom does any gliding. One of the most beautiful Pickerel Lake scenes in my memory is that of a great blue heron flying low over the water directly towards me, its wingtips, when down, nearly touching those of its image clearly reflected in the smooth surface of the lake.

The great blue heron is perhaps most often seen standing in shallow water, motionless as a statue, patiently waiting for the approach of prey. When an unwary fish, frog or crayfish comes within striking distance, it falls prey to that masterful peck. The sharp, six-inch beak shoots forward and downward with lightning speed and seldom misses its mark. Although not a swimming bird, the great blue heron sometimes is found on the

surface of deep water where, with wings outstretched, it floats while feeding. It can actually take flight from this unusual position. This versatile heron also feeds in meadows, where it stalks such prey as frogs, salamanders, mice, and even gophers.

The large nests, loosely constructed of sticks, added to and used from year to year, are built in groups sometimes numbering hundreds, usually in the tops of trees in some isolated location. If one should visit such a heronry and climb up to look into a nest the outcome might be tragic should the herons direct their aim at one's eyes. Although these herons nest in groups they usually feed alone. Spreading out from the home heronry, the parent birds sometimes fly distances that may take them several hours. At their destination they gather food until their large crops are filled to capacity and then return to feed their offspring by a process of regurgitation so violent that one may well wonder how the young can survive the ordeal.

Legislatively, the great blue heron is given full protection under the Migratory Bird Treaty. But it still has lots of trouble. Thoughtless hunters take advantage of the slow, steady flight which makes them an easy target. Like many of us, the great blue herons prefer to make their living as conveniently as possible. They are expert at locating open fish hatchery ponds, where they forget their solitary feeding habit, gather in large numbers and gobble down the valued fry voraciously. The proper solution to this problem, of course, is the screening of fish-rearing ponds against such depredation by herons, and federal funds are available for this purpose. But there still are a great number of these open ponds throughout the country which act as death traps for these birds. Armed with guns and special permits, fish hatchery attendants kill herons by the hundreds every year.

At about this time of year the young great blue herons are large enough to forage for themselves. From now until ice covers our lakes this fall many a pond, lake and stream will have its solitary, picturesque sentinel of the shallows. I hope the great blue heron never passes from the American scene.

... *Yellow-headed blackbird*

August, 1954

As we watch the blackbird clans gather for their autumn festivities we will find one species conspicuously absent. A question in the minds of many will be, Where are the yellow-heads? Although yellow-headed blackbirds, the most strikingly beautiful of all our blackbirds, were never as numerous as redwings, they were, nevertheless, very common birds in this area forty years ago. Today they have become as rare as the cattail and quill-reed sloughs in which they nested. While they nested in sloughs the yellow-heads found most of their food on the upland, where they could be seen any summer day in fields, pastures and about the farmyards. In the fall they were well represented in the flocks of blackbirds that gathered to feed in stubble fields, grain stacks and to feast on milky corn.

Yellow-headed blackbirds were much more particular in their choice of a nesting site than were redwings, although both species nested much in company. Redwings will nest in any slough. If there are no reeds or rushes, they will nest on hummocks. If there are no hummocks, they will nest in a meadow or even a grain field. Yellow-heads, however, sought a slough with fairly deep water where they could nest far out among the reeds and be neighbor to the muskrat, turtle, coot, black tern and pied-billed grebe. The draining of these sloughs for the production of cultivated crops has been the bird's undoing. With the changing habitat, the redwing has proved adaptable and is still with us in great numbers, while the yellow-head has proved sensitive and has all but disappeared.

One of my boyhood tasks was to gather and sack corn cobs from the hog lot for use as fuel in our kitchen range. This was generally a pleasant job because it gave me a chance to watch the yellow-heads walking about among the hogs picking up stray kernels as the hogs were eating their ear corn. It was a thrilling experience to see these colorful birds so near and to hear their strange song. The rich dandelion-yellow of the male bird's head, neck and chest contrasts sharply with the glossy black of the rest of its plumage. In flight, the male also shows conspicuous white wing patches. The female is brownish black with some dull yellow on its throat and upper breast.

The call note of the yellow-head is a low "krik." Its song, which is unusual to say the least, begins with a few harsh, distinct notes, then becomes jumbled with hoarse croaks and ends with a prolonged, low, rasping sound, which some say resembles the squeaking of rusty hinges. I think the last part of the song sounds like the vibration of a low-pitched violin string. The song is produced with a great deal of effort and fluffing of feathers, similar to that of a young rooster just learning to crow. I used to think the bird was purposely making its voice sound as ugly as possible. Although among the oddest of bird songs, it does have a strange musical quality which I never tire of hearing.

On our Iowa farm, about a quarter mile from the house, was a cattail slough which harbored a thriving and loud-spoken marsh-bird community. In the evenings, when most daytime noises had quieted down, one could hear the various sounds come over the hill and across the field from this sanctuary. Many of the calls were then mysterious. But there was no mystery about the song of the yellow-headed blackbirds. Every summer, a colony of them nested in the middle of this slough. I was annoyed at them for nesting in such an inaccessible place. It wasn't pleasant for bare feet to make their way through the saw-grass and other marsh vegetation. The water and oozy mud was too deep for me to venture into. I have learned later that the yellow-head's nest is a deep, thick-walled basket, woven from water-soaked marsh vegetation of the previous season and laced to the stalks of cattails or other water plants a foot or more above the water. The young birds leave the nest before they are able to fly and make their way about clinging to the reeds. Sometimes one falls into the water but will struggle up into the reeds again, unless a snapping turtle makes a meal of him.

The last time I visited our old home farm this slough had been drained and corn was growing where the yellow-heads once nested. I did not see any yellow-heads or, for that matter, any of the other numerous marsh birds that lived there.

The yellow-headed blackbird is a summer resident of the west and central prairie states. It nested as far east as Indiana when it could find a suitable place. It has been reported as a visitor further east, but few people have seen it there. When Carl W. Buchheister, vice-president of the National Audubon Society, was in Albert Lea in April, 1952, he told me he had never seen a yellow-headed blackbird and that he was very anxious to see one. Several people enroute had promised to show him one, but so far they had failed. I was not optimistic about my chances of spotting one for him since the bird had become so rare that sometimes an entire season went by without a single yellow-head crossing my path. I had my try, however, because the Missouri River flood had disrupted Mr. Buchheister's train schedule. It was necessary for me to take him to Mankato by auto to make bus connections, so we drove there leisurely the morning after his Screen Tour appearance here, birding as we drove. We saw several species of birds, but no yellow-heads. I did not feel too badly about it until, on my way home, I saw a yellow-head in a slough along Highway 16. I heard later that the Screen Tour chairman at Sioux Falls, South Dakota, had the coveted honor of showing Mr. Buchheister his first yellow-headed blackbird.

Although yellow-heads have not disappeared entirely yet, they will soon be seen no more unless we can maintain a representative suitable habitat for them.

... *The gulls*

September, 1954

Birdwatchers in the interior section of the country who have never observed a flock of gulls from a tractor seat have been missing a thrilling experience. I think that everyone who enjoys wild creatures likes to see them at close range, perhaps because they seldom get the opportunity. Some time during every spring and fall I get a chance to see gulls nearby when migrating flocks numbering hundreds of birds come to follow my plow and feast on the earthworms and insect larvae exposed on the freshly turned furrows. The mere concentration of these large birds circling so near is an impressive sight. They do not follow the plow continuously as some birds do, but come and go like the clouds in the sky. Gulls are very gregarious birds. Like a flock of merino sheep, they stay close together. Rather than a few following my plow, the whole flock comes to see me for a while. Then all of them depart for my neighbor's field or elsewhere. Sometimes there are no gulls at all in my field. Then suddenly I am surrounded with them, and while they are near I enjoy watching their aerial maneuvers.

The graceful, buoyant flight of a gull is remarkable. It is a powerful flyer and an expert glider. The ease with which it gets about is amazing. A bird may be skimming along so close to the ground that it could easily touch the plowing with its feet when, without any apparent wing effort, it will suddenly zoom skyward fifty or a hundred feet. Heading into the wind, one will set its wings just right to hold itself aloft, motionless as a kite, while looking for food. One may be flying at headlong speed, then stop suddenly in midair and plunge downward to pick up some tasty morsel. Sometimes there is quite a scramble to see who gets the worm, but in the concentrated confusion of wings I have never seen two birds collide. Occasionally, a gull will alight in the plowing to rest a while and soon the others quickly take up the idea. In no time at all the plowing is white with gulls for several rods. Most of them stand quietly, merely turning their heads to watch what is going on. Some may lower their heads to preen a feather or take a few steps with their awkward goose-like waddle. As suddenly as they alighted, they take flight again. The takeoff may be a little slow but, once in the air, they exhibit their skill, circling about the plow and tractor so near that the operator can see the plumage marking in minute detail — the hooked upper mandible, the color of the eyes, and even the scales on their legs. This is almost as good as having the bird in the hand.

As yet, only three species of gulls have followed my plow — Franklin's gull, ring-billed gull and a few herring gulls mixed in some of the flocks. Bonaparte's gulls are also plow followers, but I have not seen any in my fields yet. Herring gulls and ring-billed gulls are very similar in plumage markings. In adult plumage the head, neck, underparts and both upper and lower tail surface are white. The back and upper surface of the wings are pearl-gray, except for the black wingtips and a narrow band of white along the back edge of the upper wing surface. However, the two species can easily be distinguished, especially at close range, because the herring gull is considerably larger and has a slower wingbeat. Its feet and legs are pinkish, while those of the ring-billed are yellowish. The ring-billed also, as the name indicates, has a black ring around its bill near the tip. The brown or brownish birds one sometimes sees are the immatures.

My favorite of the three, the Franklin's gull, is a more colorful bird. In spring plumage its mantle is bluish-slate and its head and upper neck black. Against this background its conspicuous white eyelids are bewitching. The bill is crimson with a little black toward the tip. The dusky red feet and legs contrast sharply with the white underplumage. Like several species of gulls the Franklin's gull has a narrow band of white along the back edge of the upper wing surface. But the Franklin's gull is unique in that this band comes forward to separate the gray mantle from the black wingtip. In fall plumage the head is white, except for a dusky area across the back of the head reaching from eye to eye.

Gulls of any species are often referred to as sea gulls. They are not true sea birds in the sense that petrels and albatrosses are, for example, but have no doubt acquired this group name because most species of gulls congregate along coasts to feed on dead fish and other dead animal matter that has washed ashore and to follow fishing boats and feed on the offal that is thrown overboard. Gulls may eat some live fish, but they mainly serve as scavengers, performing the same duties along waterfronts as vultures do inland. It seems a shame that these beautiful birds should be given such a distasteful assignment but, on second thought, perhaps it is well that gulls, which are required in such large numbers to keep nature's house in order, are beautiful rather than ugly.

Franklin's gulls cannot be called sea birds because they are strictly an inland species that seldom visits either coast. They are birds of the northwestern prairie states and the southern prairie provinces of Canada, where they nest in large colonies among reeds in marshes and reed-grown lakeshores. Franklin's gulls are mainly insect eaters. They feed to some extent on aquatic insects and catch some on the wing in swallow fashion, but find most of their food in the fields, where they feed among the growing crops for miles around their nesting area. They are especially effective in the control of grasshopper population, eating great quantities of these harmful insects during the egg-laying stage. Without birds it would be difficult to bring any plants to maturity.

. . . *Bird migration*

When my older brothers were of air rifle age they spent an enjoyable evening taking turns shooting at the moon. They had found, to their surprise and delight, that they could see the shot travel through the air as long as it was silhouetted against the moon. When the BB lost momentum and dropped down past the edge of the shiny disc they could no longer see it. Today, ornithologists employ the same principle in making studies of bird migration. Most of our small birds do their migrating at night, frequently at elevations of 2000 to 5000 feet, and when viewed through binoculars, they, like the air rifle shots, can be seen silhouetted against the moon. It isn't like seeing birds in a tree, of course. One cannot determine the species in this way — or even the size of the bird — but can count the number of birds whose paths cross the shiny disc and observe the direction in which they fly. On almost any moonlit October night one may find many bird enthusiasts across the country watching the moon through binoculars, recording their observation and, no doubt, enjoying their vigil as much as did my brothers with their air rifle. The information is sent in to the ornithologist requesting it and, bit by bit, it adds to our knowledge about the seasonal movement of birds.

Some birds are permanent residents, staying with us throughout the year. Others, like the waxwings and crossbills, are sporadic or unpredictable migrants. However, most birds have definite summer and winter homes, and migrate between these two areas with remarkable regularity. No phase of bird life has attracted more attention or aroused more curiosity than seasonal migration.

The winter homes of most species have now been quite accurately determined. But before this information was available many strange theories were advanced to explain the disappearance of birds in the fall and their reappearance in the spring. Even today, after all the research that has been carried on, there is still so much mystery about bird migration that any discussion of the subject is likely to raise more questions than it answers and, finally, fall back on that rather vague but all-inclusive explanation: instinct. Take, for example, that perennial question: How do birds know when to migrate? What signals do they go by? It is commonly believed that birds fly south in autumn to find a more comfortable climate in which to spend the winter. A plausible reason, no doubt, if we were doing the migrating. But, if comfort is the motive, why do some birds leave us while the weather is still pleasant? A more logical reason would seem to be food supply. It is easy to understand that a rugged winter season of this latitude with its dormant insect life could not support the bird population that it does during the warmer season. If food is the sole spur to migration, however, why does the upland plover start south in August, when insects are much more numerous than they are when the bird arrives in the latter part of April? Why doesn't the bobolink stop to winter where it finds an abundance of food rather than fly all the way to Argentina? Ornithologists today generally accept the theory that the time of southward or northward migration of any species is determined by a migratory instinct.

Probably the most intriguing question about bird migration is: How are the birds able to find their way? The summer and winter homes of most of our warblers are separated by 3000 to 5000 miles. With shore birds, the distance is up to 8000 miles. And the Arctic tern travels up to 11,000 miles between its two abodes. Yet the birds not only find their home areas but, as has been proven by numbered leg bands, some individuals spend the winter in exactly the same place. Winter after winter they show up at the same window feeder. After wintering in South or Central America a bird may return to nest in the same yard as it did the previous summer. Many of the birds migrating southward are immatures that have never made the journey before. Sometimes the southward immatures do not migrate at the same time as the adults, or even use the same route. But somehow they find their way, often by flying in complete darkness.

We find this phenomenon hard to understand because we tend to judge it by our own ability. We fail to fully realize that, even though birds are a lower form of life, they do have certain powers that are much more highly developed in them than in humans. Among these powers is this instinct, or sense of direction, which keeps them from losing their bearings and guides them unerringly to their destination.

The migratory journey is not a carefree jaunt. Birds encounter many perils enroute. Storms sometimes kill thousands of birds in one ill-fated night flight. Many man-made obstacles, like telephone and electric wires, tall buildings, airplanes, monuments and lighthouses, kill night migrants that collide with them. There is also the ever present danger of natural enemies. And we know what happens to a lot of southbound game birds.

When migrating, birds tend to concentrate in certain routes or flyways. Four of these flyways cross the United States. We are in the Mississippi flyway, which is the longest flyway in the Western Hemisphere, extending from the arctic coast of Alaska to far-off Patagonia. Swelled by the throngs of southbound feathered travelers constantly converging on it, this flyway becomes very concentrated with birds as it narrows toward the mouth of the Mississippi River. I should like to spend a few hours on one of the small islands in the Gulf of Mexico, just off the Louisiana coast, where, during the height of migration, birds literally swarm.

. . . *Pied-billed grebe*

November, 1954

On one of the first days I attended country school after we had moved to Minnesota, a schoolmate told me that his older brothers had once captured a "helldiver." I had not heard this appendage before and thought at first the boy was using profane language. But, as the story unfolded, I realized that he was referring to that shy, little waterbird, the pied-billed grebe. Some birds have acquired very strange names. This particular name originated in the days of the muzzle-loading shotgun, when a wasted shot meant a great deal more than it does today. It was claimed that the reflexes of the pied-billed grebe were so fast that, after seeing the flash from a discharged gun, it could dive and be safely under the water before the charge of shot could reach it. This claim is not as fantastic as are the powers attributed to some of our wild creatures but I think it is a little exaggerated, unless the hunters of that day were using a very poor grade of gunpowder. The hunter who first used the name "helldiver" was probably annoyed at missing his mark and, feeling the need for some explanation to bolster his ego, applied a name befitting his mood. Be that as it may, the name has persisted to the present time, when one hears it as often, or perhaps more often, than the proper name, pied-billed grebe.

The particular grebe my new friend was talking about had made the mistake of staying too late one fall and so found itself in a pond that was almost completely frozen over. In fact, at the time of its capture there was only one small hole in the ice, about two feet in diameter, which the grebe had apparently kept from freezing by swimming about in it. With the pond in this condition, the little grebe was trapped, because a grebe can only take flight from water, and then only by skittering along the surface for a considerable distance, using both wings and feet to attain enough speed for a takeoff. In equipping its creatures for expertness in one element, nature sometimes makes them almost helpless in another. The capture was not easy. Even with the very limited space in which the grebe could emerge to snatch a breath of air, it emerged and dived under again so quickly and expertly that only after hours of eager watchfulness and splashy effort were the boys finally able to catch the utterly exhausted bird. With youthful enthusiasm they took the grebe home, intending to keep it over winter and release it the following spring. However, the unfortunate bird went the way of most captured wild creatures in the hands of amateurs, a fate to which it was doomed even had it not been captured. But before it died it demonstrated to its captors its helplessness out of water. Its legs were placed so far back on its body that it could only walk clumsily by holding its body upright like a penguin. When hurried, it fell on its stomach and attempted to scramble forward using both wings and feet — a poor way on land and poorer yet on linoleum floors.

The pied-billed grebe is one of nature's submarines. It is often seen swimming with only its head above the water, looking like a periscope. A diving duck can stay under water only by constant effort. When this effort is relaxed it bobs to the surface like a cork. The grebe, however, like its close relative, the loon, can change its buoyancy at will and swim with ease at any level. It can do this because it has within its body air sacs with muscular walls. When these muscles are relaxed the air sacs are large and the bird swims high in the water, like a kernel of puffed wheat. When the grebe suspects the slightest danger it contracts these muscles, the air sacs become smaller and the bird sinks lower in the water. To make itself inconspicuous and still keep an eye on things, the grebe lowers itself until only its head or sometimes only its beak and eyes are above water. If really frightened, it dives with amazing speed and does not reappear. Actually, in such cases, it swims under water to some reeds and very cautiously emerges till its beak and eyes are above water so it can breathe and watch unseen from among the reeds. Its skill in doing this disappearing act has earned it the name "water witch." This behavior is, of course, primarily for self defense. But often, while watching the antics of a pied-billed grebe, I cannot help wondering if at least part of it is not sheer playfulness.

The grebe is probably more completely at home in the water than any other bird. Its food is all gathered from the water. It consists of small fish, leeches and other small aquatic creatures, together with seeds of various waterplants. Its nest is a mere floating mass of dead vegetation anchored among the reeds. The eggs are seldom dry because the mother grebe goes directly from the water onto the nest. When she leaves the nest she pulls some of the nesting trash over the eggs to conceal them from possible enemy eyes. So effective is this camouflage that, unless one is very experienced in the ways of grebes, the nest is almost impossible to find. The young can and often do take to the water almost as soon as they hatch. The mother grebe broods the young on her back under her wing feathers. Sometimes their heads can be seen sticking up through the feathers. When the mother dives, she takes the young under the water with her. If she dives too suddenly the young are sometimes left on the surface. The little "water witches," however, can do a fairly good job of swimming and diving themselves.

Fortunately for the grebe, its flesh is distasteful, so it is not considered a game bird. Before it was given federal protection, however, great numbers were shot for their breast feathers, which were used as insulating material for muffs and as trimming for hats and coats. Today few ponds, creeks, lakes or open marshes in this area are without their nesting pair of these comedians. In the winter months they go south only far enough to find open water. Let's hope that none get trapped by a sudden freeze this fall.

... *Golden eagle*

December, 1954

A drive out along the south shore of Albert Lea Lake is always a good birding trip. With the variety of habitats encountered, one is assured of seeing a number of the common birds, and there is always the possibility of seeing unusual species. After church services last August 29th I went birding with three friends, intent on identifying shore birds. Our lakes and streams at that time are usually at a low water stage. Consequently, a strip of mudflat runs along the shore where shore birds starting on their southward migration like to gather and probe in the mud for worms, crustacea and other minute animal life. We were disappointed to find only three species. A few least sandpipers, one spotted sandpiper and one dowitcher were pattering about in some water puddles away from the lake. The heavy rains of the previous week had raised the water in the lake so the mud flats were covered and for this reason or for some other reason, the shore birds had gone elsewhere. Flying over the lake were a number of ring-billed gulls and black terns. In the shallow water near the shore stood a black-crowned night heron. Farther down along the shore we saw another. Since no more bird life was visible from this point, we started out the south shore road.

About two miles out we caught a glimpse of a large bird through the bur oaks. This looked interesting, so we stopped the car and readied our binoculars. When the bird cleared the treetops we realized it was one of the raptores and, from all appearances, one of the eagles. Presently, there were two of them, spiraling upward so rapidly that they were out of range before we could ascertain their identity. A bird watcher must often make observations quickly at a considerable distance and often be satisfied without positive identity. A mile or so farther on we saw two more birds at much closer range and identified them as immature golden eagles. They had white patches under their wings at the base of the primaries — a characteristic marking of immature goldens.

You may well ask what golden eagles were doing in this area, for they are birds of the savage mountain wilderness. Their nest (or aerie) is built in some storm-battered tree on a mountain height or on some inaccessible crag overlooking a wide expanse of countryside. The nearest place they might possibly nest would be in the Badlands of South Dakota, yet here they were near Albert Lea Lake. They have also been seen by others in this area in past years. It happens these birds have the habit of roaming widely after the nesting season has ended.

A stately bird, which takes its name from the gold-tinged feathers on its head and neck, the golden eagle is a larger, swifter and fiercer bird than our national emblem, the bald eagle. It is the species that has inspired the title, "King of Birds." The bald eagle is a fish hawk found nesting in trees near the seashore, rivers or large bodies of water. It feeds almost exclusively on dead fish and fish which it steals from that expert fisherman, the osprey. The golden eagle, on the other hand, is a bold hunter which feeds on such prey as ground squirrels, rabbits, prairie dogs, woodchucks, grouse, waterfowl and, to some extent, on foxes and coyotes. It spots its prey from almost invisible heights and plunges downward in a falcon-like powerdive to deal a death blow. It will, of course, not tolerate other eagles within its nesting territory and, when food is scarce, it will even pursue and kill such competing species as red-tailed hawks and great horned owls. It has been known to kill deer that are starving or handicapped by snow. An occasional individual or pair will get into the habit of carrying off domestic stock, such as poultry, young pigs, and unprotected newly born lambs. Extensive studies of nests indicate that this criminal behavior is rare. It is certainly no ground for condemning the species.

Individuals developing this habit, however, must be done away with, because they can be very destructive.

This swift, powerful raptore can readily be trained for falconry. Howard Cleaves, veteran wildlife photographer and Audubon Screen Tour lecturer, once told me that he had visited with a western couple who had a golden eagle trained to hunt coyotes. The strategy used was to carry the eagle, tethered to its T-shaped perch, until a coyote's den was found. The perch would then be placed upon the ground and held upright to support the bird, which would then be untethered. A smoke bomb on the end of a cable would be lit and pushed down into the coyote's den. The coyote, knowing that there were humans about, would emerge from its den at headlong speed. But before it had taken many leaps the eagle would have caught it, sunk its talons into the animal's body and pinned it helplessly to the ground until the man could dispatch it.

The golden eagle ranges over half of the land area in the world. In America, it is now found nesting almost entirely in the Rocky Mountains. It is much persecuted by embittered ranchers, who hire professional hunters to shoot the eagles from airplanes. The species must not be driven to extinction. It has a place in America. It is a part of what remains of our unspoiled wilderness. It is as much a part of "America the Beautiful" as are the mountains, glaciers, canyons, woodlands and wide open spaces.

. . . Short-eared owl

While rounding up my sheep the other day I met a welcome avian visitor from the north. A short-eared owl took flight from the ground just ahead of my pickup truck. After a short wavering flight it alighted again, as lightly as a moth, in the grain stubble about a hundred feet away and stared with curiosity. With up-stretched neck, it moved its head from side to side like a lady viewing a new hat in a mirror. The small, closely-placed, inward-curving ear tufts or horns, which ordinarily are hard to see, were raised and plainly visible. Two years ago I flushed one of these owls from this same spot and it behaved in precisely the same manner, an excellent way for an owl to conduct itself in the presence of a bird enthusiast, but an utterly stupid way to perform before an unscrupulous hunter. I like to think that these two encounters were with the same individual owl but, of course, I have no way of knowing this. It has been determined by bird banding studies, however, that some individual migratory birds spend consecutive winters in exactly the same locality.

The short-eared owl may be found throughout North America and in Europe. Our North American species nests mainly in the land of perpetual daylight during May and June. It builds its nest on the ground by merely tramping down vegetation or adding a few sticks in the shelter of a bush or clump of tall grass. The four to seven eggs are laid at two or three day intervals, with incubation starting when the first egg is laid. The result is that young, in various stages of development, live together in the same nest, as is the case with many other birds of prey. When still a young lad, I accompanied an older brother one day on a tramp along the dredge ditch on our Iowa prairie farm and discovered an American bittern's nest in which the young varied greatly in size. Thinking that this was a very ridiculous arrangement, since it seemed unfair to the smaller nestlings, I expressed my opinion, and was reminded that we had the same situation in our family.

During the winter, short-eared owls may be seen in many parts of the United States flying noiselessly over low meadows, like large bats. This day-flying ground owl — about the size of a crow — is heavily spotted and streaked with dark brown on a background of buff and lighter below. In flight, it shows large buff patches on the upper wing surface and black smudges under the wings at the base of the primaries.

If the feathers were removed from the head of one of these owls one could see that it has very large ears. It is believed that the bird depends to a great extent upon hearing in its search for mice. Although the short-eared takes some small birds and a great many insects, its principal food is mice, which it hunts by flying low over meadows and marshland like a marsh hawk, though with a more slovenly flight. Sometimes it is called marsh owl, bog owl and prairie owl. It prefers open country with plenty of mice. Perhaps that is why the one I saw the other day has taken up winter quarters in my grain stubble field.

A field of grain stubble that has been seeded to alfalfa and clover is an ideal place for field mice to spend the winter. In the process of harvesting and combining, a considerable amount of grain falls to the ground and is left in the field, so there is plenty of mouse food. The tender young alfalfa and clover plants add greens to the mouse diet, at the expense of next year's hay crop. The stubble and straw make good nesting material and protection from enemies. Given this combination, field mice gather and, in turn, short-eared owls are attracted to the area. These owls often gather in considerable numbers where there is heavy mouse infestation.

The daytime activity and relative trustfulness of the short-eared owl often puts it in the path of hunters and within easy shooting range. They used to be much more numerous than they are at the present time. Perhaps some hunters shoot these valuable mousers without thinking, or just for target practice. It is more likely, however, that they are shot because of the foolish but deep-rooted prejudice against all birds of prey. I am sure the shooting is not done because of any particular love for mice. It isn't rational to praise a domestic cat for being a good mouser and condemn a bird with the same virtue, but that is the popular attitude. One of the toughest problems with which the National Audubon Society has ever had to deal is this prejudice against birds of prey.

A farmer near Northfield, Minnesota, saw a strange sight one day several years ago. While walking through a woods on his farm he was confronted by a family of seven young owls, lined up on one branch looking at him. These were of the species called long-eared owls, which live almost exclusively on mice. The farmer — excited by his discovery — walked home after his shotgun, walked back to the woods where the owls were still perched, and shot them down one at a time at close range. The fact that this was a violation of Minnesota state law never occurred to him. This incident occurred near the city where Dr. O. S. Pettingill, prominent scientist and Audubon Screen Tour lecturer, had been teaching ornithology at Carleton College, and it was he who related the incident to me.

Old ideas are hard to change. The idea that our hawks and owls are vermin persists, in spite of the fact that much research has shown them to be highly beneficial to man's interests. Laws are not effective without enforcement, and enforcement is impossible without public support. We have a long way to go in wildlife conservation.

. . . "Black Donald"

February, 1955

A bronzed grackle hunting for corn kernels in our hog lot the other day stirred memories of Black Donald, a male bronzed grackle that stayed at our house on our Iowa prairie farm during the disagreeable winter of 1915-1916. For some reason this bird had stayed behind long after the others of his kind had hit for Dixie. Perhaps he had been temporarily disabled at the time they left. Perhaps his tardiness had been induced by the soft corn of which grackles are so fond and which, that fall, never did mature. The bangboards of our husking wagons were white-spattered and dripping with the juicy contents of smashed kernels as the milky crop was harvested. This lone grackle had often been seen feeding in the hog lot during the late fall and early winter.

One day there was a blizzard like the one immortalized by Whittier in his winter idyl "Snow-Bound." In the morning, when we had finally dug our way to the "prisoned brutes within," we found not only the hogs, huddled together for warmth, but also, perched on a partition in the hog house where he had taken refuge, the grackle. He refused to escape through a broken windowpane to brave the weather that was still acting up, so he was finally captured and brought to the house. In our family there was a rule against the capture and imprisonment of any wild creature, but circumstances alter cases, so Black Donald became a member of our household.

He acquired his name quite by circumstance. Father, at the time, was reading the Norwegian translation of *The Hidden Hand* by Mrs. Emma Southworth and enjoying the escapades of the heroine, Capitola. Since the grackle's head and neck glistened with iridescent hues of blue, green and purple, it was obviously a male and could not be christened "Capitola." But the name of the crafty villain, "Black Donald," suited him perfectly.

Every bird living in the same house with humans needs a cage in which it can be confined to keep it out of mischief. This was especially true of a roughneck like Black Donald, so the slat-work egg case was requisitioned for this purpose and eggs were taken to the store in a pail with oats packed between them to keep them from breaking.

Bothered with rheumatism, Father was obliged to spend much time indoors during the cold weather, part of the time confined to his bed. At his bedside was a small table on which he kept, within easy reach, such articles as his pipe, tobacco, ash tray, the daily mail, pencils, and a scratch tablet. A corner of this table was cleared to make room for the improvised cage, and there Black Donald spent the winter.

Black Donald was a commanding personality. He disliked being handled and resisted the indignity by pecking any hand that attempted to pick him up. When it became necessary for sanitary reasons to remove the many layers of newspapers from the floor of his cage and replace them with clean ones, the cover was removed and Black Donald was given the freedom of the house — a privilege that he enjoyed immensely and an occasion to which we youngsters looked forward with glee.

In the living room were many interesting things to perch upon. Our feathered guest shuttled about between the tops of doors, picture frames, the wall mirror and the clock on the shelf. He even tried to perch on the nickel-plated fancywork on the top of the heater stove, but found this a little too warm for comfort. We learned to put vases and other unstable objects in safer places. Once, he was turned loose after the Christmas tree had been put up. That was a mistake. We redecorated it after Black Donald was safely back in his cage. For the remainder of the holidays the living room was kept closed while Black Donald's cage was being tidied up.

Another member of our household was "Foxy," the pampered house cat. Traditional enemy of birds, she at first stalked this intruder of her domain, while Black Donald, wise in the ways of cats, scolded her vehemently from atop the huge frame of grandfather's picture. Mother, less concerned for Black Donald's safety than for the welfare of the living room curtains, slapped Foxy down until the feline begrudgingly granted Black Donald undisputed right to the upper half of the living room.

Getting Black Donald back into his cage was at first quite an ordeal, and required the cooperation of every member of the family in guarding every possible perch. However, he soon learned that the little egg case was his only place of absolute refuge, so when the fracas started — or as soon as he had had enough of it — he willingly darted into his cage and stood his ground with the dignity of a five-star general.

As the winter wore on, Black Donald became less active, paid less attention to his preening and spent more time standing dejectedly in one corner of his cage. Perhaps he was dreaming of his fellow grackles in the balmy south or brooding over his lost freedom. It was more likely, however, that his listlessness was due to a lack of some nutrients in his corn and water diet.

We would have hated to lose Black Donald. By this time we were all so attached to him that he got more attention than the family dog. Father was most concerned for his welfare and puttered about the pantry in search of some remedy for Black Donald's ills. He tried feeding rice, pearl barley, rolled oats, soaked bread and even johnny cake, but to no avail. His patient continued downcast.

Father was fond of fish, so occasionally a large frozen pickerel found its way home with the groceries. One day, as he was helping Mother with the arduous task of beheading a big fish, he was prompted to grumble about the amount of waste, when the thought struck him that perhaps Black Donald would like to pick at a fish head. Split from the underside and pried open to expose the fleshy portion, the huge thing was put into Black Donald's cage. Spread out as it was, it covered half of the cage floor. The response of Black Donald was immediate. "Check," he said, as he drove his beak forcibly into the meat and jerked hard enough to slide the slimy thing about. "Check-Check," he repeated, gulping down a tasty morsel.

In a burst of enthusiasm and excitement, he leaped upon the pickerel head, jabbing, jerking and twisting. He feasted long and furiously, with many an undignified slip, much to the delight of his audience. When finally satisfied he drank and swished his beak in the small tin cup securely fastened to one corner of his cage. Having slaked his thirst, he proceeded to preen his plumage meticulously. We never had as much pickerel, before or afterwards, as we had during the winter that Black Donald was with us.

When the weather began to moderate, Black Donald showed signs of restlessness. One day there was a faint "Boom-boom-boom" from the direction of the cow pasture. "Boys," said Father, "you better get the fanning mill started. I hear the prairie chickens calling." The hustle and bustle of getting ready for spring work was under way. Father spent more time outdoors. It was obvious that Black Donald was being more and more neglected.

From the grove came a mighty chorus of redwing and grackle voices. But, for a while, Black Donald stayed with us. There seemed to be a reluctance to part with him. Then it happened. It was quite a ceremony. With everyone gathered about, the egg case was carried to the front lawn and held at shoulder height while the cover was removed. Black Donald hopped up on the edge of it and hesitated. "Check," he said, as he looked around and flipped his tail, as though wondering if this were really true.

With another "Check" and a mighty kick, he took off, a little unsteadily, upward and southward. Then he turned westward and disappeared over the top of our windbreak. For a time we hoped he would come back and in some way identify himself. But to our knowledge we never saw him again. We could only hope that, after his ordeal of spending a winter in the north, he lived a normal, happy life and found it possible to forgive us for some of the indignities to which we had subjected him.

... *The blue jay*

March, 1955

One cannot help noticing the blue jay. Large enough to be easily seen, and one of the most strikingly beautiful of American birds, it doesn't mind coming near human habitations with its loud, sharp call notes, "Teeah — Teeah," emphatically calling attention to its whereabouts. The male and female — and even the young — sport flashy uniforms of bright blue above and whitish grey below. The crown, jaunty crest and back are clear violet-blue. The wings and tail are rich cobalt-blue and are accentuated by contrasting white and narrower black crossbars. A black ring around the neck broadens to a crescent shape on the chest.

It is amusing to watch a blue jay from an unobserved position as it sounds forth its clarion call. The flagrant rascal evidently enjoys hearing its own voice, putting forth its utmost effort to make the loudest possible noise and bowing impressively to emphasize each call. Not content with a mere call note, our vociferous friend has a variety of utterances, including a soft, conversational purr. In fact, the blue jay is a remarkable mimic. And a ventriloquist as well. While doing chores one day, I paused to look toward our windbreak as I heard the perfect screaming call of a red-tailed hawk. At so close a range, this large bird would be plainly visible among the bare-boughed trees. But all I saw was a few excited chickadees. Presently, however, a blue jay, apparently satisfied with his prank, took flight leisurely from where he had perched facing my direction, his grayish breast a perfect camouflage against an overcast sky. I don't know whether his efforts were directed toward me or the chickadees, but it certainly worked.

On the last morning of my stay at the National Audubon Society's Connecticut Nature Center in August, 1953, two other delegates and I were trying desperately to raise our bird list to 100 species. We had 97 and were returning to the dining hall when the toad-like call of an upland plover came from among the shrubbery, a strange place indeed and an odd season for an upland plover. But, since we were within three species of our goal, we started on a "will-o-the wisp" trail through the dew-drenched shrubbery, led on by a blue jay with a sense of humor, and came very near being late for our breakfast.

The blue jay is often denounced as a nest robber. It goes against our principle of fair play to see this large bird eat the eggs and even kill and eat the fledglings of smaller birds. But it must be remembered that, in the law of nature, there is no more wrong in this method of obtaining food than in eating insects. Furthermore, the blue jay is not nearly as persistent a nest robber as it is thought to be. One summer a pair of blue jays and a pair of mourning doves nested in the same juniper tree near our house. The nests were less than eight feet apart, yet these birds got along peaceably. Before we judge the blue jay too harshly let us consider our own custom in this regard. Do we not enjoy eggs for breakfast and chicken for dinner? A great many of us enjoy hunting and fishing, taking it for granted that there is nothing wrong with this method of obtaining victuals — and there isn't. We need no other justification for this than the fact that we have canine teeth. It is a perfectly natural thing to do. But why criticize the blue jay for doing the same thing?

During the summer the blue jay is predominantly insectivorous. But during the rest of the year it lives on acorns, chestnuts, hickory nuts, beechnuts, corn, etc. Blue jays are energetic, industrious workers. Like the squirrel, they store away and bury many more acorns and other nuts than they can possibly use or even find again, so they become an important agent in planting oak, beech and other forest trees. There is more blue jay character than fiction in Mark Twain's story about the blue jay that labored incessantly to fill an old deserted cabin with acorns by dropping them one at a time through a knothole in the roof while a number of other blue jays, taking turns looking in through the open door to see the acorns falling on the floor, sat about in the trees and guffawed at the joke.

When nesting time comes, the active loud-spoken blue jay becomes very quiet and sly, to avoid revealing the location of its nest. The nest may be in dense woodland or in a tree near our home, preferably in a conifer, and anywhere from five to fifty feet from the ground. The bird never flies directly to the nest. Approaching cautiously, it usually alights on one of the lower branches and, keeping a wary eye to see that it isn't being watched, hops leisurely from branch to branch until it finally reaches the nest. Male and female take turns brooding the eggs and the one that is off duty often brings food to the one on the nest. Both parents take part in the arduous task of feeding and caring for the young. They show great valor in defense of their young, driving squirrels and even cats away from the nest. The blue jay's family stays together throughout the fall and winter, the young often being fed by the parents long after they are well able to feed themselves. The family group migrates irregularly at this season, being joined by other family groups to form noisy, rollicking bands wherever food is plentiful.

Blue jays are listed as permanent residents throughout their range, which extends from southern Canada to the Gulf of Mexico. Some individuals may even spend the winter in frigid latitudes. But there is a noticeable southward movement of these hardy birds from the northern part of their range in the fall. In this latitude they are quite common throughout the winter.

We are fortunate, during this season of bird scarcity, in having blue jays to liven up our quiet winter woods with their vigorous, cheerful calls, to lend a flash of color to our drab winter landscape and to amuse us with their pranks.

...Yellow-shafted flicker

April, 1955

Several times this winter I have noticed yellow-shafted flickers in the neighborhood. They are recognizable by their size and characteristic bounding flight, even at a considerable distance. On January 4th two male birds of this species were considerate enough to appear on our front lawn where I could see them plainly. In all probability these were individuals from the northern part of their range that had chosen to spend the winter in this area. Since the food supply is the deciding factor in determining their winter sojourn, I suspect these flickers have located some trees that are riddled with wood borers or carpenter ants.

Southward bound flickers were very numerous along the north shore of Lake Superior on September 9, 1953, when I was among those who watched the hawk migration at Duluth. Afraid to fly over an expanse of water, the flickers, like the hawks, follow the shore southwestward to Duluth before fanning out again in their southward migration. A few individual flickers may winter as far north as southern Minnesota, but most of them go farther south and return to this latitude in the early part of April. Last year I heard the first one on March 28th.

The call of the flicker is one of the most welcome sounds of spring. The wind may be chilly and the ground still frozen after the long, cold monotony of winter, but that loud, long-continued and often-repeated "wick wick wick wick wick" from the windbreak expresses the spirit of spring and stirs in us thoughts of milder weather, running streams and catkins dangling from the cottonwoods.

The yellow-shafted flicker was one of my first bird acquaintances and holds a special appeal because, as a youngster, it was my thrilling experience to observe closely the domestic life of a family of flickers that occupied a dead cottonwood stump with a nesting cavity low enough for me to reach into. While the nesting cavity was being excavated I actually caught and held one of the birds in my hands. Strangely enough, this did not stop the flickers from completing their home and rearing a family there. Despite Mother's advice to the contrary, I visited the nest almost every day to count the eggs and take them, and later the young birds, from the nesting hole to look at them. What faithful, patient, tolerant and understanding birds those parent flickers were! I never succeeded in catching either of them again. They always left just before I slapped my hand over their doorway. One day I discovered that they had made a small peep-hole through the back of the stump at the nest level so they could keep an eye on what went on in their back yard. Some have suggested that this hole had been made accidently, but I am inclined to credit the flickers with this much ingenuity. All seven of the glossy, white eggs hatched and all the nestlings were successfully reared. As they neared maturity, the nesting cavity became desperately crowded, so a leather-hinged smoked-herring box was nailed to the top of the stump and all the young flickers put into it. The parent flickers, still cooperating without protest, paid no more attention to the nesting hole but went directly to the box to feed their young. Neither the nesting hole nor the box were occupied in following years, but how the flickers loved to use that resonant box for drumming their beaks during the courtship season!

The courtship antics of the flicker are extravagant and amusing to watch, especially when the competition is keen. The wooing calls are numerous, the most common being "wickup, wickup, wickup," accompanied by much bowing, nodding, peek-a-booing and feather displaying. When the matter is finally decided, both sexes take part in excavating the nesting cavity, brooding the eggs and caring for the young.

This, our only brownish colored woodpecker, is less specialized than any of the other woodpeckers. It may perch in a vertical position on a tree trunk, bracing itself with its tail feathers like other woodpeckers, or perch on a branch crosswise like other birds. Besides drilling in trees for wood-boring insects, it eats some wild fruit and feeds on many kinds of insects, some of which it may catch in flight. It spends much time on the ground and is particularly fond of ants. The greater diversity in the food habits of the flicker probably accounts for its being more numerous and more generally distributed than any of the other woodpeckers.

The red-shafted flicker of the western United States is very similar to the yellow-shafted flicker in voice, feeding habits, nesting habits and in all other respects, except for a few plumage markings. Its wing and tail linings are salmon-red rather than golden-yellow. It has no red on the back of its head and the male has red patches or whisker markings on the sides of its throat rather than black ones as in the yellow-shafted flicker species. Originally, the Great Plains, treeless as they were, served as a natural barrier separating the ranges of the two flicker species. But today, when the prairies have been settled and planted to windbreaks and shelterbelts, the range of both species has broadened so that the two not only come together but overlap. Where this occurs the two species interbreed, producing hybrids the likes of which, I doubt, ever inhabited Noah's Ark. Some have orange-yellow wing linings. Some have one black whisker and one red one. Some are yellow feathered with reddish nape. Still others are colored like the eastern species on one side and like the western species on the other side. Because these two species interbreed so freely some prominent ornithologists now question whether they are, in reality, two distinct species.

... *American bittern*

Spring has lost many of the sounds that were so characteristic of the season a generation ago. One of the most familiar of these sounds was the mating call of the American bittern. This peculiar, loud, pumping sound produced by the male bittern during the courtship and nesting season was no example of eloquence. But the very strangeness of it — and the fact that the bird was such a secretive fellow — aroused curiosity, provoked comment and often brought smiles to the faces of those who heard it. People naturally wondered how the bird looked while rendering such an odd serenade and often tried to catch him in the act. But the bittern is a very deliberate bird. Clothed in neutral colors — buffy-brown — and penciled to match the vegetation among which it dwells, the bittern is an expert at concealing itself by assuming a slender, upright posture and remaining perfectly motionless. The bittern's home was among the rank vegetation of cattail sloughs which, at that time, could be found on so many farms. There were as many courting bitterns as there were sloughs. The song, if it can be called a song, was clearly audible for at least a mile or so. From early morning until far into the night rural dwellers could hear "plum pudd'n, plum-pudd'n, plum-pudd'n," arising from the secret depths of every cattail slough in the neighborhood.

Near the schoolhouse where I attended country school was a small cattail slough that each spring, of course, harbored its pair of nesting bitterns. When school was in session the bittern's call, though muffled, could be heard even within the schoolroom. To one who was more conscious of bird calls than was sometimes to the best interest of the lessons at hand, that bittern was always answering the teacher's questions with comments that were sometimes quite as appropriate as those of Poe's "Raven." In physiology class one day the teacher asked one of the boys to describe the action of the heart. While he was scratching his head and wondering what words to use, the bittern beat him to it with his usual comment, "plum-pudd'n, plum-pudd'n", for which observation I think he should have rated an A. I suspect that the teacher sometimes wondered at the reason for some unexplained smiles.

Several of the herons are gregarious and nest in colonies, but the bittern prefers solitude. The first bittern to arrive at his favorite slough in the spring proclaims his right to it by sounding his pumping song. Other male bitterns respect his right and fly on to look for other sloughs. While the odd call repels other male bitterns, it attracts females. It serves as both a property lease and a love song. In due time arrangements are made and the bittern pair get on with the task of rearing a family in their own private slough. The nest is a platform of dead vegetation among the cattails. The eggs are brooded from the time the first egg is laid, so the young hatch at intervals, with resulting variation in size. Young bitterns have many enemies, such as minks, muskrats, snapping turtles, snakes, hawks, etc. But the mother bittern, with her courage and rapier beak, is a formidable defender.

The bittern finds such choice morsels of food as snails, frogs, crayfish, snakes, dragonflies and a number of small water animals in his own home slough. But, like other herons, it has a voracious appetite and sometimes wanders into adjoining meadows and fields in search of such game as meadow mice, moles, shrews, snakes, lizards and a variety of insects, including grasshoppers.

In the neighborhood where I grew up were two drainage ditches — one on our farm and the other a mile to the north. These open ditches were fenced, to keep livestock from trampling dirt into the watercourse. The resulting tall grass and weeds along the banks furnished cover for many forms of wildlife. Attracted by mice, frogs, minnows and crayfish, the bitterns left their sloughs and took up stations at various places along these streams where, concealed by the tall grass, they could hunt and fish all day, unobserved by passers-by. When on adventurous strolls along our ditch banks we were frequently startled by a bittern taking sudden flight from almost underfoot. The take-off always followed the same pattern. There was a sudden rapid flopping of large wings, a dangling of long, greenish-yellow legs and three or four wheezy croaks as the bird struggled for altitude. Simultaneously, the "slough pump" (as the bird was often called) never failed to register his disgust at being disturbed by discharging a splash of excrement. After attaining a height of about thirty feet the legs were locked straight back in flight position, the neck folded and the head drawn back to the shoulders in true heron flight fashion. Changing to a slow, even wingbeat, the bittern then headed for his home slough.

Bitterns living in the sloughs south of us could be seen every day flying overhead to and from their favorite fishing spots. A lady in our neighborhood hated all bitterns because of a sad Saturday experience many years ago. I don't blame her. But I cannot share her grudge, because I doubt if that bittern really aimed to give her any trouble. In anticipation of possible Sunday company, she had scrubbed her porch immaculately clean. Having poured away the wash water and stepped inside the screen door, she turned to give her porch a last critical look, when she noticed a shadow cross the yard, heard a familiar squawk overhead and then found it necessary to wash the porch again.

With the coming of tractor power and all-clear-field farming, the farm slough has disappeared and with it the bittern and his unique song. To hear a bittern now one must journey to the cattail border of some river or lake. On a field trip to White's Lake west of Albert Lea in 1952 members of the Albert Lea Audubon Society were fortunate enough to see a bittern render his remarkable courtship performance. The bird's lower neck was dilated, as though it had attempted to swallow some object about the size of an orange and was having extreme difficulty getting it either up or down. The head suddenly lowered, then shot convulsively upward and forward several times while we heard "plum-pudd'n, plum-pudd'n, plum-pudd'n."

Economically, the bittern was of neutral importance and not numerous enough to affect us much either way, but I, for one, regret his passing because of his outstanding attribute, the peculiar pumping song.

... *Upland plover*

June, 1955

It is heartening for a bird enthusiast to witness the coming back of a species that has been as seriously threatened with complete extinction as has the upland plover. I do not know if my experience with the bird is a true indication of its status in general, but, if so, there is hope that the upland plover will survive as a species, even though, with habitat limitations and other adverse factors, we can never expect to see it in such great numbers as used to populate this area in pre-market hunting days.

Every year for the past fifteen years it has been my pleasure to have at least one pair of upland plovers spend the summer on our farm here in Freeborn County. I remember vividly the first pair that came here. On April 28, 1940, as I was putting the cows into the barn for the evening milking, I paused abruptly to listen to a bird call I had not heard for at least 25 years. From dizzy heights over the pasture to the west came the prolonged, two-syllable song, starting with a bubbling, liquid-like sound and changing to a clear, mellow whistle, first rising and then falling in pitch and intensity. In modern lingo I suppose one might call it a long-drawn wolf whistle. The long-lost bird song, so mysterious in my boyhood days on our prairie farm in Winnebago County, Iowa, turned out to be the mating call of the upland plover.

Those first birds were very shy, invariably flushing before I came within sixty rods. Perhaps it was my fault for trying to approach them on foot while fetching the cows, with my dog usually following me or running on ahead. During the early part of the season they always flushed from the same area in my sweet-clover pasture, so I assumed they were nesting there, although I never found their nest. The next spring I learned to my amazement that upland plovers have little fear of the tractor or other farm machinery. Often they merely step aside far enough to avoid being covered with dirt by the disc. From the tractor seat I have had no trouble observing them at close range and enjoying their winsome ways.

Unlike the mechanical running of the killdeer, the upland plover walks with dainty grace, bobbing its head forward with every step. The enchanting call is given while flying with quivering wings several hundred feet up. When alighting, the bird always lifts its wings, holding them outstretched over its back a moment before folding them carefully. This habit flashes the lighter-colored underwing plumage, which often calls my attention to the bird's presence in a field. Several times the plovers have surprised me by remaining confidently perched on a fence post while my tractor thundered past, taking the first disc-swath along the fence.

In 1941, the upland plovers' activities had moved to the next field, which was then my pasture. They faithfully follow the crop rotation, always, presumably, nesting in the field that is being pastured that season. In 1943, while planting a field of silage corn, I had the good fortune to see two parent plovers with their brood of four newly-hatched chicks, the first definite proof that the birds were actually nesting here. I caught one of the chicks, much to the consternation of the parent birds, who hovered about feigning charges at me and uttering their discordant cries. The captive chick made my eardrums ring with its fretful cries. It had a masterful voice for such a delicate creature.

In 1944, three pairs of upland plovers nested here, each holding forth on a separate area — one in the pasture and one in each of two small, grassy waste areas. After that bonanza year, however, there has been only one nesting pair each year, although during the spring migration I have seen as many as six birds walking about my fields.

Early in June in 1948 I was plowing a field of pastured rye in preparation for planting it to soybeans when, suddenly, an upland plover charged toward the tractor with half-raised wings, then veered off and took flight. After stopping the tractor I went forward to the spot — directly ahead — from which I saw the bird start. A tractor wheel had gone within four feet of the nest on the previous round without disturbing the brooding plover. To spare the nest with its four eggs I left a small patch of rye unplowed. Having discovered the nest I went back often to check it in order, if possible, to be on hand when the eggs were hatching. The brooding plover proved unbelievably tame, never seemingly disturbed when I stopped the tractor near by or even when I stood or squatted within two feet of the nest. Lest the eggs should hatch and the young leave the nest unobserved on Sunday, I also checked the nest then. Curiosity prompted me to see how close I could get to the bird before it flushed. When my fingers were within six inches of her, the plover's eyes started shifting. I spoke a few reassuring words, whereupon my dog (which had followed me unobserved, despite my order that he stay home) evidently thought I was talking to him and bounced up to me, almost trampling on the nest. The plover left in such haste as to knock one egg against another, cracking one shell badly. The membrane under the shell, however, was not ruptured. The next day the plover was on her nest and all seemed well.

The second day after the accident the brooding plover seemed more nervous than usual and sat in a half-raised position. She left the nest a little way as I approached and found two of the eggs, including the damaged one, hatched and a third shell pipped. I immediately called a member of the Albert Lea Audubon Society who is a camera enthusiast with a flare for nature pictures. He drove out at once and took some still pictures of the nest, eggs, and young plovers. A little later, as I watched from the tractor, the mother plover returned and he took, at close range, about fifty feet of film showing the bird parading protectively between him and the nest. The following day the nest was vacated and I saw the parent plovers escorting their three young in the sweet-clover pasture, which was in the next field. I cracked the deserted egg and found it to be infertile. This is the only nest I have actually located, although I often encounter the plover family as they go about their insect-hunting in my fields during corn cultivating and haying time.

The most common date of spring arrival has been April 28th, although they have shown up as early as April 19th and as late as May 5th. This year they came on April 25th. On a field trip to Upper Twin Lake, about twenty members of the Minneapolis Bird Club and six guests from Worthington, together with three local birders, stopped at my farm to see some field and woodland birds. The upland plover put on a fine serenading demonstration for the group. Apparently they were not frightened by the presence of seven cars and thirty enthusiastic birdwatchers in my cow lane.

Every year during the upland plover's absence (from early August until the latter part of April) I keep my fingers crossed, hoping that my plovers will not fall victim to some trigger-happy Argentine gaucho or meet with disaster en route to or from their winter home. Each spring, however, I am reassured, as I was this year on April 25th, when again I heard their welcome call.

... *The spring bird count*

July, 1955

One of the favorite activities of birdwatchers is the spring bird count. Every bird club and Audubon Society chapter worthy of its name plans at least one spring bird-counting field trip, not only for the enjoyment of its members but also as a contribution to the science of ornithology. Birders in this latitude find that May is the magic month for those who long to lengthen their list. It has been my experience that, in this area, a greater variety of birds can be seen during the third week in May than at any other time of the year. While several migrants will already have gone on to their more northern nesting areas and others will not have arrived yet, the bulk of the migrants will at that time be passing through and a good birder should be able to go afield during the third week in May and count from 75 to 100 species in a single day. This isn't a simple task, however, especially in a year like 1955 when tree leaves were fully developed so early in the season. Many of the smaller woodland birds are difficult enough to identify in the treetops without being concealed by a mass of leaves. Birds instinctively try to avoid being seen lest they fall prey to some enemy. But after a night of migratory flight hunger keeps them on the move despite their awareness of one's presence, and their movements help to betray their whereabouts. In 1950, when a late spring frost killed all the leaves and trees had to rebud, birdwatchers had a heyday because spring migrants found our trees almost bare-boughed and so had very little to hide them. The composite list of the Albert Lea Audubon Society that year, in a four hour count, was 107 species — a good list for this small group in so little time. At Frontenac in 1953 the composite list of 200 birders attending the spring meeting of the Minnesota Ornithologists Union reached the remarkable total of exactly 150 species in the two-day count.

There is great variation in the migrating bird population in any given area from year to year. A species may be very numerous one year and almost (or entirely) absent the next. Wood thrushes were abundant at Frontenac in 1952. But in 1953 I failed to see or hear any. The blackpoll warbler was one of the most numerous species in the Albert Lea area in the spring of 1950. They have never been so numerous since. This year we saw only one after a considerable search for a strange whisper song. I have seen migrating warblers in such con-centration that half a dozen species were in sight in a single tree at the same time. This, in birders' lingo, would be called a "warbler wave." There was no "warbler wave" this year. We had to be content with listing only seven species. Three of these — the yellow warbler, the redstart and the northern yellow-throat — were quite numerous. But we saw only one bird of each of the other four species. Last year our list included twenty species of warblers.

While finding warblers this year was generally difficult, three of the vireos were quite numerous. I have never seen or heard warbling vireos in such concentration as they were this spring. The red-eyed and the yellow-throated vireos were also very much in evidence. Vireos are interesting birds. As they go about in-sect-hunting so leisurely and well camouflaged in the treetops, they might escape notice entirely were it not for their charac-teristic and persistent song. Most vireo songs, with variations of course, consist of short two or three syllable phrases with brief pauses between. The song is not loud and may be hard for the novice to concentrate on among the frequent calls of the car-dinal, oriole and other loud-spoken species. However, vireo songs are consistent and, with a little help from a fellow birder, should not be very hard to learn to recognize. While break-fasting at Frontenac this year, a gentleman seated across the table from me complained to the person sitting next to him, "I can't, for the life of me, see how some of these people can go out into the woods, point up into a tree and say, 'There's a vireo,' without even seeing the bird." I knew what he meant and could sympathize with him because all vireos used to be such mysterious birds for me. But the remark amused me since the Albert Lea group had just spent a half hour in pursuit of a yellow-throated vireo — led on by its song — and had several good looks at the bird. Recognizing a bird by its song is like recognizing a friend by his voice in the next room. Familiarity lends assurance. Knowing the song, one has only to follow it until he gets a chance to see the bird. This may take half an hour or more with the yellow-throated vireo, which has a habit of flying to a tree several rods away about the time one has it spotted. It also has the habit of occasionally pausing in its singing, giving the impression that it has flown away unobserved, only to resume its song in the same tree. These pauses give the birder an idea of how frustrating the search for a vireo can be without its song as a guide.

Until after the turn of the century the accepted practice among birders was to shoot the birds they wished to identify. With the dead bird in hand they could then examine it at leisure and in minute detail. They called this method "collecting." But, whatever name it went by, it was still killing birds. Thanks to the efforts of the National Audubon Society, backed by public opinion, this practice has now been outlawed. Birding today is done with the aid of binoculars and pocket-sized field guides which have, for each species, an illustration for comparison with the live bird and brief text material on field marks, voice, behavior traits and range, which help to identify the bird at a distance.

Birders use various methods in spotting birds. In attempting to reach a goal of 100 species I prefer birding by ear. One naturally hears many more birds than he can see. Birds are usually heard before they are seen. It saves a lot of time to list the familiar birds by their songs without taking time to look them up. This leaves more time to trace strange sounds to their source. However, one has to be careful in calling the birds too quickly by their songs lest he find himself in the red face department. Some of the bird songs sound much alike, and when one is birding in company he gets checked up on.

There are other compensations in birding besides the lure of the long list. There is the satisfaction of helping a fellow birder find a bird he has never seen and there is the thrill of being helped by a fellow birder in finding a bird one has not seen before. There is also the experience of meeting people from all walks of life, brought together by a common interest in birds.

Some question the accuracy of these mass field observations of birds and, no doubt, there are mistakes in the listing. But there is much of scientific value to be learned from them, nevertheless. Professional ornithologists do not take the unusual finds as authentic until one has established a reputation of reliable birding.

... *Vesper sparrow*

August, 1955

The sparrows are a confusing lot. How often, while birding, one hears the remark, "It's a sparrow. But what kind?" There are so many species and subspecies so annoyingly similar in general appearance that it is no disgrace for even an expert birder to admit that he does not know them all. In his *Field Guide to the Birds*, Roger Tory Peterson lists 62 species of sparrows for Eastern North America. Nearly all of them have plain, brown-streaked plumage which, for concealment, is so well suited to their grassy or dusty habitats. Although much alike in color, size and form, their songs, behavior traits, habitat and minor plumage markings serve to distinguish the various species so, one by one, the birder can learn to separate each species from the perplexing group.

A rather dingy, grey and brownish-streaked member of this large family that everyone should know is the vesper sparrow. It is easily recognized by the white outer tail feathers which it obligingly displays in flight. Sometimes this bird is called the bay-wing because of the small, triangular, chestnut-colored patch at the bend of the wing, a much less conspicuous but equally positive mark of identification. The emotional quality of its song, registering such satisfaction and contentment with its pastoral abode, has earned for it the title, "Poet of the Fields." From atop a fence post, weed stalk or, perhaps more often from a hidden position in the grass, it can be heard singing at any time of day, and occasionally even at night. Its simple little melody can be heard to the best advantage when the sun begins to lower and other bird songs tend to slacken. Hence its very appropriate name, vesper sparrow.

The vesper was one of the first native sparrows I knew. I frequently saw it dust-bathing or running ahead of me in the road as I walked to country school, the white outer tail feathers flashing conspicuously each time it flew to keep a safe distance ahead. When driving along dirt or gravel country roads one is almost certain to see the vespers engaged in these activities. But they can hardly be expected to compete with the modern automobile along our speedways. However, I often catch a bit of their quiet peaceful song as we whiz past. Like other sparrows, the vespers are naturally a little shy. But they can be observed at close range when one drives leisurely or parks the car near them. Apparently, the birds think man looks less dangerous in a car than on foot. The vespers are constant field companions. There are times when I do not see some of the other field birds. But from the earliest spring field work until far into November, I never fail to see a number of vesper sparrows while operating field machinery or going to and from my fields. I never see them around the farm buildings but frequently see and hear them in the field just outside my cowyard or beyond the windbreak. They avoid wooded areas and low, swampy ground, preferring rather to inhabit open upland where they are equally at home in meadows, pastures, cultivated fields and roadsides.

In the days when we cultivated corn with a single-row cultivator drawn by a team of horses we saw each and every hill of corn in the field as the work progressed, and frequently discovered a vesper sparrow's nest tucked close to a corn-hill. The neat cup, built of grass and lined with fine rootlets or hair, was sunken so the brim of the nest was even with the ground. When disturbed, the parent bird fluttered away along the ground in pretended injury to lure the intruder away from its nest. Flooding during heavy rains destroys many nests with eggs and young. But the birds readily renest and usually rear three broods in a season. The vesper sparrow also nests in pastures, meadows, stubble fields and fencerows. It is frequently parasitized by the cowbird, usually at the complete sacrifice of its own young. I once saw a vesper sparrow feeding cutworms to a young cowbird more than twice its own size. Fair play or foul, the little vesper was faithfully performing its assigned duty of ridding my fields of injurious insects.

The vesper sparrow is one of the farmer's best feathered friends. Like other sparrows, it is a seed eater, by which virtue it is enabled to exist in great numbers. During the crop-growing season its diet almost entirely consists of insect food, including many kinds of the most destructive insects, such as cutworms, click beetle (the adult of the wireworm), weevils, grasshoppers, etc. A bird that is rare may be ever so beneficial individually, yet of insignificant importance economically. The vesper sparrow, however, is so numerous and well distributed through fields of growing crops that it renders great service as a guardian against insect damage. Having adapted itself well to an intensively cultivated land habitat the vesper sparrow is very successful as a species. By virtue of its small size and modest color it has escaped much of the wanton destruction suffered by many of the larger birds but, since it is inconspicuous, it does not get credit for all the good it does. For that matter, I doubt that many people give any birds full credit for the good they do. Any bird that destroys cutworms, grasshoppers, wireworms and other injurious insects is a friend of mine, because I have had occasion to see some of the damage that these pests have brought about.

... *Bird flight*

September, 1955

The other evening, as I was looking westward over our windbreak at one of those sunsets which artists find so hard to duplicate, five ducks flew by, silhouetted against the crimson sky. My thoughts turned to the mobility of birds and the many ways in which their bodies are adapted for flight. Nature has indeed provided birds with a much more convenient and efficient means of getting about than she has the mammals. When we stop to consider that a creature as small as the ruby-throated hummingbird actually possesses the ability of spending its summer with us and its winter in South America we cannot help but marvel at it. By contrast, what chance does a mouse have of getting to South America to spend the winter? With its limited means of moving about, a mouse is destined to spend its entire lifetime within a few rods of where it is born. The fox, a larger animal that we think of as quite able to go places, spends its entire lifetime within an area about the size of one township, although it may travel farther if pursued. Even a big, burly beast like the grizzly bear spends its entire lifetime within a radius of five or, at the most, ten miles. For that matter, how far would we get if we depended solely on the mobile means nature has provided us with?

Bird flight has always attracted the attention and intrigued the imagination of man. His efforts to acquire the power of flight for himself have resulted, during the last few decades, in his mastery of the air by machines. But individual flight by his own muscular effort has always proved a failure. Every few years the press carries a story about someone who claims to have devised wings of some sort to propel himself through the air by his own muscles, like a bird. But the undertaking is doomed to failure before it starts because the human body is not designed for flight.

The body of a bird is adapted for flight in many ways besides the mere fact that it has wings. A bird is light and what weight it has is well centered. For their size and weight, feathers are the strongest structures known. Wing feathers overlap for support and are designed with a downward curve of both the shaft and branching, or barbs. The barbs are hooked together in zipper fashion. About half of the wing surface is beyond the wrist joint and can be turned downward when the wing is lifted. All of these things give strength and resistance to air on the downward beat of the wing, yet much less resistance to the air on the upward beat. Try pushing a pencil upward through the wing feathers of a chicken; then notice how much more easily the pencil can be pushed downward through the same wing feathers.

A bird's bones are hollow and thin-walled, which makes them much lighter than the bones of mammals. A bird lacks teeth and the necessarily heavy jawbones and muscling to support them, hence its head weighs little. The legs of most birds are very much reduced in size, with consequent saving in weight. A bird's wings are not heavily muscled. Instead, the muscular strength is extended to them by strong but lightweight tendons. For all its lightness, a bird's skeleton is strongly designed to support the muscular structure and to stand the strain of flight. The backbone and pelvis are rigid and the breastbone is greatly enlarged, with the ribs firmly attached to both, making a boxlike frame for the bird's internal organs. A large ridge down the middle of the breastbone serves for the attachment of the flight muscles, which are located on the under side of the body for the purpose of pulling the wings downward. This flight muscle (the white meat on a chicken) often makes up half of the weight of the entire bird.

The bird's bodily processes are much more rapid then ours and muscular energy is liberated much more rapidly, giving it the muscular power necessary for the strenuous work of flight and the endurance for long, continued flight. The golden plover, during migration, flies 2500 miles nonstop, with only the fat stored in its body to serve as fuel. It travels from the arctic regions to Argentina on about 1½ ounces of fat. That's real fuel economy!

To attain efficiency of flight some of the bird's needs are greatly suppressed. A mammal with an injured leg will hobble along on its remaining limbs until the injured leg mends, but a bird deprived of its power of flight is a pitiful thing. A broken wing often means death. A marsh hawk that fails to find as much as a mouse to eat for two days becomes too weak for flight and starves to death. There is the story of a North Dakota farmer who raised pigeons as a hobby and was inclined to boast about the homing abilities of one of his birds. When friends from various parts of the country visited him he would send the pigeon with them to be released when they reached home. When the pigeon returned to its cote the farmer would write to his friend, telling just when the pigeon got back. Each of these incidents spurred him on to greater boasting. All went well until a friend from Chicago, with a flare for pranks, plucked the pigeon's wing feathers before releasing it. No letter came, but about six months afterwards the friend chanced to meet the farmer on the street in Chicago and asked him if the pigeon ever returned. "Yes," replied the farmer. "He came back yesterday. But his feet were pretty sore."

Birds vary in their expertness of flight, all the way from the flutter of a sparrow to the graceful gliding ease of a swallow, from the weak butterfly-flight of a rail to the apparent motionless flight of an albatross, and from the flightless, waddling but expert swimming penguin to the split second powerdiving falcon.

Bird flight is indeed a wonderful adaptation, and it is our good fortune that birds are mobile enough to be present to aid us during our pest ridden crop-growing season, even though they are absent during the dormant season, when we have less need for their services and might otherwise have to provide special food for them.

. . . *Barn swallow*

October, 1955

One of the best known and probably the tamest of all our wild birds is the barn swallow. I have heard from those who have been there that the birds in the western United States are not nearly as fearful of man as the birds we have here. As yet, I have had no opportunity to observe this, but the barn swallow is certainly the tamest of all the wild birds that I know. This bird has thoroughly adapted itself to living near the habitations of man and by so doing has greatly benefited. It is much more numerous now than it was when it had to seek nesting shelter in the caves, crevices, large, hollow trees and under protruding rock ledges. In the northern wilderness the barn swallow still nests in such primitive locations. But throughout the far-flung settled area of the continent it has become so dependent on bridges, farm buildings and other man-made structures as a shelter for its nest that it is regarded by some as a sort of domesticated bird. There certainly has been a great change in its nesting location, even though the bird has made the change of its own accord and without any effort or persuasion by man, except indirectly.

When these swallows first began nesting in barns they often built their mud nests in colonies on the rafters and beams in haylofts. But after the introduction of that intruding rascal, the English sparrow, the barn swallows have moved downstairs. They still nest in colonies to some extent. One summer there were seven nests in our hog house. On a joist over the driveway through our barn is a barn swallow nest that is at present harboring its second brood of the season. The parent birds pay very little attention to me or the children as we go about the chores.

They never hesitate to bring food to their young, even though I may be so close to the nest that I could easily reach up and touch it. Sometimes they will take to dive-bombing a cat if the feline is too close and seems interested in their activities. When one of the children picks up a cat while standing near the nest the swallows do a little scolding. But usually everything is peaceful. The swallows enter the barn through a small top door that is always open during the summer. But at milking time, when the large doors are open, the birds take advantage of this more convenient entrance, even though it sometimes means flying within a few inches of our heads.

It seems only a few days ago that a tell-tale shell on the floor indicated that the eggs were hatching, and I wondered how these tardy young swallows would be able to join the southbound throngs already gathering. But so rapid is the development of young birds that today, September 11, one of the three young had taken a practice flight and was perched on a partially constructed mock nest·a few feet away. Whether by design or oversight, the parent birds kept bringing food to the two young in the nest but none to the nestling on his lone perch, even though he pleaded ardently every time they came near. After being passed up several times, the adventurous one flew back to join the other two and received his share of the groceries. Some people do not credit birds with any reasoning power, but it seems to me that this young swallow was using good logic. Young barn swallows do not leave the nest before they are fully able to fly and even then they keep returning to the nest for about a week before they break home ties.

Barn swallows are swift, strong, tireless flyers. They glide through the air with the ease and grace of Sonja Henie on ice. Their long, deeply-forked tails enable them to make the quick changes of direction so necessary for catching insects in flight and for eluding enemies. Most of their daylight hours are spent on the wing, where they obtain all their food, in the form of flying insects, and even their drink, which they secure by flying close to the surface of a pond, lake or stream and dipping down to scoop up mouthfuls of water. They also bathe in this manner.

These friendly swallows are attracted by grazing cattle and moving implements in the fields. They like to follow anything that moves, so as to feed on the disturbed insects. On cloudy days they seem to delight in flying low and swooping dangerously close to the front wheels of my tractor, where they feast till their crops are packed and their gullets are distended with insects. While mowing hay one day I saw to my dismay that European corn borer moths flew up in clouds from the alfalfa as the mower moved along. Presently, however, the air was full of barn swallows actively snapping up the destructive insects. Our colony of purple martins was also busy working at a little distance. By living near our dwellings, barn swallows help a great deal in reducing the number of flies, mosquitoes and other insect pests of man and his livestock. They are entitled to protection and encouragement. A window or door always left open during the summer will invite them to nest in any barn or outbuilding.

Like other swallows, the barn swallow migrates during the daytime, catching its food as it goes. It roosts at night in marshes and trees, sometimes using the same roosts year after year. As they move southward they congregate in flocks numbering hundreds of thousands. They encounter the same hazards en route as other birds do — shooting for sport, accidents and, the greatest of all bird hazards, the weather.

We slap mosquitoes less often now and it is time to bid our barn swallows farewell. But by the latter part of next April we can again look for their return, announced by their cheerful, conversational, musical twitter.

. . . Fall migration

November, 1955

Many of our feathered summer residents have left us, but the air, woods, lakes, marshes, fields, roadsides and fence rows are so filled with transients that, for the birdwatcher, this is an immensely satisfying time of the year. The autumn flight of birds is in full swing. It began with the gathering of some of the shore birds in the early part of July and will continue to some extent into December when the last of the arctic birds, such as the snowy owl, come to stay with us. But the greatest hustle and bustle in the southward shifting of bird populations occurs during September and October. The task of rearing young has been completed for the year. The nesting territories have been abandoned and there has been a gathering of the clans in preparation for the departure. The general movement is southward but there is always considerable shifting about.

Like children off to school, the birds are all decked out in new attire, which in many species differs so much from the spring plumage that even the most expert birder is often confused. Especially confusing are the great many species of warblers native to the United States and northward. In flashy spring plumage they are readily recognized. But in their plain, often similar, autumn garb they are hard to distinguish.

While I was plowing the old alfalfa-brome grass pasture this fall a flock of gulls, probably numbering over a thousand birds, followed my plow almost continually. Their clamor as they scrambled for earthworms and insects uncovered by the plow sounded as if the coulters and wheels of a dozen plows were all squawking for grease. With all of its virtues, the gull is not a **gifted singer. Most of these were Franklins, both mature and** juvenile, in both adult and immature plumage. The Franklins in winter plumage had gray hoods rather than the dark heads of their spring plumage.

While walking across a grain stubble field one evening I disturbed a flock of American pipits. About a hundred of them took off from a low place in the field and circled erratically overhead, constantly uttering their sharp, high-pitched call notes, "tsee-seep, tsee-seep." When I had passed, they circled down in true lark fashion to alight in the same spot from which they arose. Perhaps each bird found his same snug roosting place among the stubble. I wouldn't know how to go about making sure of this but it is an interesting thought.

For several days I have heard from among weedy fencerows an indistinct "tseet" and occasionally a faint snatch of the spring song, "old sam peabody, peabody, peabody," betraying the whereabouts of a white-throated sparrow. As I started homeward with my tractor and plow one evening, a half dozen birds flew up from some dense willow shrubbery and darted into the woods. I caught a glimpse of the chestnut sides and large white spotting on the long, rounded tail of the nearest bird and recognized it as an eastern towhee or chewink — a rare bird in this locality. They were numerous in Connecticut when I was there. But I have had only four sight records of this bird locally.

The first wave of juncos appeared suddenly a few days ago. One day there were none, and I hadn't seen any for months. The next morning dozens of them were flitting across my path, everywhere, flashing their white outer tail feathers. Like most small birds, juncos migrate at night and, with the coming of daylight, drop down to feed and rest wherever they happen to be.

Hawks are daytime migrants and interesting birds to watch. They all like to make use of thermals, or upward currents of air, where they can fly with little effort. On warm still days the sun heats the air next to the ground, causing it to rise up through the cooler, heavier air, thus creating a thermal. Although these thermals are invisible they are sometimes topped by a cumulus cloud. I have seen as many as fifty buteos in a group, circling about under such a cloud, where I could view them from my tractor seat. Mother used to call these buteos "wind-hawks," and that isn't a bad classification. When wind blows against a mountainside the air is turned upward. Hawks seek these updrafts and follow them on their migratory journey. In the Blue Ridge Mountains in eastern Pennsylvania there is a rocky ridge extending above the forested sides of the mountain. From this vantage point one can see far over the lowlands on either side. When the wind is from the northwest, hawks by the thousands glide by — many of them at close range. This place has become known throughout the ornithological world as Hawk Mountain. In past years hunters used to gather here during hawk migration and shoot hawks by the thousands as they came within range. Today, Hawk Mountain is patrolled by wardens employed by the Hawk Mountain Sanctuary Association. Birdwatchers from all over the world come with binoculars to watch the hawk flight and identify the species of each bird.

There are many other places, however, that offer equal opportunities for viewing hawk flights. I wonder how many Minnesotans are aware of the hawk flyway at Duluth. From the skyline drive above 45th Avenue three times as many hawks have been counted in a single day as have ever been counted in one day at Hawk Mountain. Furthermore, the Duluth flyway is more dependable. One can always count on seeing some hawks there every day from mid-August through November, regardless of which direction the wind is from, although here also a northwest wind brings the greatest number of hawks.

. . . Starlings

December, 1955

While the Sunday noon meal was being prepared a couple of weeks ago, I was deeply engrossed in a *Nature Magazine* article about the geological oddities of the old Apalachee region around Tallahassee, Florida. Suddenly there burst forth that startled expression so familiar at our house, "Hey Daddy! What kind of bird is this?"

"What does it look like?" I asked, thinking I might identify it without leaving my comfortable chair.

"Plump, fat birds like pigeons with green and purple spots all over" came the rapid-fire but incredible description. By now, I realized it would be a saving of time to get up and take a look out the window. A number of starlings were helping themselves to the fruit of our hackberry tree and trying in vain to get a drink from the frozen contents of a pail that we used for watering the chickens last summer.

The starling in new fall plumage is a strikingly attired bird. The white and buffy tips of its body feathers give this chunky, short-tailed blackbird a conspicuously speckled appearance, accentuated by a background of glossy-black with metallic green and purple iridescence, especially about the head and neck.

The starling is not a native of America. It is a European bird that was imported and released in this country because immigrants from Europe were lonesome for the birds they used to know. Before 1900, hundreds of foreign bird species were released in the United States, but most of these introductions have proved complete failures — largely because ecology was not taken into consideration. It is hard to duplicate exactly the conditions under which foreign birds thrive in their native home. It is disgusting to observe that, of the very few species that have caught on and prospered in this country, most of them have found in our cities and farmsteads a reasonable semblance of their native habitat, without their natural enemies, and have developed into a nuisance. Such is the case with the pigeon, the English sparrow and now, the starling.

In the early twenties I read an account of the rapid westward spread of the European starling in America. Although these birds were by that time already a nuisance in eastern cities, I had not yet seen any of them and looked forward to the arrival of starlings here with mixed feelings of curiosity and dread.

The first of these boisterous birds came to our farmstead in 1933, and promptly took over one of the English sparrow's nesting sites — the small, inaccessible, decorative tin cupola atop the silo roof. English sparrows were already nesting there, but the newcomers threw out their nest and its contents onto the silage below and — disregarding the fuss of the sparrows — made themselves at home. It seemed good to see that, at last, the troublesome sparrows had met their masters. The starlings held undisputed right to this nesting place until a couple of years ago when a strong wind blew the top off the cupola, making it unfit for either starling or sparrow nests. The starlings still do a lot of spring courting there. They also attempt to build nests on the top step of the ladder inside the silage chute, with the result that in the fall at silo filling time I find hay, straw, grass, feathers and other nesting material to a depth of two feet in my silage room below the chute. One year starlings entered a knot hole in the haymow wall and nested in the hay inside. They were safe until the hay was used and the nest exposed. This nesting was never repeated. One year rats gnawed a hole in the boxed eaves of my corncrib-granary cupola, so now the starlings have another ideal nesting place where no one can disturb them. On our lawn stands an old, dead black cherry tree with a flicker nesting hole near the top. Every year there is spirited rivalry between the flickers, the English sparrows and the starlings for the possession of this nesting site, but eventually the starlings always win. An old poplar that for two years had harbored a family of sparrow hawks blew down and I built a nesting box in the hope that the hawks might find it an acceptable substitute for their destroyed home when they returned for another season of nesting. Starlings, however, took over the convenient shelter at once. The last two years, starlings have invaded the woods out on our farm and have employed flickers as their carpenters.

Starling numbers have skyrocketed and their territory has now spread to all settled parts of North America from Hudson Bay to the Gulf of Mexico and from the Atlantic to the Pacific, with the greatest concentration in eastern cities. Even in mid-western cities, however, their noise and litter about roosts are already causing severe complaints by residents. Many attempts by various methods have been tried to discourage and break up starling roosts. The latest idea is the use of a tape recording of a starling's distress screams. It seems to work, as the starlings and other birds roosting with them promptly leave. How long this ruse will work to disperse the plucky birds is a question only time will answer. One thing is certain. The European starling is here to stay. We may not like its noisy quarrelsomeness and filth. We may not like its crowding out of our native species of birds as we Europeans crowded out the American Indian, but we have no choice. We will have to put up with the starling and hope that its population reaches a leveling off point.

Perhaps it might be well to look for some of the starling's good qualities. After all, it is not totally obnoxious, and we must remember that it is not here of its own accord but because of the unwise meddling of man.

...*The loon*

January, 1956

On Saturday, December 3rd, my wife and I motored to Minneapolis to attend the winter meeting of the Minnesota Ornithologists Union at the Museum of Natural History. The very excellent program consisted of thirteen papers on various phases of ornithological research and several colored films on bird life. The papers inspired the group to enthusiastic questions and much favorable comment.

The highlight of the afternoon business meeting was the agreement to support and recommend the loon as state bird of Minnesota. This decision did not come easily. The matter has been dangling for years, with about as many favorite bird candidates as there were people meeting to discuss the problem. At a special meeting of the M.O.U. policy committee the previous evening an attempt was made to reach agreement on one bird to submit for approval at the Saturday meeting. The committee was successful in narrowing the field to two birds, but remained deadlocked on the loon and the pileated woodpecker. It was decided to take a vote on the two birds at the Saturday meeting. At that time there were sixty members present and the first vote, quite typically, was 30 to 30. One of the members arose to suggest that, since the pileated woodpecker stayed with us throughout the year, whereas the loon skipped out for the winter months, we should give preference to the pileated woodpecker as our state bird. Dr. Dwain Warner of the museum staff then took the floor in defense of the loon and so ably phrased his plea that when a second vote was taken it turned out 46 to 14 in favor of the loon.

Many other groups also have an interest and influence in this

matter. And, of course, there will be no official state bird until the legislature passes a bill to that effect. But it is a step forward to have the M.O.U. united in support of one bird as a candidate. One might object to the loon as state bird on the ground that it does not nest in southern Minnesota, and therefore many Minnesotans have never seen one. Even more of our people have never heard one, since the loon is quiet during migration. On the other hand, the loon does typify the northern unspoiled wilderness for which Minnesota is widely known. To quote Dr. Warner, "Anyone who has heard the cry of a loon on a lonely, northern lake on a moonlit night will never forget it."

As a state bird it would be consistent with our selection of the red pine as official state tree and the moccasin flower, or showy lady's-slipper, as our state flower, both of which are found in the same general habitat as the loon. It would also be natural for Minnesota — the land of 10,000 lakes — to select a water bird as its state bird. And what water bird would be more appropriate than the common loon?

The loon is a fairly large bird, weighing from eight to twelve pounds at maturity and measuring nearly three feet in length, with a wingspread of almost five feet. It has within its body a number of large air sacs which it can inflate or deflate at will, giving it the ability to float like a cork or sink like a stone. It can dive instantly with a plunge or sink gradually without leaving a ripple. It often swims with only its head and neck above the water. When preening, it sometimes rolls on its side, exposing its white underplumage. As a swimmer and diver it is almost unexcelled. Its strong, sharply pointed beak is designed for spearing fish, which it pursues under water by using both its feet and its wings to propel itself. In this manner it can catch even the fleetest fish.

So far has nature gone in perfecting the loon for expertness in water that the bird is almost helpless on land. Its large webbed feet are placed so far back on its body that it cannot stand upright or take flight. To reach its nest — which it always places very near the water — it slides on its breast, pushing itself forward with its feet. Even on water it cannot take flight without taking a long, splashing run into the wind, using both wings and feet to attain sufficient speed for a take-off.

In contrast with many water birds that are gregarious at nesting time, the loon prefers solitude. A lake must be large to harbor more than one pair of loons. The down-covered young take to the water soon after hatching. They sometimes hitch a ride on the backs of the parents, but quickly learn to swim and dive, although at first they tire easily. On our northern lakes a loon family, consisting of the parents and two young, is a common sight during July and August. Fishing vacationists are often highly entertained by the hysterical yodeling, quavering laughter and insane acrobatics of a male loon trying to divert the intruders' attention from the mother loon and the young. These antics are quite likely responsible for the origin of the expression, "crazy like a loon."

In spring plumage the adult loon of either sex has a glossy-black head and neck with a white collar. Its back is black, thickly marked with white spots. Underparts are pure white. It may take three or four years for the young to acquire this plumage. In winter, young and old alike have gray or grayish-brown crown, neck and back and white cheeks, throat and underparts.

Loons are birds of the Northern Hemisphere. Their range is circumpolar. In the spring they follow the thawing ice northward, some of them going well above the arctic circle. They may start southward in September, although some remain until forced southward by freezing lakes and streams. Most of them winter on the oceans near the coast while some winter on inland lakes and streams as far north as water remains open.

. . . *Purple martin*

On an errand to the post office the other day I chanced to meet a local hardware dealer who is also a bird enthusiast. The subject of birds came up quite naturally and he suggested that I write on the purple martin. The weather was bitterly cold and perhaps my friend was thinking of balmier days. I must confess that, at the mention of purple martins, my thoughts wandered for a moment from the frigid, windy street corner where we stood to the tropical Amazon Valley of Brazil where the martins are now busily skimming about over the jungle, catching insects on the wing.

The purple martin, of course, is one of the best known of our birds because it has become so completely dependent upon man-made nesting sites. All members of the swallow family enjoy a good reputation. But the purple martin, the largest of our swallows, is particularly popular. More than any other wild bird, it enjoys a selected, sympathetic audience. Since it nests almost exclusively in shelters specially designed for martin nesting, it naturally comes only to those dooryards and parks where someone has thought enough of the bird to make it welcome by taking the trouble to build and put up a martin house. It does not follow that martins will immediately occupy a new martin house. When Howard Cleaves, the naturalist, last stayed at our house he said, "I have news for you! For twenty-five years I have had a martin house in my yard and last summer martins occupied it for the first time." My luck was better. Seeing a couple of martins scouting about our place one spring day two years ago, I went to the basement after a sixteen-compartment martin house I had built during the winter. The martins showed considerable interest in the structure as it stood on the ground before being erected on a sixteen foot pipe. Four pairs of martins occupied it the first season and were back to claim it again last year, even though I had neglected to take it down during the winter, with the result that it was thoroughly occupied by English sparrows when the martins returned. Somehow the martins made themselves at home and, after a few initial passes and squabbles, got on peacefully with their sparrow neighbors.

The practice of putting up martin houses is not a recent or passing fad. Long before Europeans came to this continent, American Indians were attracting martins to their homes by hanging hallowed gourds on saplings or poles. Early settlers observed this and copied the idea from the Indians. The Negroes of the southern states were great at providing places for martins to nest near their cabins. Martin houses may vary from these simple one-room affairs to elaborate structures with several hundred compartments. Some cities have become famous for their martin populations by arousing community interest in martin housing. Martins are sometimes thought of as city birds, but this is merely because more people there put up nesting for them. Actually, these birds prefer open country, though they may be induced to develop thriving colonies on the busiest streets.

A colony of martins adds life to any dooryard. An occupied martin house is always a scene of great activity. Although each pair occupy a separate compartment the whole group is very sociable. Every time a martin arrives at the house all of the birds present exchange greetings with friendly chirruping and a variety of low-pitched gurgling sounds. Since birds are continually coming and going, the martin colony is constantly noisy throughout the daylight hours. They are enthusiastic but not especially gifted songsters. Martins seem to enjoy cruising about leisurely over the tree tops, and especially near water or open meadows, ranging widely in search of food but can, if necessary, fly fast, maneuvering expertly to catch such quick-dodging insects as dragonflies or zooming down in divebombing attacks on any enemy venturing near their home. When they think their home is endangered martins attack en masse. My dog is well aware that she cannot go near our martin house in summer without losing dignity.

The young of most altricial birds go through a period of relative helplessness, even after leaving the nest. The first feeble attempt at flight is likely to send them fluttering to the ground or, at best, to a branch of a tree or bush where the parents continue to feed them. This is a precarious time for the young birds. Many are killed by wandering cats, skunks, weasles, owls and other predators. Young martins, however, like the young of other species of swallows, fly very well, even at the first takeoff. They naturally tire quickly at first, but wisely return to the nest for periods of rest and to spend the night for a considerable period after starting to fly. In the southern states martins usually have two broods per year, but in this latitude only one brood is reared and the young may continue to return to their nesting box until the middle of September or later, when they start gathering in large flocks in preparation for their southward migration. While most small passerines or perching birds migrate at night and stop to rest and feed during the day, martins and other swallows migrate leisurely during the daytime and feed as they go. En route to their South American winter home they follow the shore through Mexico and Central America rather than crossing the Gulf of Mexico as many of the night migrants do.

Martins are entirely beneficial birds, deserving every protection and encouragement. It is unfortunate that they must compete for nesting sites with such gangsters as English sparrows and starlings. With a little care on our part, however, they can enjoy relative freedom from these usurpers. The simplest way to accomplish this is to take down the martin house after the occupants leave in the fall and delay putting it up again until the martins return in the spring in about the middle of April. The sparrows and starlings will by this time have nested elsewhere. Some people vary this by putting the houses up again immediately after cleaning them but keep the entrances covered until the martins return. Naturalist Howard Cleaves was highly amused by one martin enthusiast's solution to this problem. A large cork was fitted into each compartment entrance. Attached to each cork was a string that passed over a pulley and was fastened to a stouter string that extended down the pole, where it could be reached from the ground. After watching the thwarted sparrows and starlings all spring this ingenious fellow at last saw martins around the house one morning, went to the pole, gave the string a jerk and, to his joy, sixteen corks popped out in unison and dangled in the breeze while the happy martins moved in.

. . . *The robin*

March, 1956

While doing the morning chores on January 28th I caught just a fleeting glimpse of a bird about the size of a blue jay as it flew into the box elder thicket in my neighbor's hog pasture across the road from our farmstead. At that distance, and looking towards the sun, I could not see any plumage color but the flight pattern strongly suggested a robin. The next morning I was not too surprised when I saw a robust-looking robin feeding on the scanty, shriveled fruit still clinging to the hackberry tree on our lawn. While I watched, the bird picked loose a few pieces of crusted snow and swallowed them, his only way of quenching thirst at this season.

I doubt if my visitor had any plans for establishing a nesting territory hereabouts. His summer home is very likely much farther north, perhaps even in Alaska, because robins do nest northward to the very limit of trees. There are several subspecies or geographical races of robins, with minor variations in size and in shade of plumage. Along the Atlantic seaboard these differences in plumage help to establish the robin's migration pattern. In our area robin migration is not so apparent because we see only the eastern robin, which has by far the most extensive breeding range. Nevertheless, the migration pattern is the same. Most, if not all, of the robins nesting in this latitude leave for the southern states before the end of October. Some of the birds nesting farthest north may spend the winter as far north as southern Canada.

While wintering in the southern states, robins sometimes gather in enormous numbers to roost at night in trees or among reeds in some secluded swamp and scatter during the day to feed individually or in small flocks. From the warm south, robins start northward early in the year, often in vast flocks. But before they reach this latitude the great gatherings have thinned out. A great many wild, wary males appear in this area during March. These birds do not sing, but sometimes express themselves in loud, nervous exclamations. Not until early April do male robins, by a sudden, noticeable change in behavior, show evidence of being birds that plan to select nesting territories here. They suddenly become very tame, run about our lawns as though they owned the place, sing jubilantly and are sometimes seen in conflict over a boundary. Sometimes one will dash himself against a basement window fighting his image, which he thinks is a rival male intruding on his territory. When the females arrive from the south the excitement of the courtship antics of the robin begins.

In the United States and southern Canada the robin is very tame during the nesting season. Because the robin, throughout most of its nesting range, has so thoroughly accepted man as a neighbor, it is probably more numerous now than it was before this country was settled. The bird is certainly much more numerous in populated areas than in the wilderness. Some ornithologists believe that the robin prefers to nest near our homes because of the relative freedom from wild predators. Others feel that the greater abundance of earthworms attracts them.

Whatever the reason for their affinity, robins seem to consider the concealment of their nests a matter of minor importance. Despite our domestic cats and other threats, the trustful birds build their nests on our very window sills, on clothes-line posts, shutters, rain pipes, fire escapes, on beams outside and inside buildings, on railroad signal gates, inside broken street lights, on trolley wires, statues and, of course, in trees around our homes and on the busiest streets. Having selected their nesting site, robins are persistent in their nest building.

Early in June robins reach their highest pitch of excitement, for then the first brood is ready to leave the nest and enter the most dangerous period of their lives. The squat, stub-tailed fledglings, with heavily spotted breasts and some natal down still sticking through the feathers on their head, are at first unaware of their danger. As they glory in their new freedom their loud and oft-repeated "seech-ook" betrays their whereabouts and their feeble flight makes them easy prey for cats. Anxiously, the parents watch for possible danger while working hard to feed their hungry, scattered brood. Any threat is greeted with loud screams of protest which quickly bring every robin in the neighborhood to join in the rumpus and defend the young vigorously. After a few days the female, who is the nest-builder, prepares the nest for a second clutch of eggs and leaves the male to care for the first brood alone. Male robins may start to gather in summer roosts as early as July. Later in the season they are joined by the young of the first brood. As soon as the young of the second brood are able to care for themselves we see little of the robins because they again become shy, elusive birds, shifting about the countryside, living on wild fruit until their southward journey.

Any discussion of the robin would be incomplete without mentioning albinism. White plumage is quite common in robins. A bird may be fully albino or just partly so. Melanism — the excess of black pigment in the plumage — is much less common, but occasionally does occur. A couple of years ago there was quite a furor about a white robin on Frank Avenue in Albert Lea. A resident phoned to tell me that he had seen such a bird near his home several times. Although I drove down Frank Avenue several times I had no luck spotting the attraction. Several others saw the bird, however, and later another resident said that the bird was among a brood of robins that hatched in her yard.

Economically speaking, the robin has its faults. It seems he takes some beetles that we consider beneficial. Earthworms, which we consider valuable as soil builders, are a favorite with the robin. Haven't we all seen robins on our lawns cock their head sideways and then jab into the ground and pull out an earthworm? It is unclear whether they hear, see or feel the presence of earthworms underground, but they have in some way been equipped to detect them and I feel that they are entitled to them. The robin's fondness for fruit is well known to commercial fruit growers — especially in sections where there is little or no wild fruit. With all its faults, however, the robin is almost universally loved for its beauty, its cheerful carolling and especially for its neighborliness during the nesting season.

...*Cedar waxwing*

April, 1956

If you have a mountain ash or some other tree that retains its fruit throughout the winter you have probably seen cedar waxwings at some time or other as they stopped to feed during their winter wanderings. If there are mulberry trees in your vicinity you have quite likely had these gentle-mannered birds nesting near your home. Unless you are an avid birder, however, the chances are that you have never heard or taken notice of their song, for their vocal powers are limited to a faint high-pitched, vibrant lisp, as though the birds were saying "three—three—three" in a slowly whispered monotone. These notes may be uttered in flight or when perching but cannot be heard very far. Often the birds make no sound at all. I usually see cedar waxwings at irregular intervals every year but hear their songs so seldom that I sometimes have difficulty associating it with the bird. While walking to the mail box the other day I was puzzled by the strange song and took a few steps toward the trees from which the sound was coming. The mystery was solved when three cedar waxwings took flight from the top of a juniper tree.

I recall distinctly the first cedar waxwings I ever saw. On one of those bleak, mid-winter days when Mother thought it best for little tots like myself to stay indoors, I was looking longingly out the north window at our two crab apple trees, still heavily loaded with fruit, when suddenly there descended into the tops of the two trees about thirty crested, brownish-colored birds with sleek, silky plumage. Immediately, the hungry birds began devouring the frozen spoiled apples. Of course, I had to know what kind of birds they were, so Mother, who was busy frying salt pork for dinner, stepped to the window for a quick glance and, to satisfy my curiosity, invented the name "winter king." And it was by that name I knew these beautiful birds for several years.

When we planted our windbreak in 1937 we included 150 mulberry trees for the purpose of attracting birds, especially cedar waxwings. The project has been successful. Many of the trees are now bearing and a great many birds of several species are attracted in berry season. Cedar waxwings have nested here several summers. The waxwings are late nesters, rearing their young from late June into August. One fall, after the leaves had fallen, I could plainly see an abandoned waxwing nest from the barn while doing chores. A dangling leaf clinging tenaciously to the nest, even in high wind, aroused my curiosity, so I investigated the next time I walked through the windbreak on my way to fetch the cows. What had from a distance appeared to be a leaf was actually the dried remains of a fledgling that had become entangled in a loop of string used in building the nest.

The food of the cedar waxwing consists largely of fruit, much of it wild and of little value to man. These fruit-loving birds also eat quantities of insects in season. A flock will alight on an apple tree and clean it completely of cankerworms before moving on to the next tree. Last fall I saw some birds flying out from the tops of some ash trees in our windbreak to catch insects in mid-air and return to their perch in flycatcher style. When near enough I saw that they were cedar waxwings. The young are fed insects at first, but as they grow larger are fed fruit. The parents carry fruit in their gullets and regurgitate it into the mouths of the young. At one of our Audubon Society meetings a member told about observing this process. As he put it, "A stream of berries passed from the beak of the parent bird into the mouth of the young like a string of beads." In the fall, when plenty of wild fruit is available, waxwings often gorge themselves and have been known to become intoxicated on occasion.

Cedar waxwings are very easygoing, friendly, sociable birds. They have the unusual habit of sometimes perching close together facing the same way and passing a berry or caterpillar from beak to beak up and down the line until one of them finally swallows the morsel. Interesting also is their habit of freezing or perching motionless in an upright position when they think they are being noticed. I once saw one of them in such a pose on a light wire while a strong side wind kept blowing the bird's crest into a twisted "rooster tail."

Some of the individuals in this species have on their secondary wing feathers flattened and expanded prolongations of shafts that are scarlet, giving the appearance of having been dipped in sealing wax, and it is from this peculiarity that the bird gets its name.

Cedar waxwings winter irregularly throughout the United States. In the fall the families join in groups ranging in size from a few birds to flocks numbering hundreds and roam the countryside in a carefree manner. There is a general migratory movement, but they are such roving, unpredictable birds that the sight of them is always a thrill to birdwatchers.

In February 1955 a Minneapolis Bird Club member and I were planning a field trip for his group to Upper Twin Lake and Albert Lea Lake. Sticking my neck out, I ventured to predict that upland plovers would return by April 28th and would be on hand for the group to see on May 1st, the date of the proposed field trip. The plovers showed up on April 25th and on May 1st two male plovers dutifully serenaded the highly pleased Minneapolis group parked in my cow lane. I wish that I might make a similar prediction this year about the cedar waxwings, but the appearance of this bird is far too uncertain.

... *Brown thrasher*

One of the most delightful bird songs is that of the brown thrasher. Perhaps we should expect this from such a close relative of the celebrated mockingbird. Although not the sweetest of bird songs, it is loud, clear, emphatic, pleasingly musical and greatly varied. Most bird songs are short and simple, consisting of a few notes or short phrases repeated in the same order, with pauses between each song. The brown thrasher, on the other hand, has a great vocabulary of notes and phrases that he utters, usually in pairs but otherwise in no particular order. One can never tell what kind of sound will come from the bird next. I sometimes wonder how the bird himself can decide so quickly. This may be one of his reasons for repeating each note. It gives him twice as much time to think of what to say next. The brown thrasher may sing continuously for fifteen or twenty minutes at a stretch, then pause to rest, look about or preen briefly before resuming his song. At any disturbance, such as the bark of a dog or the slam of a door, he will stop abruptly in the middle of a note. If the disturbance is nearby, and particularly if some person seems too interested in the singer, he will leap from his perch and plummet headlong into a thicket and disappear. But not for long. The urge to sing seems irresistible. In a few moments he will be back on his conspicuous perch singing for all the world to hear. Under favorable conditions the song can be heard for half a mile. Occasionally he lapses into mimicry, imitating the songs of other birds. Ordinarily, however, he sticks to his own lingo. But what a lingo it is! Some people refer to the brown thrasher as the "planting bird" because he arrives about corn planting time and part of his song seems to say, "drop it, drop it, cover it up, cover it up."

Every year, beginning about the first of May, I can expect to be pleasantly awakened early each morning by one of these cinnamon brown minstrels singing fervently from the topmost branch of a walnut tree just outside my bedroom window. Judging from its bold rollicking song, one would never suspect that the brown thrasher is, in reality, a shy, retiring bird, spending most of its time among shadowy thickets where it finds most of its food on the ground in the leaf-mold, throwing old leaves aside with its beak and probing in the soil for insects. Insects make up two-thirds of its food. The vegetable portion — one-third — is made up of mast (mostly acorns), a little waste grain and berries in season. The thrasher is not as destructive of cultivated fruit as either the robin or the catbird but does take some as wages for its spirited song.

The brown thrasher may be found in all the states east of the Rocky Mountains and in the southern part of the bordering Canadian provinces. It winters in the southern United States, but an occasional individual may winter even as far north as Minnesota, where it is dependent on bird feeders for a winter livelihood.

Memory seems to associate a bird with the place where it was first seen. One day, as a youngster, I was exploring a rarely frequented portion of our windbreak when a brush pile attracted my attention. It was the only brush pile we had. Wood was scarce on the prairie. When a wind storm broke down a tree or a branch we gathered every stick and saved the twigs as fuel for the kitchen range. Ordinarily, we did not cut down any trees, but in the rush of a day's work the previous summer we had the misfortune of breaking a wagon bolster. We had no car and, rather than take the time to drive to town with horses to get a new bolster, Dad decided to cut down a box elder tree and hew out a makeshift bolster. While the bolster was being prepared, the remainder of the tree was hurriedly trimmed and the branches thrown into a pile for future attention. On my carefree exploration I decided to look into this branch pile to see what might be there. At first I could see nothing. But as I continued peering in and waiting for my eyes to get accustomed to the dim light there was a sudden commotion in the depths of the pile and a cinnamon brown bird flew out and started scolding me very excitedly. Its loud, emphatic "tzuk, tzuk, tzuk" soon brought its mate to join the scolding. Birds are altruistic, at least to the extent that they recognize and respond to each other's distress calls. First, all the robins in the vicinity, and then the grackles, gathered to protest. In the rapidly increasing hubbub I soon withdrew, but not before I had taken a good look at the bulky, twiggy nest lined with rootlets and the five eggs densely covered with small brown dots.

When I described the bird I had seen I was told that it was a "brown thrush", a name that many people apply to this bird. However, the bird is not a thrush. It belongs to the family Mimidae (the mimics), which includes also the mockingbird and the catbird. The name thrasher may seem to be an odd name for a bird, but birds acquire their names in strange ways. The thrasher gets this name from its habit of shuffling its long tail feathers when angry or excited. Some people say this tail action suggests the swinging of a flail that was used for threshing grain in those bygone days when the brown thrasher was first named.

The brown thrasher does not seem very abundant but, as is the case with many small songbirds, is probably more numerous today than it was before this country was settled. By disturbing the land, man has created much brushy growth, wood openings and so-called edge, thus making the countryside a much more favorable habitat for many songbirds, including the brown thrasher. Bird songs add much to the enchantment of spring. We are fortunate indeed to have the shy, furtive brown thrasher forget his bashfulness as the spell of spring stirs him to eloquent expression of his vocal ability.

...White pelican

June, 1956

En route from their Florida home to their nesting grounds in North Dakota, Montana, and western Canada, several hundred white pelicans took time this spring to rest and feed in the various lakes around Albert Lea. These peculiar-looking birds have stopped here in previous seasons but not in such great numbers as this spring, when one could see flocks of up to 200 birds. From a window of his new home on the shore of Pickerel Lake, a neighbor of mine looked out across the water, thinking he might see the flock of whistling swans that habitually came to the lake every evening. Suddenly the air was filled with white pelicans gliding down to plow into the surface of the lake. He estimated this flock to number 200 birds. Many Albert Lea people had opportunities this spring to see these large, picturesque water birds as they cruised about on our lakes, perched grotesquely on shore or engaged in their spectacular aerial maneuvers (often directly over the city) while flying from one body of water to another. A standard greeting last April was, "Have you seen the pelicans yet?"

White pelicans are large birds weighing up to 15 pounds at maturity and having a wingspread at times approaching ten feet. They are very gregarious birds. Like a flock of merino sheep they stay close together. On shore they appear sluggish, awkward and ill-proportioned with their goose-like bodies, short, squatty legs, over-sized, pouched beaks and kinked necks. These shore gatherings are interesting to watch. Each bird looks soberly down its long nose at the others, clumsily preens its spick-and-span plumage and yawns. What a yawn!

Although awkward in other attitudes, white pelicans are

graceful aerialists. Alternately flapping and sailing, they wheel and turn as they glide with downward slanting wings, each bird synchronizing its actions with the other birds in the flock. Each turn, wingbeat or slight movement is executed in unison with military precision. The flight formation, whether a V or a straight line, is rigidly maintained. There is true beauty in pelican flight.

As I watched the pelicans at various times throughout April, I could not help thinking about the part played by the National Audubon Society in the survival of the species. A bird as large and conspicuous as the white pelican, needing so much time for its eggs to hatch and its young to reach flight stage, requires a safe place in which to rear its young. They nest only on isolated, sandy or reed-grown islands in large lakes. It is on record that pelicans formerly nested in southern Minnesota. But settlement has long since driven them out. We are indebted to the National Audubon Society for their wise and timely action in seeking out the nesting grounds of the white pelican and working to have the areas set aside as wild bird reservations. This zealous organization has also secured protection for these birds in their winter range. Without this protection the white pelican could not have survived up to the present time. Now we are enjoying the rewards of this action. White pelicans responded to protection, increased in numbers and are again being seen on their ancient ancestral migratory flyways. Folks who are unfamiliar with their story think that the appearance of these great white birds in Freeborn County is unusual because they do not remember their former abundance.

White pelican history follows the same pattern as that of our other large white birds. At first there is direct persecution by man, coupled with the drainage of breeding areas and the consequent decrease of bird numbers to near extinction. Then comes the warning cry of interested people and an aroused public demanding protective legislation and vigilant enforcement. Then follows the eventual increase in numbers of the endangered species. The American egret has responded wonderfully. The whistling swans are coming back. Their larger relative, the trumpeter swan, is still in danger. The story of another of our great white birds, the whooping crane, is well known. Public interest is greatly aroused and protection is rigid, but the species is still in desperate circumstances. Their breeding grounds, now restricted and virtually inaccessible, are near Great Slave Lake in northern Canada. Their wintering range is the Aransas government refuge in southern Texas. The small remaining colony must migrate precariously over hundreds of miles of settled areas every spring and fall. Authorities disagree on the possibility of the whooper's survival.

Not all species respond to efforts at preservation. The heath hen, Carolina paroquet and ivory-billed woodpecker disappeared in spite of all-out efforts to preserve them. Only time will tell which way the balance will swing for the whooping crane. We laud the National Audubon Society's efforts, however, and cheer the return of such species as the American egret, the upland plover, the whistling swan and the white pelican. Whoever contributes to the National Audubon Society's funds by direct contribution, by membership, by supporting projects such as the Audubon Screen Tours or by bequests can rightly feel that he has a part in this worthwhile work. He can feel that he is contributing to the survival of the white pelican and other threatened species.

. . . The kingbird

If birds were rated according to their display of courage the kingbird would probably top the list. The utter fearlessness with which it attacks much larger birds, such as hawks, crows and even eagles, is truly amazing. Other small birds harass hawks and crows that venture too near their nesting territory, but no other bird attacks them as ferociously as the kingbird, which sometimes even alights on the larger bird's back, jabbing savagely with its pointed beak to inflict as much punishment as it can. There is, of course, no real danger for the larger bird but the irritation is so severe as to force it into undignified gyrations of flight in futile attempts to shake off the determined little assailant.

Every summer a pair of kingbirds nested high in the European poplar towering over the boxelder windbreak of our Iowa home. While his mate brooded, the little guardian kept constant watch from his perch on the topmost branch. Any crow that unwittingly or deliberately came within a quarter of a mile was due for humiliation. Taking off from his perch, the little feathered policeman sped swiftly away until he was a mere speck, or even disappeared from sight. I could easily tell when he reached his goal, however, because the crow suddenly started swerving and dipping in flight and screaming in distress while beating a hasty retreat for safer territory. Having driven off his giant adversary the little hero returned to his mate, gloating and bragging in his most enthusiastic kingbird language. I always envied the kingbirds for their wisdom of placing their nest near the top of this tree. Climbing the big tree was out of the question for a youngster. But, while on an errand to the field with drinking water, I chanced to notice a movement in the top of a small willow tree leaning out over the water in our dredge ditch. It proved to be a kingbird, and closer observation revealed a nest. The tree was much too small and limber to be climbed safely. Its position over the water could bring about an embarrassing fall, to say the least. Mother would object, because a dunked offspring is a mess to clean up. Older brothers, awaiting a drink of cool water, might complain if the water was unusually warmed by delayed arrival. But for a young bird enthusiast there was only one answer. I climbed the tree and had a good look at the nest and eggs while the mother kingbird perched quite unruffled on the pasture fence near by. After seeing the fuss that robins and grackles made when their nests were threatened, I was quite surprised at this calm attitude on the part of a bird that could be so belligerent.

In classifying this bird, ornithologists unfortunately chose to call it tyrant flycatcher, strongly suggesting cruel oppression. This is unfair to the kingbird because it lives in harmony with its smaller bird neighbors, permitting them even to nest in the same tree. The kingbird is also burdened with the uncomplimentary name "bee martin," implying that it destroys honeybees, which are valuable, domesticated insects. This charge has been pretty well blasted by subsequent biological studies. One day a friend and I were birding when a small beetle flew into the car and alighted on the windshield. Unhesitatingly, my friend reached up and killed the insect.

"Was it harmful or beneficial?" I asked.

"I haven't the slightest idea," was the reply. How absurd then to expect a bird to distinguish between insects on this basis!

The kingbird prefers open country — especially where there is water near by. It is probably the best known of the flycatchers. It is often seen about farms in meadows, pastures and cultivated fields. Perching on fence wires or any weed or cornstalk, it dashes out to catch flying insects and returns to its same perch. It is an effective moth catcher and, as is well known, many moths are among the most destructive insects in their larval stage. The kingbird also picks up many insects from the ground and perches on the ground when no convenient elevated perches are available. A number of kingbirds stayed about the fields where I was planting corn this spring. In fact, they followed the planter closely and didn't mind hopping over the planter wire as it whipped toward the planter.

Many of our eastern bird species have corresponding or closely related species inhabiting western United States — roughly west of the 100th meridian. The line of separation is not clear-cut, and in Minnesota and for some distance westward both eastern and western species of many birds may be seen. On May 16th I had the very thrilling experience of seeing a western kingbird for the first time. For about two hours it stayed about the field where I was planting corn, so I saw both the eastern and the western kingbirds side by side at close range. The western kingbird seems to be extending its range eastward, but it is still a rare bird. It is a much more beautiful bird than our plain, black and white eastern species. Its gray head, dark back, bright **lemon-yellow underparts and black tail with white outer tail** feathers present a very pleasing appearance. I did not hear the bird utter any sound, but kingbird songs are nothing fancy. A bird as beautiful as the western kingbird does not need a song to make it captivating. Both eastern and western kingbirds are very interesting and highly beneficial birds. May their tribes increase.

...*The hummingbird*

My electric fencer wasn't working properly the other day. The machine was clicking but the wire wasn't delivering any shock. With only one strand of wire separating my cows from my neighbor's corn field it is important that the cows have respect for that wire, so I started walking along the fence, inspecting it closely to find the place where it was grounded. Suddenly I was looking directly at a ruby-throated hummingbird perched on the wire less than two feet away from me. Naturally I stopped to admire the tiny, feathered gem. The diminutive creature seemed more like an insect than a bird. I have seen hummingbirds at close range before but always when they were in flight. The little bird appeared quite fearless, although its tiny, bright eyes were watching me constantly as it perched with its back toward me, its bronze-green plumage glistening in the sunlight. Ruby-throats have been known to feed from flowers held in the hand and even perch on an extended finger. I could not have seen this bird any better if it had perched on my finger. It was a female. Its throat was white. Only the male has the ruby throat. The needle-like beak and individual wing feathers were plainly visible. For about two minutes I watched the hummer, but when I stooped to get a look at the tiny feet grasping the wire madam hummingbird evidently thought I was getting too personal and took off. She perched again momentarily on a dry twig of a chokecherry tree and then disappeared among the foliage.

In flight, the hummingbird's wings appear only as a blur. The hummer is also able to turn its wings so that it leads with the forewing in both the forward and backward strokes. This makes it a virtual helicopter, flying forward and backward with equal ease, maneuvering expertly while probing deep-throated flowers, hovering motionless in mid air or speeding away at more than 50 miles per hour. It is the only bird that can actually fly backward. A hummingbird may be extremely small but it certainly is not delicate. For its size it has more strength than any other bird. Its flight muscles are relatively immense. It seems incredible that this tiny bird, weighing but a small fraction of an ounce, can actually spend its summer with us and its winter in South or Central America, flying across the Gulf of Mexico to Yucatan, a distance of over 500 miles, in a single night without stopping to eat or rest. By contrast, consider the relative immobility of a mouse that must spend its entire lifetime within a few rods of where it is born.

Hummingbirds are fond of bathing. They do not get into the water as other birds do but bathe in the rain, in dew-drenched foliage, in the spray of waterfalls, fountains, lawn sprinklers and even in the shower from a garden hose held in the hand. One day I dashed into the woodshed as the quickest escape from a sudden downpour of rain. A low-toned buzz attracted my attention and I turned to see a hummingbird hovering motionless directly in the stream of water running off the roof. Its whirring wings sprayed water in my face. The hummingbird is so named because of the sound made by its rapidly-beating wings. Despite their wee size and exquisite beauty, hummingbirds are fierce-tempered, fighting much among themselves and attacking larger birds in a foolhardy manner. They seem to have few natural enemies, perhaps because of their swiftness and agility.

The food of hummingbirds consists of small insects found entrapped in sap exuding from the bark of trees. They frequently visit trees where sapsuckers have punctured the bark. They are best known for their fondness of nectar sipped from deep-throated flowers by means of their tubular tongues which they can extend far beyond the tip of their long beak. By planting such flowers as salvia and delphinium, hummingbirds may be attracted to our homes. Some people have also had very good luck attracting them with sugar water in brightly colored vials.

The nest of the hummingbird, as one might expect, is a very dainty affair constructed from soft plant downs matted and bound together with spider web. The little cup, about the size of a marshmallow, is laced with spider web, usually to a downward-sloping branch and camouflaged by a covering of small pieces of lichens held on with spider web. The lining is made of plant hairs taken from the stems of plants or the under side of tree leaves. Nests are hard to find because they look like a knot or natural growth on the branch. The eggs, usually two, are pure white and about the size of navy beans. Since the male rubythroat is a wandering, carefree creature, the female does all the work of building the nest and rearing the young. The young are at first fed partially-digested insects regurgitated by the mother hummer in a violent sort of sword-swallowing, squirt gun performance. Later they are fed whole insects.

Hummingbirds cannot be mistaken for any other bird. But they are sometimes confused with the larger hawk moths that visit flowers and feed in much the same manner as hummingbirds, moving forward and backward while probing deep-throated flowers to sip nectar with their long tongues. The hawk moths, however, visit flowers only at dusk while the hummers confine their activities to daylight hours. A little care in observation will enable one to easily distinguish the birds from the moths.

If usefulness to man, other than aesthetic value, is necessary, then their aid in pollenating certain flowers may be cited. But who could fail to accept hummingbirds solely as the most **brilliantly charming of all birds?**

. . . *Mourning dove*

No matter how long or how well one has known a bird, there is always the possibility of discovering in it some peculiar trait of behavior that one has never happened to notice. I thought that I was pretty well acquainted with all the ways of the mourning dove, having known it intimately since childhood. But early one May morning last year I was both surprised and amused by a pair of these familiar birds walking about very contentedly side by side on the dew-drenched lawn just outside my bedroom window. They seemed to be feeding. But there was something so oddly deliberate about their movements that I was curious to see what they were eating. Putting their beaks down into the grass they would hold them still for a moment before lifting their heads and taking a step or two to repeat the performance. After watching them closely for some time I saw that they were not eating at all, but drinking dewdrops from the blades of grass. The sunlight was reflected brightly from each dewdrop and every time a bird's beak went down and paused, a tiny reflection would disappear. The mourning dove, like the rest of the dove clan, does not drink in the customary bird fashion by lifting its head to let each beakful of water trickle down its gullet but holds its beak in the water and drinks steadily, as a cow does. This was the first time, however, that I had seen mourning doves bother with a drink as small as a dewdrop. How long the devoted pair kept sipping the bits of refreshing beverage before quenching their thirst I do not know because I had chores to do and had to get going.

The mourning dove gets its name from its slow, melancholy mating song, "coo-ah-coooo-coooo," which suggests unconsolable sorrow. As a youngster I used to watch and listen, but found it hard to believe that so doleful a song could come from such a pleasant and contented-looking bird. Through the years, as I learned more about the bird, the song has seemed less and less forlorn. I now find it a pleasant dooryard sound.

It has been hard to get used to what the mourning dove considers a nest. To me it still looks like a half-finished job. There are birds, of course, that do not build any nest at all, as for example those that lay their eggs on a sandy beach or on a bare rock. But for a bird that builds its nest in a tree, the mourning dove gets along with closer to nothing than any bird I know. A few sticks, carelessly laid crisscross, form a flat-topped, flimsy platform that is scarcely enough to keep the eggs from falling through or rolling off. There must be some reason for the scanty design. Some bird students claim that the beak and feet of the mourning dove are so ill-suited for nest building that the bird cannot do any better, but this seems a poor excuse. Any bird could certainly build a more substantial nest if it had a mind to. A more logical explanation is the idea of concealment. A bulky nest would be conspicuous, but a slight structure, even with the neutral-colored bird on nesting duty, may escape notice, even though it may be in plain sight of a much traveled path. Often the nest is first discovered when the brooding bird becomes frightened for some reason and explodes from the nest to flop hysterically along the ground feigning injury in an attempt to lure its enemy away. Though crudely constructed, the mourning dove nest serves its purpose well. Two or more broods are reared in a single season, all in the same nest. The heavy-bodied young are slow in attaining the power of flight. On rare occasions fresh eggs have been found in a nest before the squabs of the previous brood were mature enough to fly. In such cases of overlapping broods the nest serves double duty. A common, comical sight is that of a parent dove trying to brood the two fat squabs, as large as herself, with their heads sticking out on one side and their tails sticking out on the other side. The young are at first fed on pigeon's milk, a secretion which is formed in the parent dove's crop and regurgitated at feeding time. Later, they are fed seeds and insects. The adult birds are almost exclusively seed eaters.

Mourning doves are found in every state of the union. They are listed as permanent residents throughout the United States. But this is misleading because only a very few of them remain in the North during the winter months. These gentle, peace-loving birds are much more numerous in the southern states, where their reproductive rate is higher and losses from natural causes are lower. During the winter months the northern-hatched birds go south to increase the total number there.

It seems strange that a bird weighing only about four ounces should be considered a game bird, but such is the case. Mourning doves are much hunted in the South. In the North they are protected by federal law as migratory birds. The species could not maintain even its modest numbers in the North if shooting was permitted. Northern hunters seem to feel that this arrangement is unfair, and there is constant pressure by that group to have hunting restrictions lifted. Wildlife conservationists are pushing hard for the full protection of mourning doves everywhere in an effort to improve the status of this valuable weed-seed eater and symbol of peace.

... *Nighthawk*

October, 1956

Many strange superstitions have been associated with various birds. One of the most ridiculous of these beliefs was the idea, prevalent in early European times, that nighthawks obtained their nourishment by sucking goats. One can only guess at the reason for the origin of this warped notion. Certainly no one ever saw one of these birds in the act. The nighthawk's deeply cleft mouth opens far back to its ears. When held open it appears grotesquely large for a bird smaller than a robin, and this may have suggested that the bird was able to suck a goat if it chose to. Nighthawks flying near goat herds at night or during evening hours in search of insects disturbed by the grazing animals may have helped bring on the accusation. It is quite possible also that the idea was first advanced by someone who made a practice of snitching milk from his neighbor's goats during the night and needed an explanation for the resulting deficiency in the morning milk yield. Be that as it may, so widespread and persistent was this superstition that, in naming this group of birds, ornithologists adopted the term "goatsuckers."

Nighthawks feed entirely on flying insects, which they catch by flying about with their mouths open during any hour of the day or night. They most often fly at dusk, however, with daylight hours being spent in rest and sleep. When perching, the bird sits horizontally on a branch or rail and, being well camouflaged by its dark grey and white mottled plumage, is easily mistaken for a knot or a gall. Relying on their protective coloration, the birds remain motionless, even when approached closely. Several times I have tried to catch nighthawks that I have happened to come upon. Although they appeared to be sleeping they always took flight just before my hand could clasp over them. Nighthawks sometimes perch on the ground. I have come upon them while walking across a field, unaware of the bird's presence until it flew up suddenly from underfoot.

The songs of the various species of goatsuckers are very distinctive. The most celebrated is the three-syllable call of the whippoorwill. Then there is the four-syllable song of the southern bird for which it is named, "chuck-will's widow." The call of the nighthawk is a very unmusical, nasal screech, "spee-irk," uttered intermittently in flight, but sometimes also while perching. At Frontenac in 1952 I was birding along with a Minneapolis industrialist who is an ardent birder by hobby. He stopped suddenly with the remark, "I heard a nighthawk somewhere," and looked skyward, thinking the bird was in flight. I heard the call too and spied a nighthawk perched on a branch no larger than an inch in diameter. The bird was turned at an angle of about 45 degrees. When I called my friend's attention to it he exclaimed, "Well! That's the first time I have seen a nighthawk perched crosswise on a branch!" To my suggestion that perhaps the bird could not find room for both its feet on so small a branch without turning slightly, he replied, "It could have found a larger branch."

The flight pattern of the nighthawk is interesting in that it consists of short, jerky, erratic and apparently aimless wandering — forward, upward, to the right or left and downward, without any rhythm or regularity. A flock of migrating nighthawks is a strange sight. Each bird gyrates independently of the others in an angle-intersecting mixup which makes one think that the birds must indeed be skillful flyers to avoid colliding.

The nighthawk is known by several other names such as nightjar, bullbat, mosquito hawk, etc. But nighthawk is the name most commonly used. The term "hawk" is ill chosen. We think of a hawk as a bird of prey, with strong talons and a hooked beak for tearing apart its food. The nighthawk's beak is small and weak. Its feet and legs are almost rudimentary, being used only for grasping onto its perch while resting. A nighthawk couldn't walk if it tried to. It is not a woodland bird like its close relative, the whippoorwill. Originally it preferred open country, laying its eggs on a patch of gravel covered ground and depending for safety upon the protective coloration of itself, its eggs and young. With the advent of flat gravel roofs, however, the nighthawk has become largely a city bird, laying its eggs on the roofs of city buildings. This is another good example of a native bird adapting itself to a world changed by the settlement of man.

Because nighthawks nest in locations seldom visited by predators, and are usually on the wing during the time that night prowlers are about, they usually live longer than most small birds. A new threat may be the peregrine falcon, or duck hawk, another bird that is becoming a city resident in order to enable it to prey on pigeons, and which might prefer an occasional nighthawk for variety.

These entirely useful birds start their southward journey in August when food is still abundant and, feeding as they make their leisurely way, may be seen in loose flocks throughout September. They fly only with others of their own kind. Perhaps this is because no other bird flies like a nighthawk.

These birds are no strangers in Albert Lea. I don't know on whose roof they nest. But I see and hear them every time I come to town from April into September. Considering our mosquito problem, they should be welcome residents. Their appetites are voracious. Stomachs examined have been found to be packed with a variety of insects. Mosquitoes rate high on their menu. And we can rest assured that our nighthawks will not suck goats or, for that matter, dairy cows.

...*Blue-winged teal*

November, 1956

While down in my woods the other day, selecting a few trees to buzz up for winter fuel, I came upon the remains of a wild duck. The predator that devoured the bird had left one wing intact, so it was easily identified as that of a male blue-winged teal.

The duck season had just opened, and it was not hard to imagine the fate of this particular bird. It had very likely been wounded by shot but had continued flying until forced by its misery to land. It then either died as a result of its wound or had its agony mercifully ended by a predator out looking for food. The teal may have landed in the woods or the predator may have brought its prey there to enjoy its meal in privacy. Shortly after the shooting started that first morning I saw a great flock of ducks, which must have numbered thousands of birds, flying toward Albert Lea Lake. Perhaps this teal was one of those which had left for this sanctuary that morning. Had it not been for sanctuaries such as Albert Lea Lake, wild ducks would long since have gone the way of the prairie chicken.

The blue-winged teal is the first of all wild ducks to migrate southward each fall, and is thus favored by a late opening of the hunting season. Its habit of flying in compact flocks, however, makes it easier to shoot than most species.

The blue-wing is the common summer teal of the northwest section of the country, and is still quite common in this area. It is very prolific, and with reasonable protection will maintain its numbers. This protection, however, must also be provided by our Latin-American neighbors because the majority of blue-wings winter south of our borders into Brazil and Chile. It should be added, in fairness to our southern neighbors, that most of the duck shooting there is not done by natives but by United States gunners who go there to enjoy shooting ducks under more liberal regulations.

The blue-wings are among the latest ducks to arrive in the spring. The nest is placed on the ground, usually near water but sometimes far from it, and at times confidingly near traffic lanes and human habitations. I have often found blue-winged teal nests on our farm. Once I left a small area unplowed to spare a nest with eleven eggs only to find the next morning that some night prowler had found and devoured, not only the eggs, but the brooding duck as well. Another nest in a grass-grown stump patch fared better, despite the presence of over twenty cows turned in to graze before the teal eggs hatched. These ducks must hatch and leave the nest quickly because I have never been able to catch them in the process.

One spring, willow roots had so completely plugged a drain tile that a five acre field area was covered with water until far into summer. As a consequence, I had a whole array of migrating shore birds and water birds next to my cow yard. The shore birds included the least, spotted, solitary and pectoral sandpipers, Wilson's snipe, greater yellowlegs — and even a western willet. Among the ducks were scaups, shovelers, pintails, canvasbacks, mallards, redheads, ring-necked, and of course, blue-winged teals.

While preparing a field for corn planting that spring I happened to see a female blue-winged teal alight on the ground among the trees of our windbreak. Thinking there might be a nest, I kept my eye on the spot where the duck alighted. When I reached that end of the field I stopped to search the area, without success. Some birds, including the blue-winged teal, employ the trick of alighting at a distance from their nest and approaching it cautiously on foot. Since the next day was Sunday I took time after noon to search the area inch by inch. But I finally gave up hope of finding a nest. A couple of days later I was walking through the windbreak on my way to fetch the cows. My dog, loping ahead of me, suddenly stopped to sniff and point at a spot near where I had seen the teal alight. Suspecting that the dog had discovered the duck on her nest I tried to call the dog away. At that instant, the duck exploded from under the dog's nose, and the nest location was a secret no longer. With the dog's aid I found the nest and twelve eggs, disgustingly covered with a splash of excrement. At first I thought that this might have been accidentally caused by fright at the dog's nearness. But when it happened again later as I approached it without the dog's presence, I was led to believe that it was a safety measure employed as a last resort to protect the eggs from being devoured by making them as distasteful as possible. Except in such emergencies the usual way of protecting the eggs from predators during the duck's absence is to cover them with a plentiful nest-lining of down, plucked from the brooding duck's breast.

How this bird, measuring 16 inches in length, could so expertly conceal herself and her nest as to escape my discovery during that first thorough search is still a mystery to me. I guess it was just an example of "those who have eyes and see not." When I approached the nest later, knowing the exact tuft of grass it was in, the duck's eye was the first thing to reveal her presence. I visited this nest often, not to disturb the duck, but to be on hand if possible when the eggs hatched.However, even this eluded me. On one visit the mother teal sat as snugly as ever, and on the next visit there was nothing but the downy nest filled with empty eggshells. If I had been a naturalist by profession rather than by hobby, I probably would have built a blind close to the nest and remained in it continuously. But, as it is, I should be thankful that a wild creature chose to make its home so near my home as to permit this close observation of its domestic life.

...*The wild turkey*

December, 1956

On an errand to Albert Lea some days ago I chanced to see five large truckloads of turkeys—about 1000 birds in all—being delivered to a local poultry dressing plant in preparation for the festive days ahead. In the United States, Thanksgiving Day and roast turkey are synonymous. Since the first Thanksgiving Day of the Pilgrims when friendly, visiting Indians brought wild turkeys for the feast no Thanksgiving menu has been complete without its roast turkey.

Domesticated turkeys are all descendants of that grandest of all American game birds, the wild turkey. The name turkey has no connection with the Middle East nation of Turkey but was probably suggested by the bird's call, "turk, turk, turk." The wild turkey is strictly a North American bird. There are several regional species, which vary somewhat in plumage. These species were formerly abundant throughout temperate North America. They used to gather in the fall in flocks of a hundred or more birds and migrate on foot in search of food, which consisted for the most part of acorns, chestnuts, beechnuts, hickory nuts and other mast. However, they ate a great variety of foods, adapting themselves readily to the available supply, such as berries, buds, weed seeds, grass and insects. Wild turkeys are woodland birds. They roost high in tall, dense timber but prefer open woodlands for feeding. They also frequent meadows and fields, especially during the season of grasshoppers, on which they are fond of gorging themselves.

During the mating season the males engage in a spectacular courtship display. Spreading their tails fanwise and upright, fluffing their feathers and dragging their wing tips on the ground, they strut, gobble and fight in the same familiar manner of the domestic variety. Turkeys, like other members of the pheasant family, are polygamous, with one gobbler maintaining a harem of several hens. The hens hide their nests skillfully in grass or bushy thickets, not only to protect them from predatory animals but also to conceal them from the gobbler, who may destroy the eggs or newly hatched young if he comes upon a nest. After the eggs hatch, several hens and their poults usually stay together. Perhaps this is nature's plan for better protection of the poults from the cannibalistic gobbler. As is well known about domestic turkeys, young wild turkeys are very delicate when first hatched, and will die from a good soaking. But the wild turkey hen usually manages to rear her brood quite well. The fox is probably their worst enemy at this time. But when the young are old enough to roost in trees the great horned owl takes its toll.

Speaking of enemies, man has been the wild turkey's undoing. Continued shooting and trapping at all times inevitably spelled the bird's doom. Over most of their former vast range these grand birds have long since been killed off. Through unwise treatment, the great flocks roaming every North American woodland have been reduced to a few small flocks in fragmentary areas of the South and Southwest, where they are now rigidly protected. Attempts to reestablish wild turkeys in Minnesota have failed.

When, in the infant years of our nation, the time came to select a national bird, some persons strongly advocated adopting the wild turkey. But more dramatic-minded men of influence held out for the majestic bald eagle, and won the decision, making the bald eagle our national emblem. In another sense, however, the turkey is our national bird. Thanksgiving is as distinctly a United States holiday as the turkey is strictly an American bird. And what American would want to separate the two or dispense with either one? So well rooted is this tradition that the turkey raising industry has grown to gigantic volume. As a farm enterprise and source of income it ranks as a substitute for hog raising. Roast turkey is also rapidly becoming customary food for the Christmas season. For this most toothsome of domestic fowls we thank the native Indians of Mexico who first domesticated it.

...The bald eagle

January, 1957

There is something awe-inspiring about the sight of a mature bald eagle on the wing in complete wild freedom. The size! The strength! The regal bearing! The mastery of flight! Little wonder that the founders of our nation chose the bald eagle as our national emblem and symbol of American liberty.

My uncle, Andrew Brones, who served in the War Between the States, knew the tame eagle that was the mascot of the Wisconsin 8th Regiment. He often spoke of the contempt of the Confederate soldiers for this bird and of the morale it aroused among Union soldiers. During a battle the eagle would soar overhead screaming. Needless to say it was shot at a great deal. But it came through the war safely, died a natural death and was mounted in the state capitol in Madison, Wisconsin, but was lost when the building was later destroyed by fire.

Although the population of bald eagles in North America today is but a pitiful remnant of the original number, since it breeds only in scattered localities in its former range, this majestic bird can occasionally be seen during migration almost anywhere on the continent. I have seen mature bald eagles several times in this area. On one clear day in May of 1948 I glanced skyward as I left the house after dinner. Poised motionless at a dizzy height was what I first thought to be the local-nesting red-tailed hawk. There was something unusual about this bird, however. From observing its upward-curving wingtips I thought it must be a bald eagle, and I called my family to come to see it. There was no doubt about the bird's identity when it suddenly went into a glide and shot in a straight line like an arrow to some spot a couple of miles away. While seeding rye in

BRECKENRIDGE

early September, two years later, I saw another mature bald eagle high overhead, motionless as a kite, riding the breeze on pinions spanning nearly eight feet. I watched this bird for several minutes before it went into a spectacular power dive and came to the ground less than a quarter of a mile away, where it remained for some time, perhaps feeding on an unfortunate cottontail.

The bald eagle is primarily a scavenger. Its staple food is fish, most of which it finds dead or dying. It is more successful at snitching fish from that skillful fisherman, the osprey, by frightening it into dropping its prey. During the nesting season bald eagles are seldom seen far from lakes, large rivers or areas along the seacoast. Immature bald eagles, which do not acquire the adult white head and tail for some years and are thus rather uniformly dark colored, can often be seen around Albert Lea Lake during the fall and winter performing the useful and humane duty of eliminating dead and ailing ducks. One-third of the wild ducks shot are never retrieved, and a great many more are victims of lead poisoning.

Years ago in my hometown of Thompson, Iowa, a farm boy about my age, while out hunting on his home farm, chanced to see a bald eagle, the first one he had ever seen. He aimed his gun at the big bird and fired, without considering whether the act was right or wrong, legally or aesthetically. By a rare chance the eagle was killed. I remember the stir in the community. The town paper played up the incident as a sort of heroic deed. The eagle was mounted and, the last I heard, adorned a wall of the local bank as a trophy of local prowess. Despite federal and state laws forbidding it, this sort of thing is still going on and accounts for the loss of many bald eagles. If reported, the cases are dealt with leniently on the grounds of being first offenses. Will there be enough eagles to go around? Why is there such a temptation to shoot large, rare birds? Every American certainly knows that the bald eagle is our national bird. Would these people be dealt with so leniently if they went about shooting at the American Flag, which is also a national emblem?

The bald eagles of Alaska had a bounty on their heads for

years. There is a strongly ingrained prejudice that the great birds are injuring the salmon fishing industry by feeding on these fish. The truth is that the salmon which the eagles are taking are the spent salmon, dead or dying from spawning. This can be proven. But there are always those in the gunning fraternity who are willing to overlook the truth to find an excuse for targets. The bounty on eagles has been removed and bald eagles have been declared a protected species in Alaska, but there is still plenty of eagle sniping going on, and the eagle population is dropping alarmingly.

A new threat to the eagle's survival is the use of DDT, which accumulates in the bird's body from eating poisoned fish. This causes the eagle to lay thin-shelled eggs that easily break before hatching. It is downright disheartening to find these large, impressive and generally harmless birds getting such a raw deal on every hand, despite laws — with heavy penalties attached — giving full protection legislatively. One hope for the survival of the species is the longevity of the adult bald eagles, who have learned from experience to be extremely wary of man. Some ornithologists think the life span of a bald eagle may exceed 100 years. Others are more conservative in their opinion.

Will the American public wake up to the responsibility of safeguarding our national bird, the bald eagle? Or will we soon be the only nation with an extinct national emblem, with a destroyed symbol of freedom?

. . . The Christmas bird count

February, 1957

Sometime between Christmas and New Year's every winter, several thousand bird watchers, well scattered throughout the United States and adjoining Canadian provinces, go afield for a whole day to count birds. This project, known as the Audubon Christmas Bird Count, was started in 1900 by Frank Chapman, who was then president of the National Association of Audubon Societies. In starting this annual census Mr. Chapman's idea was to interest people in an activity that he hoped would to some extent take the place of hunting birds with a gun. Since that time, however, rules have been set up to make these bird counts more valuable to ornithology. The temperature, direction and velocity of the wind, clouds, condition of the fields, area covered, percentage of various habitats visited, number of observers, mode of travel and other factors are all recorded, in addition to the number of species and the actual count (in the case of large numbers, an estimate) of individual birds observed.

The hustle and bustle of the holiday season and the discomforts of the weather limit the participants in this activity to a few ardent birders in each of the many bird clubs and local Audubon societies. This is especially true in an area like ours where the winter birds are limited to a few species. A club may have 200 members yet have only half a dozen take part in the Christmas Bird Count. In areas along the Atlantic and Pacific coasts, where wintering oceanic birds add to the list, there is more enthusiasm for the project. Areas along the Gulf coast record winter bird counts that equal or surpass our local counts during the high tide of the spring migration.

It has been hard to stir up any interest in the Christmas Bird

Count among members of the Albert Lea Audubon Society. Some years ago a friend of mine who was attending St. Olaf College in Northfield drove down here one day during Christmas vacation, and the two of us drove out towards Conger and Manchester and back to Albert Lea in search of hawks. I wonder what some of those farmers thought when they saw a station wagon drive into their yard to park while the two occupants dashed out through the windbreak searching the treetops with binoculars, then dashed back into the car and took off without any explanation. Fox hunting tactics are familiar, but this must have looked like something different. Our luck was good. I believe our count was 26 species, including the ones that my friend had counted around Albert Lea before coming here.

The first Christmas Bird Count, officially a project of the Albert Lea Audubon Society, was made on Dec. 30, 1956. Two birding friends and I went as one party in a station wagon. The day started with a London fog. As rarely happens, I drove from home to Albert Lea without seeing or hearing a single bird. While waiting a few minutes for the third man to show up, two of us counted six species. First was the distinct "wist" of the cardinal. Then in succession: English sparrow, chickadee, nuthatch, blue jay and downy woodpecker. We planned to circle Albert Lea Lake, with the first stop being the disposal plant. But while driving through town we decided to stop at a railroad trestle, where we counted 200 mallards and one pair of black ducks. At the disposal plant we got into estimating practice and decided on 2000 mallards and a scattering of black ducks. Looking across the lake toward a local packing plant we saw a flock that appeared to be black ducks. We drove around to the plant and ran our count of black ducks to 162 and pintails to 16.

From the plant we drove to Big Island. Searching a weed patch before reaching the park entrance we saw four chickadees and flushed 10 ring-necked pheasants. I let myself in for a little kidding by saying I thought I heard tree sparrows. At Big Island we added to our count of nuthatches, downy woodpeckers and chickadees. We also saw two brown creepers on one tree. We spotted a hairy woodpecker, the first for the day, then turned to see a spike buck watching us curiously from a distance of fifteen rods. The crows were getting vociferous, but we didn't realize why until, nearing them, we flushed a great horned owl. That was about the extent of it at Big Island. While we were driving around the east end of the lake at a good clip, one of my friends suddenly yelled, "Whoa! Back!", as if he were driving a team of horses. He had spotted a hawk. After we had maneuvered into position we agreed that our hawk was a redtail. Just before we drove on, the hawk obliged by flying to another tree so we could see its red tail, the mark of the mature bird of the species. At a farmstead we saw a flock of starlings that we estimated at 200 birds. East of Juglan we drove into a private driveway to explore a brushy patch of woods and were rewarded with a few juncos and 25 tree sparrows, both firsts for the day. At Juglan we looked across the lake toward Big Island. Near the point of the island in some open water (and on the nearby ice) we saw a raft of ducks that we estimated at 3000 — a very conservative estimate. There might well have been 5000. They appeared to be mallards. It was high noon and we had 19 species, only one short of the morning's predicted minimum, so we felt confident of reaching our goal.

After a refreshing lunch we struck out again, stopping to pick up another friend who had indicated that he wanted to take part in the bird count. The sky had cleared and the temperature moderated to thawing. We drove out through a local nursery and past the city dump, then westward on the old Alden road, stopping first at White Lake, then on again to Armstrong where we drove south and around Upper Twin Lakes. Believe it or not, in all this distance we didn't see a single new species. We saw lots of countryside, a good many crows and English sparrows, a few starlings, but nary a hawk. In desperation, we headed for my place, driving across a muddy cornfield to my ten acre woods where I had seen a red-bellied woodpecker about three weeks before. After tramping through the entire woods and scaring out the old faithful great horned owl, we heard the telltale, "churrd-churrd-churrd," and finally spotted what we had come for: the zebra-backed rarity that is very strangely called the red-bellied woodpecker. This bird is numerous in the South, but in recent years it has been extending its range northward. We were glad the South could spare us one so our whole afternoon did not turn out to be a wild goose chase. It was five minutes to four, the time set for the close of the count. During the evening another birder called up to say that she had been birding out at a neighbor's farm and had seen several species, including one new bird to our list, the yellow-shafted flicker. At our meeting on Jan. 8th, our assembled list totaled 23 species, which will be the official count sent in to the National Audubon Society. We were disappointed with the hawks and gulls, but otherwise our bird count was not bad for this area.

. . .Yellow-bellied sapsucker

March, 1957

It seems strange to be writing about a bird that I have never seen. Stranger still is the fact that I have never happened to see it, because it has been seen locally by others, and I know its trademark well. The elusive rascal has left his indelible inscription on the Scotch pines growing near our house. There were many Scotch pines in the windbreak of our Iowa prairie farm home, and the trunks of most of them showed the work of this bird. In my early explorations of nature's wonders I was puzzled by the numerous small holes so closely spaced in the bark of these trees. The orderly rows of pits certainly didn't look like natural bark formation. Whenever I had an opportunity to see pine trees in a neighbor's windbreak I noticed these same bark deformities. I still look for these borings whenever I get close enough to a pine to inspect its bark. But the mystery of the culprit responsible for the oddity has long since been cleared up. Ornithologists have long known that these peculiar bark perforations are made by a bird that has been appropriately named the sapsucker. The species whose range includes our area is the common, or yellow-bellied, sapsucker.

Sapsuckers are a degenerate form of woodpecker that obtain a considerable part of their nourishment by feeding on the nutritious cambium or inner bark of trees and the sap that flows from the bark punctures. The holes are drilled through the outer bark into the tender, embryonic (or growing) part of the tree called the cambium layer. After making an extensive series of pits and eating the portion of cambium exposed, the bird goes from hole to hole and from tree to tree, drinking the sap as it collects. It does not suck up the sap as the name indicates but licks it up with its specially adapted tongue. The true wood-peckers have extremely long, sharp, spear-like tongues equipped with barbs for the purpose of fishing wood-boring insects from their tunnels. The other day I chanced to see a demonstration of the length of a woodpecker's tongue. Perhaps the red-bellied woodpecker visiting our suet feeder did not like our brand of suet. At any rate, the bird stuck its tongue out about three inches beyond the tip of its bill. I wondered where it all came from and where it all went to when it was pulled back. The tongue of the sapsucker, however, is short and split (or brush-like) at the end, entirely unsuited for reaching into insect tunnels to retrieve larvae but ideally suited for sweeping up sap. How wonderfully the Creator has designed the various birds for the particular manner in which each secures its food.

Fruit trees, birch, willows and other trees, in addition to pines, are worked on by sapsuckers. One might think that this extensive pitting would injure or even kill a tree by girdling it, and there have been occasional reports of trees killed in this manner, but sapsuckers are not common enough to cause much damage. Usually the trees show no ill effects. After all, does not man employ the same method successfully in tapping trees for maple syrup, turpentine, rubber, etc?

Sometimes a sapsucker drills more holes than he needs. In hot weather the exuded sap ferments quickly, and there have been many reports of these birds behaving in a very questionable manner, flying erratically among the trees, dashing themselves against the sides of houses and otherwise disporting themselves. With so many drillings to watch, the sapsucker is unable to guard them all against snitchers. Many other creatures also like to feast on sap — squirrels, chipmunks, hummingbirds, insects, etc. The insects — especially ants — become stuck in the sap, where the sapsucker finds them and adds them to its diet. It also varies its menu with fruit.

On its nesting grounds in the spring the yellow-bellied sap-sucker is reportedly a very noisy bird, uttering a variety of squeaks, whines and cat-like mews. It is sometimes referred to as the yellow-bellied squealer. In addition to its vocal expressions, its loud drumming on any resonant object, such as a hollow tree limb, tin roof, eavestrough or telephone wire, calls attention to its presence. This tapping is easily distinguished from that of other woodpeckers because of its peculiarly irregular timing. With all of these characteristic sounds, the yellow-bellied sapsucker should be easily spotted on its nesting grounds. In the fall, however, it unfortunately becomes mute as an oyster while migrating southward. It is the most migratory of all woodpeckers, wintering in southern United States and south to Central America.

...A mid-winter field trip to the north shore

April, 1957

For several years the Minnesota Ornithologists Union has sponsored a birding field trip up the north shore of Lake Superior in mid-winter, climaxed by a joint meeting with the Thunder Bay Field Naturalists Club of the Canadian Lakehead. Even though this trip often coincides with severe weather, it has grown in popularity until participants now number well into the second hundred. This year the attendance was 134. The lure of this trip is the opportunity of seeing unusual birds. It is also a chance to see many northern-breeding birds, who consider themselves down south when they get to Superior's north shore. Many of these birds are unpredictable — a situation which only adds to the zest of ardent birders.

Another incentive for braving the weather to join this excursion is the opportunity of meeting in jovial fellowship with other birders, who can get as excited about seeing a new bird as an angler can get in hooking a muskie. This fraternity of kindred spirits is best attained when several birders travel in a group, as was the case on February 22, 23, and 24 this year when 39 of us went by chartered bus from Minneapolis to Grand Marais and back. This was my first north shore winter field trip, and it was a very rewarding experience indeed.

The driver was cooperative and exceedingly patient with us. When anyone saw a bird and yelled, the bus would stop and people, with binoculars in hand, would pour out to get a good look at the bird. As we filed back into the bus he counted noses to make sure that no one was left. There was no opportunity for birding on the way to Duluth on Friday evening because of darkness but there was continual chatter and getting acquainted activity, with the social atmosphere leaning heavily to birds, both seriously and in a lighter vein. Boxes of candy and cookies were passed over the seats and soon we were in Duluth.

At 6:45 Saturday morning the bus left Hotel Arrowhead for a full day of birding. We had gone only a few blocks when someone yelled, "Bird!" The bus stopped and we got a good look at several pine grosbeaks, including one bright, rose-colored mature male. This was one of the unpredictable species and a new bird on my list. Our next stop, still within Duluth, was at the home of a local birder who has gone "all out" in providing winter facilities for birds. There were feeders galore with seeds, grit, suet, and even an electrically heated water trough. The place was swarming with birds — evening grosbeaks, black-capped chickadees, downy woodpeckers, hairy

woodpeckers, white-breasted nuthatches, blue jays and many others. The musical warbling of the evening grosbeaks was continuous. Our host said that instead of his customary 100 evening grosbeaks he had only about 60 this year but, even so, they had finished 150 pounds of sunflower seeds.

The thermometer registered 15 below (not to mention a strong wind off the lake), so our stops were usually brief. At Encampment Forest we took time to hike up the scenic road a little way, but found no new birds. We did get a look at a raven soaring beautifully. Farther on we stopped the bus for a cold hike down a road to a residence near the shore. Here we encountered that coveted rarity, the Hudsonian chickadee. This was a new bird for me and also for many of the other birders. It was hard to get the group back on the bus at this stop. Herring gulls were fairly numerous, especially around fishing establishments. We looked each flock over carefully for individuals of other species. One flock included an immature ring-billed gull and one glaucous gull. The glaucous was another new bird on my list. We made several stops in order to set up the spotting scope to identify ducks out on the lake beyond the ice. They turned out to be goldeneyes, American mergansers, and especially oldsquaws, the extensively white, long-tailed Arctic Ocean ducks that are usually found wintering on Lake Superior. At one stop we saw a flock of cedar waxwings. With these frequent stops the ride from Duluth to Grand Marais was something like the old game of "fruit-basket upset." The last birders to get back on the bus took whatever seats were vacant, with the result that I found myself seated beside a different person after almost every stop. A mixer if there ever was one! Skirting the Superior National Forest we saw several deer. There was laughter when we spotted a young buck close by the road in a snowbank squatting on its haunches with its front legs extended while watching us curiously.

At Grand Marais I had just entered the hotel lobby to arrange for a room when an avid birder from Canada grabbed my arm and exclaimed excitedly, "There's a harlequin duck in a little open water at the Cascade River outlet, the third sight record for

Minnesota! It's the chance of a lifetime! Get in my car and we'll drive back!" Outside the hotel we hailed three other birders, who hurriedly got into the car. We sped back to the Cascade River to find the open water, but no duck. However, two other birders were there when the harlequin duck alighted in the water among a few oldsquaw ducks. Both men saw the rarity at close range, so it will go on record officially.

On Saturday evening we joined 30 of our Canadian friends and the other 65 Minnesota birders at the new Grand Marais High School for a splendid dinner served by the Congregational Ladies Aid. A Grand Marais lodge owner lectured and showed excellent colored slides of birds, plants and scenery from the Gunflint Lake area.

Just as some of us were coming out the door of the Shoreline Hotel on Sunday morning, a pileated woodpecker flew across

our path about 50 feet away. Another flew across the street about a block away as the bus was about to take off for a five mile swing up the Gunflint Trail. The Gunflint Trail jaunt proved to be very rewarding. The scenery was grand, and I added two more birds to my list, the red-breasted nuthatch and the white-winged crossbill. Some of the people in our party went off searching for an unidentified little bird that flew up the street at one stop. They gathered in a little knot and watched something that brought forth chuckles. I didn't want to miss anything, so I went over to them and saw a man's hand held out through a window while chickadees were feeding from it as if it were a bird feeder. We were surprised to see a white-throated sparrow scratching contentedly under a spruce tree near a bird feeder. At this season he should have been south of the Ohio River at least.

On our way back the birding was not so good. We did see a white-winged scoter, which brought forth some argument as to identity, and a horned grebe. At Beaver Bay we stopped to see some ruffed grouse at twilight. The bus group had seen a total of

28 species. I added seven species to my list, which is not bad for one trip. We did not get back to Minneapolis until 9:00 p.m., but the time seemed short because when birding people get to visiting they seem to forget about time. As the group broke up at the Minneapolis bus depot all agreed that the trip had been rewarding and that a similar trip next winter was a strong possibility.

...*The rails*

One of the most fascinating of bird communities is that of the marsh dwellers. A surprising number of widely differing species make their summer home in a cattail slough habitat and live together as neighbors. To most people, many of these birds remain mysterious creatures, known only by their strange call, since few birders are ardent enough to don high boots and spend hours wading through water, mud and tall, dense, tangled vegetation in search of all the marsh's secrets. From the middle of April to the first of June the marsh is at its best in this latitude, for it is then teeming with birds engaged in their courtship and nesting activities.

Any slough, of course, will resound with the music of red-wings, who can be seen flaunting their bright epaulettes and alternately singing and scolding. In too few sloughs these days the yellow-headed blackbirds add to the chorus their odd, rasping, yet strangely musical, refrain. Both marsh wrens are always there with their guttural rattle and dry staccato chatter. Black terns fly over the cattails, keeping vigilant guard over their nests on the top of muskrat houses or on improvised dead reed platforms. Try disturbing one of their nests and observe how belligerent these peaceful-looking birds become. In every slough there is that sober, deliberate recluse, the American bittern (or slough pump), with its well known "plum pudding" courtship call. Present also, but rarely seen, is the slough pump's midget relative, the least bittern, which is only about the size of a meadow lark. One must almost step on this fellow before he will flush from his hiding place. Experienced birders may detect his presence in a marsh by a low, cuckoo-like call coming from far out in the cattails. If there is open water there will be coots and pied-billed grebes nesting. Sooner or later one will flush a crow-sized, dark-colored bird, the little green heron, which takes off suddenly with a loud, startled "skyowk." Though not nesting in the slough, the little green's larger relative, the great blue heron, will be in the open water stalking frogs and crayfish. In the grass and shrubbery near the shore the swamp sparrows will chink and trill to the accompaniment of the northern yellowthroat's "witchity, witchity, witchity." There is always the possibility of stumbling onto the nest of a marsh hawk, especially if the pale gray male has been seen flying low over the fields near the marsh. In the wet meadow near by we may hear the alder fly-catcher's characteristic three-syllable song, "wee-be'-o." From the cattails near by comes a loud, clear, rapid, descending whinny, the song of the sora, a member of that interesting group of birds, the rails.

Rails are shy, secretive marsh birds, much more often heard than seen. Their plumage blends well with dead grass and rushes, and the chicken-like birds are experts at keeping well hidden under marsh vegetation. If pursued they will swim and

hide under water with only their beaks above the surface. Their bodies are narrow, or compressed, enabling them to run readily through dense vegetation without disturbing it enough to betray their course. Strong legged and fleet, they run rather than fly to escape danger. When cornered and forced to fly, they flutter feebly with legs dangling for only a short distance before dropping abruptly into the cattails again. One may well wonder how the rails are able to accomplish their long migratory flights.

Rails become particularly active and loudspoken after sun-down. As a youngster I wondered a great deal about the many strange sounds coming from the slough in the far corner of our farm and from the neighbors' sloughs to the north and south on spring and early summer nights. I recognized the peculiar pumping call of the bittern, but not the loud, spooky clamor starting after sundown and continuing far into the night. This variety of eerie sounds was mostly the serenade of the various species of rails. There was the low, grunting, "bup, bup, bup, bup, bup" of the largest of the group, the king rail, a chicken-sized bird of fresh-water marshes. Intermingled with weird grunts were the shrill squeals and the metallic "ticket, ticket, ticket, ticket" courtship call of the much smaller Virginia rail. Most often heard was the bewitching whinny of the little sora. Sometimes the rails will leave the marsh and venture into surrounding fields in search of food. It does not take long for them to get back to cover if danger threatens. I have, on rare occasions, seen each of these three species in the open.

I recall distinctly the first time I saw a king rail. I was ac-companying my dad on a trip to town after a load of drain tile. Horse drawn wagons may be outdated now, at least in this area, but a spring seat atop a triple box on a lumber wagon had it all over an automobile seat as a place from which to see things along the road. The elevated position, with an unobstructed view, and the leisurely gait of a team of farm workhorses permitted careful scrutiny of the roadsides and adjoining fields. As we approached a small slough I noticed a slender, brownish, chicken-like bird sneaking through the meadow grass toward the tall reeds, and called Dad's attention to it. At that tender age I naturally assumed that Dad knew everything, so I was surprised when he asked me what kind of bird it was. I felt honored, however, to have him seek the information from me. I had never heard the name, rail, applied to a bird. Judging from the bird's long legs and bill, I guessed that it was a stork. In the presence of his seventh offspring, Dad tried unsuccessfully to hide a smile. I realized that I had pulled a boner in bird identification, but did not catch the significance of it because I was not yet aware of the traditional powers attributed to the stork. I did not know till long afterwards that I had, by good fortune, seen one of the choristers of the eerie nocturnal symphony, and that our very errand after drain tile was contributing to the king rail's doom, and also the doom of its relatives, the Virginia and sora rails.

...*Valuable allies*

June, 1957

A lot of soil has been stirred here since the middle of April as farmers, alert to the change of season, have been preparing the fields and planting crops. Tilling the soil is a way of livelihood requiring long hours in the open fields giving one's crops the best possible chance. While thus engaged, one becomes aware of the many other creatures making their living from the same fields. Some of these work to our advantage, while others thwart our efforts. One cannot help seeing the hoards of destructive insects infesting the soil in which his crops must grow. Neither can one fail to see the ruinous rodents that live there. How obviously helpful are the birds that are always present during the crop-growing season. What effective allies they are in man's battle against his crop enemies!

Horned larks, vesper sparrows, killdeers, meadow larks, upland plovers and others spend the summer months in our fields, and work wonders in insect control. Brewer's blackbirds grackles, cowbirds, and black terns follow implements that stir the soil in order to take advantage of the easily garnered food. Sometimes great flocks of Franklin's gulls follow the farmer's plow to gobble up great numbers of exposed insects. Tree swallows, barn swallows, purple martins and other swallows skim over the fields to capture flying insects. Highly beneficial, too, is the rodent patrol, our birds of prey.

The faithful red-tailed hawks are again nesting in my woods, and woe to the mouse that ventures forth in the fields during daylight hours. These large birds require a lot of meat for themselves and their growing young. After a lapse of a few years sparrow hawks are again living at our place and helping the red-tails keep our fields mouse-free. I have often been disgusted with a certain red oak tree. In the first place, it stood so near the farm boundary that I could not be sure whether it belonged to my neighbor or to me, so it was left standing when I was clearing my farm for more efficient field operations years ago. From time to time, it has been dropping dead branches into my field to hinder my work. But this spring all its faults have been forgiven because its rotted heartwood has provided a cavity which a pair of sparrow hawks have chosen as a home. To show their appreciation these little falcons captured and devoured eleven field mice in one day while I was discing an adjoining field. A marsh hawk, whose nest I suspect is quite nearby, sailed over the field on the same day, and dropped down to pick up a mouse. The mousing was good that day. A pair of crows even got in on the act and made off with three of these destructive rodents.

A flurry of palm warblers peek-a-booing at me from a grass-grown fence row reminded me that warbler time was here and that not all birding can be done from the tractor seat. The tail-bobbing palm is one of over fifty species of American wood warblers that spend the summer months north of the Mexican border. Only a few species, such as the yellow warbler, redstart and northern yellowthroat, nest in this area. Most of them go on to Canada, pausing only briefly here on their journey northward. Enroute, however, they render a great service by searching out and devouring uncounted hoards of tiny insects that feed on the tender, growing, new tree leaves. The total population of wood warblers is tremendous.

Because of their great variety of bright plumage, their restless activity, small size, and brief, unpredictable stay, wood warblers lend a great deal of spice to birding. Without binoculars it is difficult to see them distinctly enough to identify the species. Spotting warblers is quite a sport in itself. Each species has its own characteristic song. But before one can become familiar with the various songs the warblers are gone for another year. They pass through again in the fall, of course, but they sing very little at that season and their brilliant breeding plumage has been replaced with plain garb which bears no resemblance to the spring plumage. Many species are confusingly similar. Adding to the confusion are the immatures in juvenile apparel. Even in their springtime splendor, warblers readily escape notice. Tree leaves conceal them and wind-stirred foliage diverts attention from bird movement. Warblers travel more in mixed company than any other group of birds. During the height of the northward movement, which in this area occurs around May 20, the woods and thickets may be suddenly filled with several species of warblers, together with thrushes, sparrows, flycatchers, vireos and other birds that have been in migratory flight during the night and have stopped to feed and rest during the day. There may be half a dozen species of warblers in the same tree. How birders relish these warbler waves!

... *An Iowa field trip*

From a friend — a retired rural mail carrier and lifetime naturalist by hobby, whose acquaintance I had made through this column — I learned that the Iowa Ornithologists Union would hold its annual spring convention at Estherville, Iowa, on May 18-19. Even though this time coincided with the Albert Lea Audubon Society's spring bird-counting field trip I decided to drive the 85 miles to Estherville for the I.O.U.gathering. Estherville — located on the west fork of the Des Moines River in the heart of Iowa's prairie lakes country — promised excellent birding, and the possibility of seeing some western birds. Last summer my friend and a birding companion who is a park warden in Estherville saw a painted bunting and a scissor-tailed flycatcher in the park area. I did not expect to duplicate this. But one can hope. I also thought it would be interesting to meet some of the birding people of our neighboring state, and in this I was not disappointed.

Enroute to Estherville I drove past my old stamping ground. For several miles near Thompson, Iowa, I knew every road, field and farmstead. Nostalgia reached its height as I passed the site of the old Combs school which I attended through the seventh grade. The schoolhouse had disappeared, as had the woodshed in which the ill-fated Iowa Bird Club, in the agony of organization, collapsed because of violent disagreement among the prospective members as to whether or not red-winged blackbirds should be put on a protected list. The last of the schoolyard trees were bulldozed into a heap. I was glad that the huge cottonwood which towered over the schoolhouse in my schooldays had not met such a fate. Planted by my older brothers one Arbor Day, it was named George Washington, and grew to dominate the schoolyard until 1921 when it blew down in a violent windstorm.

An area in the cornfield east of the schoolyard gave no indication that it had once been the cattail slough from which American bitterns pumped in answer to our teacher's questions. Schoolday reminiscing continued until a road sign announced that Estherville was just ahead.

While registering in the lobby of my hotel I heard rumors about a snowy egret at Ingham Lake. This find was later verified, since the bird was considerate enough to remain during the two days for all to see. I missed the early Saturday morning field trips but went out to Fort Defiance State Park later in the morning. When I returned for dinner at the hotel other birders were returning from their morning trips and recent comers were registering. There were people from Nebraska and birders from Wisconsin, including some that I had met on Minnesota field trips. Saturday afternoon was taken up by a short program and the annual business meeting. After the banquet on Saturday evening we were entertained with a lecture, accompanied by breath-taking color motion pictures of the wildlife of Alaska.

Three guided field trips were scheduled for Sunday morning. After hearing comments on the possibilities of the various trips, I chose one. Among the stops we made were Cheever Lake, Mini Wakan State Park, Okoboji Lake and Spirit Lake. Cheever Lake was the best area for water birds and shore birds. This lake was really a marsh — a very unusual marsh, with open, shallow water and scattered bunches of reeds. The ground, almost to the edge of the water, was firm enough to walk on, even without rubber footwear. We saw a Canadian goose and several species of ducks swimming about. An American bittern stood among the reeds. Near by was a mixed group of shore birds, including various sandpipers, both greater and lesser yellowlegs, dowitchers, and most interesting for me and a new bird on my list, the Wilson's phalarope. There, the most beautiful of our shore birds, are sometimes called swimming sandpipers. Their plumage is thick and ducklike, so they ride on the water buoyantly. Although they often wade while feeding (like true sandpipers)

they characteristically spin while swimming, supposedly to disturb aquatic life on which they feed. Another characteristic of all phalaropes is the reversal of the sex roles. The females are larger, more highly colored and more aggressive in courtship, while the male assumes the task of building the nest and incubating the eggs. The female, of course, lays the eggs. She could not shift this biological task to her faithful spouse.

After dinner on Sunday the group met to compile the list of all species seen during the two-day stay. The remarkable total was 169 species.

. . . *Peregrine falcon*

August, 1957

That prince of predators, the peregrine falcon (or duck hawk, as the American race of the peregrine is often called), is seldom seen in this part of the country. It is seen here occasionally, but only in passage to and from more northerly abodes. We have no cliffs on which it delights to nest. And, when migrating, it usually flies too high to be seen by human eyes. Our only chance of seeing it is to spot it on the ground when it is feeding. In April 1956, thanks to the good birding eye of a companion, I saw a peregrine falcon on the north shore of Bancroft Creek near a local mink farm. This bird had been feeding on a mud hen, but began watching us intently when we spied it and, distrusting our scrutiny, soon took flight. When perching, the peregrine falcon is easily identified by its crow size, dark upper plumage, white throat and face, with black mustache markings extending down from its eyes and curving forward. On May 19th this year I chanced to see another peregrine falcon perched in a cultivated field near Estherville, Iowa.

The peregrine falcon of various races is world-wide in distribution but comparatively limited in numbers. It is the bird that was (and, to some extent, still is) most commonly trained and used in falconry, the oldest of sports. The peregrine falcon's characteristic method of taking its prey is by what falconers call the "stoop," in which it descends from several hundred feet overhead, with partially folded wings, in a power dive at speeds exceeding 200 miles per hour to strike its selected target with its clenched talons, or fists, sending its victim dead and hurtling to the ground.

In recent years peregrine falcons, as well as other birds, have

been captured and banded for identification. In September 1953 I saw a captive peregrine falcon that had been taken at Two Harbors, Minnesota, by an employee of the Minnesota Department of Conservation. In capturing this peregrine he used a fine-strand net extended between two stakes set upright in the ground, a tethered pigeon for bait, and a tethered sparrow hawk. Watching the sparrow hawk from a blind, he saw it look up suddenly and appear frightened, indicating that with its telescopic eyesight it had spotted a larger hawk, possibly a peregrine. By pulling a string he released the pigeon from a concealed box to flutter at the end of its tether near the net. Lured by the apparently crippled pigeon, the migrating peregrine descended and became entangled in the net as the supporting stakes tipped toward each other, folding the net above the unsuspecting bird.

Even more exciting was the older, cruder, "buried in the sand" method so ably described to me by a New Jersey woman I know, who was one of the interesting birding people I met at the Wilson Ornithological Society's annual meeting at Duluth last June. This lady has the narrative touch, with appropriate gestures, tone of voice and laughter, to lend spice to any incident being related. She bands birds, is chairwoman of the endowment committee of the American Ornithologists Union, and knows and enjoys birds and birding people.

She once persuaded a couple of experienced bird banders to show her how to capture peregrines. Even though the appointed day brought pouring rain, she and her husband, whose protests proved futile, drove the seventy miles, only to find that said birders were unexpectedly entertaining foreign birders, who clearly resented "women seeking dickey birds." Despite excuse pleas, however, she declared: "This is the day!" Soon the group was crammed into an army jeep headed for the seashore, with her husband sprawled atop cameras, tripods and banding equipment in the back seat. At the beach the professional banders tried halfheartedly to catch a couple of peregrines, then decided it was a bad day. My friend, still hopeful, pointed to a large female peregrine perched on the beach some distance away and said, "I want to catch that one." With the jeep maneuvered closer to the bird, the men worked on the side opposite the falcon, and soon my friend was buried in wet sands. An old orange crate, made to resemble debris, was tipped over her exposed face and hands as she held a string tied to the pigeon's feet. With compassion for the pigeon, she held it close. She had sand in her eyes, ears, nose and in her mouth, clear to her tonsils. Her clothing was not as waterproof as it might have been. Miserable but determined, she waited and watched the apparently unconcerned falcon. Finally, the coveted bird came within fifty feet and showed interest in the lure. However, after goggling and gesturing endlessly, it took flight and disappeared. "Failure," she thought, "after all this effort and after bulldogging these men into an undertaking they clearly wanted to escape." Then: "Bang!" The peregrine struck! She grasped both its legs and hung on, thrilled beyond composure. The men came to take the struggling bird, but she yelled, "Leave it alone! It's mine! Get this wet sand off me! I can't move!"

"But you can't band a peregrine alone," they protested.

"We'll see about that," she replied. She then reached into her pocket for a nylon stocking and slipped the peregrine into it head first. Held snuggly in this straight-jacket the peregrine was helpless but unhurt. Having fastened the band around the bird's leg, she cut the foot-end off the stocking and pulled it until the peregrine emerged from the cut end without a single feather ruffled.

. . . Great blue heron

October, 1957

When I stopped at a local hardware store one day, the proprietor told me about an unusual experience with great blue herons. These large birds usually keep their distance and mind their own business. But on a recent fishing trip to northern Minnesota he had encountered a group of sociable great blues that were so interested in his fishing operations that they made a nuisance of themselves. One of them was so foolhardy that it collided with his car. When he launched his boat to try his luck at angling, dozens of the large birds stood along the shore watching every move. Others circled overhead, eager to plunge into the water and retrieve any small fish that were thrown back into the lake. His wife didn't enjoy having the large herons so near, and I don't blame her. Though picturesque at a distance, great blue herons are not particularly handsome at close range. When they all but perch on one's boat they can look formidable. And, besides, they are not very tidy. The boat had to be thoroughly washed before the homeward trip.

The resort owner had had an explanation for the heron's strange behavior. He said there was a large rookery near by with many hungry young, and that the high water in the lake this year was in some way interfering with the normal fishing habits of the great blues. Perhaps the open water in which they like to stand and watch for fish was too deep for even these long-legged birds. At any rate, the resourceful herons were seeking the fisherman's help.

Fortunately, the bird that clashed with the car survived the ordeal. My friend thought the bird had been killed, but when he stopped to examine the limp form in the road he had to dodge a jab by the sword-like beak. The groggy bird was put into the car trunk to recover. Some time later a vacationer stopped to ask the couple about their fishing luck, and was told that it was excellent. When the man expressed doubt, he was told to search the trunk for evidence. As soon as the lid was opened the revived heron scrambled out and took flight while the curious angler took off for a tall tree.

Speaking of odd blue heron behavior reminds me of the one that flew over our farm this spring carrying in its beak a stick that I judged to be at least three feet long. I knew there was a great blue heron rookery among the treetops on Big Island, and thither this heron was heading, but it certainly seemed unnecessary to carry such unwieldy nesting material from a distance of eight miles, and who knows how much further.

Great blue herons eat many kinds of small animal life, such as insects, frogs, salamanders, snakes, crayfish, mice, gophers, and sometimes small marsh birds, but they are primarily fish-eaters. Many birds other than herons are also fish-eaters — loons, cormorants, terns, pelicans, ibises, mergansers and gannets, to name only a few. Fish-eaters serve a vital purpose in the web of life by culling or weeding out excess fish. It is good garden practice, for example, to plant vegetable seed in excess of what is needed, and thin out the small plants later to the desirable stand so that each plant can get its full requirement of plant food, moisture and sunlight. The same principle applies to fish. Fish hatch in countless numbers, only a few of which can hope to mature. Natural fish-food in any body of water is always limited. The size of the fish is determined not so much by age as by the amount of food it can find. Over-population means small fish. The heavier the predation, the smaller the number but the larger the fish in a body of water. Left undisturbed, fish-eaters increase in population to a point beyond which they are unable to catch enough fish to meet their food needs. This is the point of population balance between fish-eaters and the fish on which they feed. In such areas man will find the fishing excellent. Man's take of game fish is highly selective, thereby creating an unbalanced condition which natural fish predation would tend to correct. Man would profit from a greater abundance of fish-eating birds.

In his efforts to create good fishing man has built many fish-rearing establishments for stocking lakes and streams with desirable game fish. In the light of recent research the effectiveness of this practice has been seriously questioned by game biologists. A more effective approach to the problem would be to improve the fish habitat. Ironically, these fish hatchery pools, being crowded with small fish, have attracted great numbers of herons, who feast on the easily obtained food. Hatchery managers, armed with guns and special permits, shoot the valuable birds by the hundreds, despite the fact that herons are fully protected by the Federal Migratory Bird Treaty. This reduction of the heron population injures the habitat in our natural lakes and streams. It is not the only factor involved, of course, but it is an important one. If fish hatcheries are to be continued they should be screened to prevent herons from getting to the officially reared fish. This will mean a substantial outlay of money, but it will be more effective, and is certainly wiser than destroying the herons.

...The loon

November, 1957

At the annual hawk count of the M.O.U. at Duluth this year, a lone bird flying in the distance was identified as a loon. Although too far away to permit seeing any plumage markings, even with aid of binoculars, its silhouetted hunchbacked profile marked it unmistakably. Far from expert in flight and quite unconcerned about thermals or updraft air currents so eagerly sought by others, it did not follow the path of the migrants, along the shore, but headed straight for its most accommodating element, the open water.

In equipping its creatures for expertness in one element, nature sometimes leaves them almost helpless in others, so we find the loon grotesquely awkward on land and very ordinary in air, but exceedingly skillful at swimming and diving. The loon's large webbed feet are placed so far back on his body that on land the bird must push itself along on its breast. To avoid land travel the loon places its nest very near water on a small island anchored in a bed of reeds, sometimes atop a muskrat house. The loon cannot take flight from land. It cannot even take flight from water without splattering along the surface for a considerable distance, preferably running into the wind, using both feet and wings to attain enough speed for take-off. Once in the air it can fly with considerable speed. But its wings are too small in proportion to the bird's weight to permit anything but labored flight. When alighting it seems unable to check its speed to any extent. Alighting on land would very likely prove fatal. When alighting on water it plunges in at headlong speed and sails about until its momentum is checked. The loon — nature's submarine—is thoroughly at home in water and is a master performer. By expanding or contracting the large air sacs within its body it can change its specific gravity at will and swim with ease at any level. It normally rides low in the water, often swimming with only its head and neck above the surface — the original periscope. The loon must have inspired the designers of the first man-made sub. It can sink from sight gradually, without leaving a ripple, or it can drop under like a stone. Its chief food is fish, which it skillfully pursues, using its feet, and sometimes its wings, to propel itself.

During migration loons often gather in large numbers in favorable feeding areas. But in the breeding season they prefer solitude. Only a large lake will harbor more than one pair. A family of loons — the adults and two young — is a familiar sight on northern Minnesota lakes during July and August. What fisherman has not tantalized one of these family groups — especially when the young are small — for the sheer joy of seeing the antics resorted to by the parents in safeguarding their offspring? Ask any fisherman. He'll smile, and tell essentially the same story. The male separates himself from the group and tries to draw the intruder's attention by carrying on in a manner very likely responsible for the phrase, "crazy as a loon." Meanwhile, the female has managed to get the young to climb onto her back. Then she submerges with them. When she appears again far out in the lake there is no trace of the young. A thorough search of the lake's surface, if the weather is calm, may reveal two tiny dots near the spot where the female submerged. These are the young, swimming with only their beaks and eyes showing above water. If the young are pursued the parents quickly return to put on another frenzy of acrobatics.

The greatest charm of the loon, however, is its strange call. To those who love the wilderness, the loud, resonant, quavering cry of the loon ringing out across the lake is a delightful sound, rising then falling, echoing and reverberating along the shore, before fading away. Anyone who has heard the call of the loon from the snugness of a camp by a northern lake will never forget the thrill of this commanding sound of wild, free nature. It lures one to return again to hear the call of the untamed wilderness.

Minnesota, with nearly 300 species to choose from, is still without an official state bird. It seeks as its symbol a bird that is a resident of the state, is colorful, and one that no other state has claimed. The loon, it is argued, is seldom seen in some parts of the state. But is it more difficult to find than our symbolic flower, the showy lady's-slipper or, for that matter, our state tree, the red pine?

Members of the Minnesota Ornithologists Union have at long last buried the hatchet and gone on record as unanimously favoring the loon for state bird, and the Federated Garden Clubs of Minnesota now favor backing the M.O.U. in its choice. Minnesota has reason to be proud of the remaining unspoiled lakes and woods of its widely known vacation mecca, of which the loon, in season, is a living part. We can do no better than to adopt the common loon, or great northern diver, with its magnetic attributes, as our official state bird.

...American osprey

December, 1957

The American osprey, or "fish hawk," as it is often appropriately called, does not nest in this area as it did before extensive settlement, but is sometimes seen here during migration.
Because it shows little fear of man it has been an easy target for
hunters and has been greatly reduced in numbers. The first
osprey I ever saw was perched on a telephone pole near Waseca
on April 23, 1952. I was in good birding company that day, for
with me was Carl W. Buchheister, vice president of the National
Audubon Society. We were enroute to Mankato, where Mr.
Buchheister was to catch a bus following his Audubon Screen
Tour presentation in Albert Lea. Since that time I have seen
several of these picturesque birds. It was one of the 98 species
that we saw at the Connecticut Audubon Nature Center in
August, 1953. One day last September when I stopped in to see a
friend he took me for a delightful cruise on Albert Lea Lake. We
saw several kinds of birds, including a Caspian tern. Just before
we docked, an osprey flew directly over us carrying a good sized
goldfish in its talons. There are goldfish in Albert Lea Lake, but
I was not aware that the osprey included such aristrocratic items
on its menu. The goldfish, however, is only a carp, and this one
had made the mistake of swimming too near the surface.

Impressively large and eagle-like, with a wingspread of up to
six feet, the osprey can readily be identified, even at a distance,
because it flies with a distinct crook in its wings. At closer range
one can see that its plumage, unlike that of any other large
hawk, is blackish above and almost clear white below. The head
is mostly white, with black cheek patches.

Many kinds of birds catch live fish for food but their method of capture varies. Pelicans scoop up fish in their capacious mouths. Loons, grebes and penguins pursue and overtake fish, even at considerable depth. Herons wade into shallow water and wait for fish to come within spearing distance. Kingfishers and terns plunge into the water head first and spear the fish with their sharp beaks. The osprey is ill-suited for using any of these tactics, but nature has equipped it for being the most spectacular fisherman of all. Its talons are strong and sharp, and the soles of its feet have horny tubercles, so helpful in holding onto slippery fish. Spotting its quarry from 30 to 100 feet or more overhead, the osprey hovers for a moment, then folds its wings and drops, plunging into the water with a splash that sends water flying in all directions. Entering the water feet first with wings extended upward, the bird may go down until only the tips of its wings show above the water, or it may disappear entirely for an instant, then rise heavily with the fish in its talons, shake the water from its plumage and head for its nest or a feeding perch.

Despite its skill, however, the osprey, like any fisherman, has its troubles and hazards. It can capture and carry off a fish considerably heavier than itself, but occasionally one overestimates its ability and sinks its talons into a fish that is too large for it to handle, in which case it is drawn deep into the water where, in its surprise and confusion, it sometimes drowns before it can detach itself. Even after a successful catch the osprey is often robbed of its prey by the larger, fiercer but far less skillful fisherman, the bald eagle. Soaring overhead and watching for an opportunity, the bald eagle swoops threateningly at the burdened osprey until, screaming in frightened protest, the smaller bird drops its fish, whereupon the eagle seizes the falling fish in mid-air and makes off with it, leaving the osprey to hunt for another fish.

Ospreys are most numerous along the seacoast, large lakes and rivers, especially where protection is rigidly enforced. They always nest near water. They return year after year to the same nest, adding material to it until, like an eagle's nest, it becomes a huge affair weighing tons.

. . . Rough-legged hawk

While harvesting corn this year, I have seen quite a number of rabbits in my fields. Cottontails are beautiful creatures, but they have played so many tricks on me that I have no particular love for them. Their keen appetite for the bark of young fruit trees has ruined their reputation. Their great trouble lies in becoming too numerous. Like other rodents, they seem able to keep up their numbers despite all the natural population controls. There is the story of the rabbit that got such a low grade in arithmetic because he couldn't add, subtract or divide. He could only multiply. The rabbits unwisely introduced into Australia, a land where their natural enemies are few, have amply demonstrated their fecundity. From this costly example we can feel fortunate that in this country we have a number of natural population checks on them. Some of these have also been evident in my cornfields. Fox tracks are numerous, and I have no doubt that these predators have found the table well set.

After sundown one evening I turned to look at my corn load and saw my good friend, the great horned owl, hovering over the standing corn a few rods away in the area toward which a cottontail had run a moment before. While I watched, the big owl lifted her wings upward and plunged down among the cornstalks. I did not actually see the bird capture the rabbit but I am sure she had a good meal. One afternoon I noticed a large black bird overhead giving my cornfields the once over. I hope he stays, because his size, habit of flight and large white underwing patches marked him as an American rough-legged hawk — *Buteo lagopus s. johannis* (if you like Latin). This individual was of the dark, or melanistic, phase. Most roughlegs are of the light phase and are easily identified by their white tails with a wide black band at the end and also by the conspicuous black wrist patches as viewed from below. American rough-legged hawks are arctic birds that come southward to this area during the winter months. This is fortunate because most of the red-tailed hawks that nest in this area migrate southward at this season and without the roughlegs to take their place our rabbit-ridden fields would go unpoliced during the daytime.

I frequently get telephone calls from people who want help in identifying birds that they have seen or found crippled or dead. A year ago last fall a friend called to tell me that a neighbor had a large crippled bird in his otherwise unoccupied henhouse. The neighbor's son had found the wounded bird floundering about on the ice out on the lake. The bird was being fed rabbits, but had such a voracious appetite that keeping it supplied was getting to be quite a chore and they were about ready to release it. He asked me to drive over and identify it before it was released. There was the possibility that it could be an eagle, although I doubted this from the description. There seemed to be no convenient time to get away and the errand was put off until I was sure they had released the bird and the matter was dropped. This fall my friend called me again and said that his neighbor still had the bird and that both men were still curious about its identity, so I drove over to have a look at the mysterious captive. I took my Peterson's *Bird Guide* along, but the book was quite unnecessary because the hawk dancing a hopwaltz before me was unmistakably an American rough-legged hawk of the light phase. The hawk had been wounded by gunshot and one wing, though completely healed, was distorted and entirely useless. Birds are equipped with the most convenient and efficient means of mobility possessed by any of the many forms of life with which we share the earth, but a bird deprived of its power of flight is a helpless, miserable creature and a pitiful sight.

At the Duluth meeting of the M.O.U. policy committee last fall members were taken on a tour of the new science building of the University of Minnesota Duluth Branch. The head of the Biology Department was complaining about the inadequacy of bird skins for use in the laboratory work when I thought of the crippled rough-legged hawk and suggested that this bird might be used to fulfill the need. "Yes," replied the professor, "if you will prepare the skin." I'm afraid that my hobby does not include this branch of ornithology, so my friend's hawk will probably never come to serve this useful purpose.

At the annual hawk count, held in conjunction with the meeting referred to, one American rough-legged hawk was observed by several of the hawk-watchers because it was cooperative enough to perch for a while on a highline pole within easy binocular inspection range. The bird was quite a surprise this early in the season (Sept. 21), late October being more timely for this species.

Many states have now passed model hawk laws giving legislative protection to all birds of prey, with the stipulation that a farmer who actually sees a criminal hawk take poultry may himself kill that individual hawk. Minnesota can take no pride in being one of the states that, so far, has not passed such a law. As long as certain species of hawks are not on the protected list, unscrupulous gunners may shoot any hawk and claim that they thought it was an unprotected raptor. With all species protected, this alibi could not be used and enforcement would be much less complicated. The fact that some species are unprotected implies that those species are bad. This is not true. No species are destructive, only rare individual hawks.

Not so long ago, the migrant hawks nearing Duluth were met with a barrage of shot. Now, Duluth Bird Club members are deputized to patrol the flyway, and binoculars have replaced guns as birdwatchers from all over the state gather each fall to watch and count hawks as they safely pass this bottleneck in their southward journey. This conservation project saves thousands of much-needed hawks to help us in our battle with rodents.

. . . Attracting birds

February, 1958

This is seed catalog and nursery catalog time. At this bleak season, who doesn't enjoy relaxing in a comfortable chair some evening with a lavishly-illustrated seed catalog and dreaming of such unbelievable beauty growing in his own garden or yard? Some wag has said that the first thing one gets in his garden is tired. There is as much truth as humor in that observation, but there are examples to prove that gardening and yard planting are not yet lost arts. Certainly anyone can dream, and dreams are the things from which plans and projects evolve.

For those who like to have birds about, it is well to keep these fellow creatures in mind while scrutinizing the colorful pages. Planting and proper arrangement of food-bearing trees, shrubs, vines and flowers is just as effective for attracting birds as is winter feeding or the placing of nesting boxes. Scattered clumps of shrubbery will attract more nesting songbirds than solid plantings because most songbirds like the edge between dense growth and open spaces. By selecting plants which differ in time of fruit maturity, one can provide birds with an almost continuous food supply throughout the entire year. Hummingbirds are partial to the nectar of certain species of flowers. Flowers left to mature their seed will provide welcome food for many seed-eating migrants. Folks who like to see birds gather like teen-agers around an ice cream counter should by all means plant shrubs like blackberry, raspberry and elderberry, which appeal to the appetite of more than a hundred species. Blackberries and raspberries prefer a sunny location, while elderberries are excellent for shaded areas. Elderberries bear profusely, the red-berried variety maturing in June and the black-berried variety from August to October. Among the tree fruits, cherries and mulberries prove the most appetizing.

Near our house is a scrubby cluster of cherry trees planted by some previous occupant of the place. During the fruiting season the heavy crops of rather sour cherries lure robins, catbirds, brown thrashers and other birds from daybreak till dark. When planting our windbreak in 1937, I included 150 mulberry trees, with the idea of attracting birds — especially cedar waxwings. I have not been disappointed. Waxwings have nested here nearly every summer since the trees reached bearing age. Long before the fruit is ripe, goldfinches and other fruit-loving birds swarm like bees among the mulberries. Mulberries are indeed one of the best bird foods.

Suburban and country homes can provide a hidden place for a small, tangled, impenetrable thicket, so attractive to both nesting and migrating songbirds. For such a thicket one might plant chokecherry, speckled alder, gray dogwood, elderberry, wild grape and Virginia creeper, with blackberry at the edge. One could even include a good brush pile to advantage. A tangle like this could exist very innocently behind a twelve-foot screening hedge of black haw, a viburnum so excellent for both nesting sites and palatable bird-food which clings to the shrub all winter. Tartarian honeysuckle is also excellent for screening and nesting, but its fruit matures early in the summer. Dogwood bushes add greatly to home beauty and variety of summer bird-food. Mountain ash and Japanese barberry add beauty but, like sumac and hackberry, their fruit is rather unpalatable. However, for this very reason, their tenaciously clinging fruit serves birds well in a pinch.

One must not forget the value of evergreens for attracting birds. A bird will fly several miles, if necessary, to reach a favorite conifer in which to roost during the night. Have you ever stood close to the leeward side of a Colorado spruce on a cold, windy winter day and felt how completely it breaks the wind? Small songbirds roosting in the dense growth of an evergreen are not only protected from wind, snow and sleet, but from attacks by owls as well. A large planting is unnecessary. A small clump, or even one evergreen, will serve the purpose. The juniper tree near my den window is especially attractive to many birds at every season. The small, blue berries are eaten by more than 50 species. The tree harbors insects that attract warblers and other birds. Blue jays and mourning doves usually nest there, sometimes simultaneously. Its value as a roosting place for migrants was brought sharply to my attention in the spring of 1948 when we started building our new house. At about 5:30 every evening several dozen Harris's sparrows started voicing their annoyance at our presence, and kept up the scolding until we put aside our tools for the day, whereupon they flew into the juniper to roost.

Birds often prefer to perch in the open on a dead branch, where their view is unobstructed and where, incidentally, they can be readily seen. Leave some dead branches for their use. A continuously available supply of water is just as important as providing food and cover. Birds like to have water to drink and bathe in near their living quarters.

This may seem like a farfetched dream and an expensive project. But it needn't be. Neither does it need to be completed at one time. Some material will need to be purchased, but the higher priced plants can be used sparingly and many hardy, native plants can be used.

. . . *Shore birds at Park Point*

March, 1958

The St. Louis River widens as it enters the tip end of Lake Superior. It is hard to tell where the river ends and the lake begins. Through the years, the sand and silt carried in the river water has settled to the bottom as the current slackened upon entering the lake. The action of the waves and the ice pushing against the deposited soil has formed a sand bar extending almost entirely across the lake from the Minnesota to the Wisconsin shore, forming the Bay of St. Louis. The longest section of the sand bar is on the Minnesota side, extending outward from Lake Avenue, and is known as Minnesota Point. This sand bar has been developed into a residential section. A surfaced street, complete with curbs and sidewalks and lined with homes on both sides, extends almost the entire length and terminates in a recreation area called Park Point. The area beyond Park Point is sand dune terrain and accessible only on foot.

Most birdwatchers who visit Duluth make a trip to Park Point. The birdlife there is unpredictable but, since birds are such mobile creatures, there is always the possibility of seeing unusual species, especially shore birds and water birds during migration. Last June, members of the Wilson Ornithological Society found a piping plover's nest on the St. Louis Bay side, a new experience for many of them. Spotted sandpipers and yellowlegs ran along shore and flew over the water. A small island, separated from the main bar by only a few yards of water, used to be the nesting ground for hundreds of common terns, but is now completely covered with grass and willow shrubbery and not suitable for tern nesting. As a member of the M.O.U. projects committee I should perhaps suggest that the vegetation be removed from the island, leaving it sandy again and ideal for common tern nesting.

A good surfaced road, with ample parking space, completely encircles Park Point, which is level, grassed, and kept smooth as a lawn. Black-bellied plovers like this area and can be seen in flocks numbering hundreds of birds. Scanning these flocks closely with binoculars often results in spotting other species like golden plovers, dowitchers, Wilson's snipe and any other of several species of sandpipers. Turnstones and oyster-catchers are sometimes reported, and this usually starts a birdwatcher's stampede from the hawkwatch toward Park Point. Also, there is always the rare chance of seeing some of the larger shore birds, such as godwits and curlews. Across the road from the recreation area one may walk over the pine-studded sand dune ridge to the steep sand beach of Lake Superior proper. While watching the gulls and terns or searching the shore for sandpipers and listening to the wind in the pines and the breakers whipping upon the beach, it is easy to imagine that Longfellow might have stood here when he coined those lines of Hiawatha's childhood: "'Wawa tassie' said the pine trees, 'Mudweosca' said the water."

At the hawkwatch on Duluth's skyline drive last September there were reports that two birdwatchers had seen a parasitic jaeger on Minnesota Point. Upon hearing this news, I accompanied a couple of friends to Park Point, where we saw several species of birds, but no parasitic jaeger. Saturday afternoon turned cold and rainy and hawkwatching became dull. So dull indeed that the organizer of the project was not on hand to help count the few hawks that passed. A miserable-looking chap with his inadequate coat collar turned up and his hands in his pockets turned out to be a reporter from the *St. Paul Dispatch* who had been assigned to get a story on the hawk count. I sympathized with the poor fellow and helped him as best I could. I haven't seen the write-up yet, but I understand he did write a story. He should have been there the next day when the count rose to more than 2700 hawks.

After hawk-counting hours on Saturday I accompanied some

Canadian friends to Minnesota Point, so for the second time that day I found myself there. We were coming back to the car after some time on the shore when we heard a gull overhead screaming in distress. Looking up quickly, we saw a gull-like bird chasing a ring-billed gull. As the birds turned upward, the profile of the darker, pursuing bird, clearly silhouetted against the sky with its conspicuously longer and pointed center tail feathers, betrayed its identity unmistakably as a parasitic jaeger.

Jaegers are dark, hawk-like sea birds that nest in northern latitudes and migrate along our coasts but are rarely seen inland. They have sharp, curved claws and hooked beaks. Although they are well able to capture their own food, their characteristic method is to harass a gull or tern until the victim disgorges a fish, whereupon the jaeger catches the booty in mid-air. I do not envy the jaeger this method of obtaining nourishment. I was glad to enter on my life list a bird that the experts say one must go to the sea in order to find.

... Spring migration

One reason why birds are such appealing creatures is that we associate them with the pleasantness of returning spring. After the lingering monotony and inconvenience of our cold, dormant winter we long for balmier days and welcome joyfully any hint that a more agreeable season is near. Long before the first bloodroot punches up through the leafmold and air becomes fragrant with awakening plant life, even before the temperature begins to moderate, birds begin returning from their winter sojourn to herald the approaching season. In keeping with the buoyancy of spring the birds enroute northward to their nesting grounds appear in their most radiant beauty of plumage and utter their most eloquent and impassioned song.

The first birds to arrive are those that can subsist on weed seeds, since insect life is not yet astir. By the middle of February horned larks may be seen on gravel shoulders along the highway. They are birds of the open fields. However, when arriving this early, they are most often encountered along the road, where they are attracted by bare ground, gravel (to be used for grit) and perhaps also by scattered grain spilled or blown from trucks. When these, our earliest harbingers of spring, take flight at our approach, one may see their black outer tail feathers and hear their high-pitched, musical twittering. Last year I saw my first horned lark on February 8th; this year on February 13th.

Next to arrive may be small flocks of tree sparrows bound for the arctic timber line. They have spent the winter just south of us feeding on weed seeds so incidental to crop production. Returning slate-colored juncos may also show up before the end of February. Some morning, about the first of March, we may expect to be greeted by that conspicuous figure of meadows and grassy fields, the western meadow lark. His repertoire includes several different songs, each a series of loud, clear, full-throated whistles that add much to our enjoyment of the countryside. With the arrival of the great flocks of male red-winged black-

birds and grackles, who quickly blend their harmony in the leaf-less windbreak, spring is ushered in with gusto. As I step outside my door some blustery morning near the middle of March, I hear, "olit, olit, olit,—chip, chip, chip, che-char-che-wis, wis, wis" from the weedy fencerow by the hog yard, and know that the song sparrow is back for another summer. A killdeer calls plaintively overhead and a yellow-shafted flicker sounds off with an emphatic "wick, wick, wick, wick" and drums a tattoo on a dead limb.

Canada geese migrate northward leisurely with the advance of spring, stopping occasionally wherever they find some open water in which to alight and swim. The first skein of Canada geese gabbling overhead is a signal for birders in this area to grab binoculars and strike out for Albert Lea Lake to get a better close-range look at various species of waterfowl than is possible at any other time of year. When the ice goes out of our lakes it thaws first along the shore where the water is shallow. When swimming waterfowl are confined to this narrow strip their plumage markings can be seen clearly. When observed walking on the ice near the open water the entire bird can be seen to even better advantage than when swimming, half submerged.

On March 17th last spring my wife and I took advantage of this seasonal situation and spent an enjoyable afternoon along the south shore of Albert Lea Lake looking over the great rafts of migrating ducks gathered there. Most numerous, of course, were the mallards, of which there were thousands. Next in num-ber were the scaups, canvasbacks and redheads, which num-bered in the hundreds. There were dozens of black ducks. Scattered through the flotilla were a few pair of pintails, shovelers, ring-necks, American mergansers, American golden-eyes, blue-winged teal, bald-pates, gadwalls and hooded mergansers. The beau brummel of the party was, without a doubt, the male hooded merganser, a show-off if there ever was one. From our car we watched one of these elegant drakes dis-porting himself beside his ladylove. The clean-cut bill, the sharply contrasting white chest and black head and neck, and especially the black-bordered, white, fan-shaped crest — opening and closing in grand display — was a treat for any birder to see. As ducks walked about on the ice there was an opportunity to see how the various species were adapted for their particular method of feeding. The pond, or puddle, ducks had long necks and small feet, placed well forward, as best exemplified by the pintails. The bay ducks, or diving ducks, best represented by the canvasbacks, had relatively short necks and noticeably large feet placed far back. The mergansers, or fish-eating ducks, had narrow and conspicuously toothed bills. Although the ducks did not seem to mind our binocular study of them, there was some shifting about. On taking flight from either ice or water the pond ducks sprang up easily, while the divers pattered along the surface in a gradual take-off.

April offers a wealth of enjoyment to those who are keenly aware of the bird life about them. During this month a great many of our birds, including many of the insect-eaters, return to animate the landscape, cheer us with their familiar songs and entice us to search for a glimpse of their beauty.

... *Experiences in bluebird housing*

May, 1958

It is discouraging for a bird enthusiast to witness the decline and disappearance of one after another of our native species of birds, as a result of the activities of man, when so often all one can offer is sympathy. Therefore, it is heartening under these circumstances to find a threatened species that will respond to one's efforts at rehabilitation. Especially rewarding is such assistance when the species responding is such a gem of beauty as that symbol of happiness, the eastern bluebird. For his friendly, contented warble, for his radiant beauty and as an economic asset the bluebird is tops.

The bluebird's problem is not direct persecution. It is much too small to have culinary appeal and much too beautiful for even the most calloused to find pleasure in shooting. Its difficulty is an acute housing shortage. In the days of wooden rail fences, replete with deserted downy and hairy woodpecker nesting cavities and old-fashioned, sadly neglected family orchards with their abundance of dead limbs and decaying heartwood, bluebirds were in their glory. But barbed wire fences with steel posts and large-scale, well pruned and expertly tended commercial orchards offer no haven. To make matters worse, man has introduced such aggressive, exotic species as the English sparrow and the starling to compete with the bluebird for the precious few nesting sites remaining. The bluebird's only hope now appears to be the provision of man-made nesting boxes, specifically designed and located for its use.

The Albert Lea Audubon Society constructed and put up 114 bluebird houses in the spring of 1949. The project had a two-fold purpose. The few members, previously strangers, were badly in need of a morale-boosting project to show some purpose for getting together, something in which they could all take part and have a common interest. One member commented at the close of a meeting, "Will this thing hang together for another meeting or will it fold up?" The bluebird housing project was the ideal solution. Here was a chance for everyone to work at constructing the houses and a chance to measure our joint accomplishment by observing bluebird response. There was some lag in getting the project underway. The first effective action was setting our goal at 100 houses ready to put up by March 1. The next constructive step was designating our January meeting as the house-building session. Members were to come dressed for the occasion and equipped with tools and materials for making the bluebird houses. The meeting turned out to be a memorable one. There had been some doubt about our ability to construct 100 bluebird houses at one meeting, and the closer it got to meeting time the more fearful I became of the possibility that my pet project might fall short of its goal. As it happened, I had been dismantling our old house, using as much of the material as possible in building our new house. There were, of course, a great many lumber pieces, such as window frames, door frames and broken cornice boards, that could not be used, but that would be good material for bluebird houses. The power saw was set up for use in finishing work on our new house, so one day when the weather was bad I started sawing material for the proposed bluebird houses. With the power saw the work went fast, and before I realized it there were parts for 95 complete bluebird houses. I brought this material and five pounds of galvanized nails to the meeting. The design of the houses was very simple: a 4" x 4" inside measurement, 9" deep with a slanted top and a 1½" entrance hole 6" above the floor. The back side extended both above and below the rest of the house for convenience in nailing to a post. I planned to help nail these houses together but, with eight hammers beating out a steady tattoo, I found myself unable to keep up, though my only task was the drilling of entrance holes. At the close of the meeting the 114 bluebird houses, in a gay assortment of colors, were parceled out to the various members, who had agreed to put them up on fence posts.

The houses were all erected, but there the accuracy of record ended. We had reports of experiences, and some pictures, but no exact data on bluebird occupancy. One member reported that a pair of black-capped chickadees nested in one of his boxes and used as nesting material strands taken from the previous year's corn stalks. It has been interesting to note some of the public reaction to this bluebird housing project. There has been very little vandalism. One of our members fastened one of his houses to a telephone pole. On checking the houses later, he found that the telephone pole had been replaced with a new one, but that the workmen had sawed off the section of the old pole to which the bluebird house had been attached and had wired it securely to the new pole. One of my houses was nailed to a post along a railroad right-of-way. During the summer this fence was taken down and replaced with a new one. However, the section men had nailed up the bluebird house again on one of the new posts.

Of the 114 houses, I had 41 on my own individual bluebird trail. Each time these houses were checked my family and I drove 20 miles, making 41 stops and spending up to three and one-half hours on the trail. These houses were not studied as intensively as they would have been by a professional ornithologist, but I do have the following records on them for the years 1949, 1950, 1951, and again in 1953.

Year	Blue-birds	Wrens	Eng. Spar-rows	Tree Swal-lows	Mice	Nothing
1949	18	3	4	0	2	14
1950	26	6	6	1	0	2
1951	2	9	8	8	2	12
1953	3	7	7	8	0	6

After 1953 I have made no check of bluebird houses on the original trail, except as I have happened to drive past where they were located. Several of the houses had been destroyed by road-building operations in 1952 or had been ruined by squirrels gnawing into them to get at acorns stored there by white-footed mice. The severe drop in bluebird occupancy in 1951 has never been recovered. Occupancy by wrens, English sparrows and especially by tree swallows has increased. Our bluebird trails have become predominantly tree swallow trails. Tree swallows are welcome, of course, but they are very untidy housekeepers, and this may be a partial explanation of the drop in bluebird tenants. Bluebirds seem reluctant to accept a dirty house, and this might be expected of such excellent housekeepers as they. To attract bluebirds to my own farm I have been putting up some new houses there every year. I have had bluebird tenants every year, usually two families. I now have ten houses on my farm and, of these, two were occupied by bluebirds in 1956, one by wrens, three by English sparrows and four by tree swallows. In 1955 a male bluebird staunchly defended a new house, although for some reason no spouse responded to his selection of territory. One day a male tree swallow, frustrated by this bluebird's vigilance, tried coaxing his partner to nest in the exhaust pipe of my tractor, parked with the corn planter near by. The enthusiastic swallow perched and kept looking into the exhaust pipe until the tractor motor started.

On the original bluebird trail I sometimes found a wren nest on top of a bluebird nest. From this, I suspected that both bluebird parents had accompanied their young for a time after they left the nest and that during this time the wrens moved into the house, preventing the female bluebird from returning to make preparations for a second brood. An experience during the summer of 1956 verified this suspicion. A pair of English sparrows took to making a great fuss around one of the bluebird houses in my cow lane, even though the house contained young bluebirds almost ready to fly. On my way to the fields one day I saw the five young and two adult bluebirds perched on posts near my cow yard. When I stopped at the house I saw hay sticking out of the entrance hole, indicating that the sparrows had already completed a nest inside. I removed the cover, intending to throw out the nest, but found the female sparrow stubbornly sitting on the nest, even while I was looking in. I reached in, caught and killed her, reasoning that the male sparrow would not be able to find another spouse to take over the house before the female bluebird returned to prepare for a second brood. There were no sparrow eggs and, out of curiosity, I left the nest intact to see what the female bluebird would do with it when she returned. Three days later I inspected the house when I saw the female bluebird fly from it as I approached. The sparrow nest had been completely removed and a neat bluebird nest containing one egg occupied the house. A second brood of bluebirds was reared successfully, without further sparrow annoyance, because I had intervened in the bluebird's favor, shall we say, in the interest of science.

I feel that the bluebird housing project has been a success. There is a wealth of satisfaction in knowing that birds are living near you which would not have been there but for your invitation. One cannot always get two beautiful birds by providing facilities for one. Before I put up any bluebird houses I saw and heard bluebirds and tree swallows only during the spring and fall migration. Now I have them near me every day during their summer sojourn. Bluebird families leapfrog along the fence post tops and tree swallows skim over the fields along with barn swallows, catching insects disturbed by my tractor during field work.

. . . European skylark

July, 1958

One evening in March my wife and I were at the home of a neighbor to assist with the rehearsal of a play to be given at the 4-H talent contest. After the young people had gone home we stayed awhile to visit. During the previous fall this couple had taken a trip to their native Denmark. When the conversation turned to birds my neighbor waxed eloquent in telling about a small field bird that he had known well during childhood. Hearing this bird's song again on the homeland visit brought back nostalgic memories. He felt that there were no words to adequately describe this song, but beamed as he said repeatedly, "Oh! They can sing!"

The sparrow-sized bird he was telling about was, of course, the European skylark, whose vocal powers have taxed the vocabulary of many a poet and prose writer, including Shakespeare, Browning, Wordsworth and, especially, Percy Bysshe Shelley. If we are to believe these authors — and there is no reason to doubt them — no other bird is so literally the embodiment of song as the European skylark. The skylark sings for six or seven months of the year, and in midsummer may be heard from the early morning hours until dark. It may sing while near the ground but, characteristically, it pours forth its flood of song from far overhead. What could be more natural for a bird of the open fields, where there are no elevated perches, than to mount into the sky to render its song for all to hear?

To Shelley, however, goes the credit for all out effort in describing the celebrated bird. In fact, the European skylark is sometimes called the bird of Shelley because of the enthusiasm with which it is portrayed in this poet's classic poem, "To A Skylark."

Referring to the skylark as a "blithe spirit," "unbodied joy" and "scorner of the ground," he calls its song a "profuse strain of unpremeditated art," "a rain of melody," "a flood of rapture so divine" and "notes that flow in a crystal stream." But read the poem again, as I did after returning from the visit with our neighbors.

Because he was a poet, Shelley recorded his experience in rhythmic meter for all to enjoy. A great many people of both high and low rank have, nevertheless, had the same experience. European immigrants to America missed the touch of their homeland countryside which only the skylark could give them, so several attempts were made to introduce the bird to their new home. Most American ventures were failures. Our Canadian friends were more successful in their efforts in establishing a thriving colony on Vancouver Island in British Columbia.

The skylark is no fancy dresser. It is just a plain brownish, sparrow-colored bird, whose plumage is designed for concealment in the grassy fields where it lives. However, there is nothing reserved about the song that has delighted millions. The gifted songster is common throughout Europe, and allied races exist in other areas of the world. Although birds of the lark family are found mostly in the Eastern Hemisphere, our own native horned larks and pipits are closely related species.

Again I am writing about a bird that I have never seen nor heard. I have, however, longed to hear the skylark's song ever since first reading Shelley's poem in the sixth grade. It was not assigned reading at that stage, but the poem was in the same reader, and what was to stop me from scanning through the book to read interesting material?

It is often said that the older one gets the fewer new birds there are to be seen for the first time. I already feel this way about Minnesota birds, and wish that I might find an opportunity to spend some time west of the 100th meridian where many new bird species await me. Meeting the skylark in its native home is, for the foreseeable future, out of the question, but the skylarks of Vancouver Island are near enough to present realistic possibilities for adventure.

...Golden plover

Although binoculars and bird guides are standard birding equipment, I do much of my birding without either. It would be inconvenient (and impractical) for me to carry these aids with me on the tractor, from which vantage point I do a great deal of my birdwatching. During the hundreds of hours that I spend driving my tractor each crop growing season there is opportunity to see and enjoy much bird life. Residents and transients alike contribute to the pageant. There is an extra thrill when a bird shows up far out of its usual migratory path.

Western kingbirds are as scarce as hen's teeth in this area, but on May 16, 1956, I saw one while planting corn. Its lemon-yellow breast and grey head were a pleasing contrast to the familiar black and white of the eastern kingbird that was perched on the ground near my western guest. As the corn planter drew near them the check wire whipped sideways and both birds hopped nimbly over it.

In October of the same year I was even more surprised by another westerner, and again its eastern counterpart was on hand for comparison. Homeward bound from plowing one day, I saw about a dozen yellow-shafter flickers feeding on the ground near my field road. They took flight as the tractor approached and in their midst was a red-shafted flicker. At a distance of five rods there could be no mistaking that salmon-red color under the wings. Red-shafted flickers are native to the western United States. Before the Great Plains were settled and planted to windbreaks, the wide expanse of grassland kept these two species separated, since woodpeckers must have trees, or at least some telephone poles. With the coming of trees and poles the ranges of both species have expanded so that they now overlap. The sight of a red-shafted flicker in Minnesota, however, is still unusual.

On May 14th I had visitors from Argentina. Resplendent in flashy springtime attire, they came far out of their way to spend a whole day with me. Golden plovers are not new on my life list. While plowing on October 27, 1952, I saw seven, and later, on Minnesota Point at Duluth, I had seen a few. Not until this spring, however, had I seen these globe-trotting shorebirds in their exquisite breeding plumage — coal black underparts from beak to tip of tail, brownish spangled with bright golden spots above and a broad white strip across the forehead, over the eye and down the side of the neck to the shoulder. One might think that these bright colors would make the bird very conspicuous, but they were actually harder to spot on the plowing than those in somber autumn plumage. The sharply contrasting colors act as camouflage by breaking up the bird's outline. In true plover style the goldens would stand motionless for a while, then take a few steps and stop. It was easy to see the bird after it had moved, but as long as it remained motionless it might be in plain sight and near by without being noticed. It was impossible to get a count of the birds until they took flight. On the ground each bird moved individually, but in flight all took off together. Flying in close formation they circled about the field at high speed and usually alighted near the place they started from. They spent most of their time on low ground where they feasted on root worms and other insect larvae that I was glad to relinquish.

The usual northward migration route of golden plovers is through Nebraska and the Dakotas, but it was nice of this flock of 50 to deviate from their path and put on a full day show for me. By the next day they had resumed their 8000 mile journey to the arctic tundra. Golden plovers have one of the most interesting of all bird migration routes, traveling a different way in the fall than they do in the spring. Starting from their arctic nesting grounds, they fly eastward to the Labrador coast and work leisurely southward to Nova Scotia, feeding on marine life, crickets and other insects. From here they take off southward over the Atlantic for a 2500 mile non-stop flight to the coast of Venezuela, then over the jungles of Brazil to Argentina, where they spend the winter. In the spring they complete the ellipse by flying over the Andes Mountains to the Pacific coast and work northward, crossing the Isthmus of Panama and the Gulf of Mexico to reach the United States at the Louisiana border, then move leisurely northward to Missouri where, for some reason, they swing westward to go through Kansas, Nebraska, the Dakotas and on north.

History records that Columbus, on one of his voyages across the Atlantic, was persuaded by his near mutinous crew to turn his course southward to follow the path of migrating land birds. It is quite likely that at least part of these land birds were golden plovers. Any golden plovers that Columbus may have seen from the *Santa Maria*, however, would have been in their plain autumn garb, and far less beautiful than those I saw from my tractor last May. Even if he had come over in the spring Columbus would not have seen the goldens in their striking plumage, since their spring route is 2000 miles farther west. If he did observe golden plovers he probably saw a great many more than I have seen, since all shore birds were much more numerous at that time than now.

... Birds have troubles, too

September, 1958

I came upon our hawk quite unawares one day while planting corn this spring. The nest was in a leaning oak tree near the field road bordering the ten-acre woods on our farm. This is the same tree, by the way, in which a pair of Swainson's hawks built their nest in the spring of 1951. It was time to refill my corn planter with fertilizer, so I stopped the tractor motor and started walking around the woods to where my fertilizer supply rig was parked for the last filling. As I approached the nest tree I saw the female redtail perched on the edge of her nest with her back toward me. I slackened my pace to watch her tenderly caring for her newly-hatched young. Of course, I could not see exactly what she was doing, but I knew the eggs had hatched because a day or two earlier I had seen a small, downy, wobbly head above the edge of the nest. The mother hawk's head was down in the nest and she was making slight movements, as though she might be patiently feeding her fumbling offspring. So engrossed was she in her domestic task that she failed to notice my approach. She very likely thought that I was still by my corn planter at the far side of the woods. When I was fully abreast of the nest she gave a short, startled scream and dove off into the woods. A moment later she was soaring grandly overhead, screaming disapproval of my stealthy intrusion.

I believe that at least the female of the redtail pair nesting here this year is a different bird than the one that was here last year. She is larger, more white underneath and far less alert. It was impossible to approach last year's wary matron unnoticed. I have often wondered why our woodlot appeals to nesting hawks. Whatever conditions determine a hawk's decision to nest in a certain patch of woodland, our ten-acre woods must possess them because, of the twenty-nine years that I have lived here, three species of buteos have in turn nested in this woods for a total of twenty-three years. One requirement, of course, is assurance of an adequate food supply, but I hope this does not mean that my farm is more rodent-ridden than adjoining property. Another condition is freedom from interference by competing species, and here is an interesting situation. Great horned owls have nested in this woods every year as long as I have lived here, and they are considered the dominant nesting species because of their large size and fierceness and also because they start nesting in February, a full two months earlier than the hawks. These powerful raptores are permanent residents and usually take over a hawk's nest in the hawk's absence rather than build a nest of their own. The red-tailed and red-shouldered hawks nesting here, however, have successfully reared their broods despite the large owls. The great horned owls' presence, however, may explain why the pair of Swainson's hawks were unsuccessful in rearing their brood in 1951. There is no reason to believe that an unguarded young hawk is not fair prey for great horned owls. Young horned owls are even known to be cannibalistic. The young do not all hatch at the same time and sometimes the older ones devour their younger nestmates.

Birds do have their troubles. In fact, this is the usual thing rather than the exception. While cultivating corn on June 14th this year, I chanced to see a horned lark fly up from ahead of my tractor and flutter along the ground feigning injury. This strongly suggested a nest, and presently I spied one close to a corn plant in the row I was keeping my eye on to guide my four-row cultivator. I pulled the clutch, but just as the implement stopped, a lump of dirt rolled into the nest. The two eggs that were in the nest were not broken, but I noticed that they were not alike. One was densely peppered with tiny brown dots. The other was a little larger, more sparsely dotted with brown, and I recognized it as the egg of that culprit, the cowbird. I left the intruding egg for the lark to handle in her own way. This experience brought to mind an incident which happened at the meeting of the Iowa Ornithologists Union at Estherville, Iowa last year. There was a session for the exchange of birding experiences. A lady from Nebraska arose to tell about a robin nest on the porch of her home that had, in addition to its quota of robin eggs, one egg laid by a cowbird. Friends told her to throw the cowbird egg out, but she left it there, thinking that if the Lord did not want it there He would not have permitted it to get there.

"What I want to know," she inquired, "is, did I do right or did I do wrong?"

"Well," replied the moderator, "if you have made your peace with the Lord, who am I to say whether you did right or wrong? Certainly robins would not be made extinct by leaving the cowbird egg where it was, and neither would cowbirds be made extinct by throwing the egg out."

One question has always puzzled me concerning cowbirds. How do young cowbirds, having known only foster parents, know that they are cowbirds and, so, gather with their kind in the fall? Some bird people claim adult cowbirds recognize their offspring and claim them after the rearing job has been completed. This theory will need more research before being accepted as authentic, but at least it is an attempted explanation. Judging by human standards, how fraudulent can they get?

...*The shore birds*

October, 1958

In the haste and scramble of present day living we miss much of what is beautiful around us. Caught up in speeding highway traffic, we see the roadside as little more than a blur. With so much emphasis on speed in our routine of making a livelihood, how seldom we pause to observe and enjoy the many forms of life with which we share the earth. It was different when a driver could sit in a spring seat atop a triple box on a lumber wagon drawn by a leisurely moving team of farm work horses. There was ample time to view the roadside, with the added advantage of an elevated position with no obstructions and no danger from other vehicles.

To birdwatchers the first sign of autumn is not the turning color of leaves but the appearance of shore birds returning from their northern breeding grounds. On my way to town one day in late July I noticed a number of small birds gathered in the shallow water of the slough across the highway from Pickerel Lake and suspected that they were shore birds. Their identity, however, had to wait, because the driver's seat of a car in motion is a bad place from which to watch birds. At the first opportunity, which was August 3rd, I parked my car on the road shoulder and, with binoculars, identified pectoral, semi-palmated and least sandpipers, lesser yellowlegs and killdeer. There were also the familiar water birds, black tern and blue-winged teal. I stopped there again on August 24th and saw 14 species. In addition to the seven species just listed, there were semipalmated plovers, dowitchers, little green herons, great blue herons, one pied-billed grebe, several mallards and one ring-billed gull.

I was about to leave when a big semi roared past. The air disturbance rocked my car and scared the birds into momentary flight. Three dowitchers that had been feeding so near the road that they were hidden by the vegetation now moved into plain sight and continued their feeding. These odd-looking birds kept sticking their extremely long beaks full length straight down into the mud. There were perhaps a hundred black terns already in their winter plumage — white below and gray above, with white heads and dark markings by the eyes and back of the neck. Only in breeding plumage do the mature birds have black heads and underparts. I was not surprised to see half a dozen great blue herons, since there is now a sizable nesting colony of these birds on Big Island.

The first two weeks of August brought some real old fashioned summer weather — excellent for the corn crop, but far too hot and humid for the comfort of man or beast. Taking my cue from the cats one Sunday afternoon, I stretched out on our lawn beside a lilac bush and enjoyed the blessings of shade. When, as a lad, I lay gazing into the blue, wondering about the infinity of space, my thoughts were always interrupted by those wayfarers of the atmosphere, the birds. Now, as I reminisced, a number of chimney swifts were feeding and chattering excitedly as they wheeled and criss-crossed far overhead. A small flock of black terns flew with swooping wing-beats across the sky. A red-tailed hawk circled leisurely. Weather like this creates thermals, and how the hawks love to ride these upward currents of air in effortless flight! A young cardinal flew into the lilac bush and repeated his sharp "wist-wist," as if protesting my presence. Blackbirds, already flocking, flew informally, redwings in undulating flight, grackles straight. Over the house and just clearing the tree tops came a little green heron. I thought it was headed for Upper Twin Lake but it disappeared into the top of our windbreak. This suggested a nest and stirred memories of the first green heron whose domestic affairs I investigated.

I was hoeing in the garden one day when a strange-looking water bird flew overhead and disappeared over the top of our windbreak. When the bird took exactly the same route and at

the same time on the third successive day my ten-year-old birding curiosity got the better of my garden duty, so I dropped my
hoe and went searching, hopefully, for a strange nest. As I
peered into the densely leafed tops of the box elders the heron
became frightened and left its nest with a squawk. Climbing a
tree with a straw hat was not easy, but leaving the hat on the
ground was not wise because this was the calf pasture. Having at
last satisfied my curiosity about the nest and eggs in the precariously elevated position, I discovered that descending a tree with
a straw hat was even more difficult. Several times I caught it as a
twig flipped it off my head, but at last it got away. I watched it
sail down between the branches, hoping it would not get hung
up. About two rods away stood a calf dropping dung. What a
mess my hat would be if it fell into that, I thought, but that isn't
even remotely possible. It would be more likely that the calf, out
of curiosity, might start chewing on my hat before I could get
down to retrieve it. Just as the hat cleared the lowest branches a
sudden gust of wind caught it and set it top down squarely in the
soft manure. The startled calf sprinted away while I, relieved by
the humor of the situation, cleaned my hat as best I could and
went back to hoeing, satisfied that the reward had been worth
the price.

...*Bird banding*

One evening last July we came home late and found, stuck into the door latch, a small paper bag containing a little dead bird and a note saying that a neighbor had brought the bird and was wondering what kind it was. When we telephoned her the next morning to say that the bird was a chimney swift, she said that when she found the dead bird in her yard she had been particularly curious about a numbered metal band fitted around one of the bird's legs. If this was an official bird band, we told her, it should have instructions on returning it to the United States Fish and Wildlife Service. Our neighbor said she had not noticed any such directions, so I drove over to look at the band. After the telephone conversation she looked more closely at the band and found stamped on the inner side the following inscription: Ret. U.S. Fish Wildlife Serv. Wash. D.C.

I told her to include in her report the number of the band, the date and place the bird was found and also that the bird was found dead. In return she would be sent information as to when and where the bird was banded and who had done the banding. In due time this information came through. The swift had been banded as an adult at Memphis, Tennessee, on Sept. 17, 1955. From this information we know that this particular chimney swift was at least 3 years old when found on July 7, 1958. We know also that in its southward migration it had passed through Memphis, Tennessee, and that it had returned to Minnesota to nest this summer, probably in the Albert Lea area. Additional information sent to my neighbor included these items on known ages of banded birds: chimney swift 13 years, purple martin 14 years, mallard and pintail ducks 21 years. I'll bet those ducks took some cooking!

Of course, only a small percentage of banded birds are ever recovered. But it is also true that many more are recovered than are reported. The failure to report is due generally to lack of information about the procedure. When a banded bird is found dead its band or the number on its band should be sent to Washington, with appropriate details concerning the finding. If the bird is captured alive, the number of its band should be noted, the bird released, and the information reported. Through its bird banding work, the United States Fish and Wildlife Service has accumulated a great deal of information about birds — their migration routes, dates of migration, speed and habits of flight, age, winter range, etc.

One circumstance exasperating to ornithologists was the fact that up until 1942 no one knew where chimney swifts stayed during the winter. No one had reported seeing any at that season and no bands had been returned, despite the fact that thousands of these birds had been banded. To get this much desired information, the banding of chimney swifts was stepped up tremendously. Swifts are the easiest of all birds to band. During migration they gather in flocks sometimes numbering several thousand and roost at night in large chimneys, into which they descend at twilight like a funnel cloud. After dark the chimney is covered to prevent their leaving at daybreak. A trap is then placed over the chimney to collect the birds as they leave. Following this mass banding of chimney swifts, the riddle of where chimney swifts spend their winter was solved when among the bands being returned was one from Peru, South America. Ornithologists dispatched to the area found the swifts there in great numbers.

At the winter meeting of the Minnesota Ornithologists Union in December, 1955, a member of the faculty at St. Cloud Teachers College reported on swift banding work carried on in that city from 1952 to 1955. A total of 3,085 chimney swifts were handled. Of these, 398 had been previously banded. Most of these had been banded at St. Cloud, but of the 11 that had been banded elsewhere, one had been banded at Bemidji, Minnesota, and all the rest in Tennessee, one in Chattanooga and 9 in Memphis. One swift was banded at St. Cloud on August 29, 1952, captured and banded on the other leg at Memphis on October 11, 1952, and recaptured at St. Cloud on August 17, 1955. The Tennessee recoveries were all in the fall, indicating that although St. Cloud swifts migrate southward through Tennessee — near Memphis — they apparently return northward in spring by another route. The professor concluded his paper with this plea to people interested in birds: "Tell others about bird banding and how to report recoveries, won't you? Recorded information about birds will be increased manifold if you do."

...*Screech owl*

I look out through my den window at a scene that today is completely devoid of bird life. But wait! There is something in the bird feeder that I put up this fall to replace the weather-beaten one that fell apart last summer. My tardiness in providing food has no doubt contributed to the scarcity of birds, but I notice that the feeder has been used nevertheless. A screech owl has brought her own food and dined there, leaving two bunches of sparrow feathers as mute evidence. I'll venture a guess, also, as to where the little predator found those sparrows, because I caught her in the act one evening when we returned home and drove the car into the garage. I warmly welcome the nocturnal hunter and heartily approve her menu. The hood and top of our car has lately shown less of the unsavory indication that English sparrows have slumbered overhead.

The screech owl, like so many birds, is poorly named. In some parts of the South it is more appropriately called the shivering owl. Its call is not a screech but a series of short whistles — a mournful, tremulous wail usually running down the scale, but sometimes uttered at the same pitch. Because of its doleful call and its silent nocturnal flight the screech owl has, through the ages, been unfortunately regarded by ignorant and superstitious people as a bird of ill omen.

As a youngster I used to dread the sound. To me it was the threatening voice of the vast mystery of darkness. The call of the bittern, the killdeer and the rails sounded good in the dark. But the call of a screech owl made my skin crawl. Someone at our house was always subscribing for the *Youth's Companion,* a weekly magazine that was always filled with hair-raising yarns for teenagers. In addition to the stories of Indian threats of scalpings and burnings, there were the accounts of terrifying encounters with savage, wild beasts, always on a lonely trail after dark. At that age I did not read those stories but saw the blood-curdling illustrations and listened open-mouthed while older members of our family recounted the most frightening situations. Of course, the stories always had a happy ending, but that did not prevent nightmares or hinder a lively imagination from populating our box elder windbreak with all kinds of ferocious creatures after dark. My fear was not allayed, either, by such admonitions as, "Better watch out, or the owl will get you!" It was not always possible to avoid the dark entirely. There was no indoor plumbing at our house, so it was standard practice for small fry to make a trip outdoors just before bedtime. When the time came to venture forth on these errands alone, even with mother's assurance that nothing would get me, I went in high gear. And, if a screech owl let go an eerie whinny, I shifted to overdrive.

As I grew older and more enlightened on natural history I realized the foolishness of such fear, and found consolation in learning that others older than I also had misgivings about the screech owl's call. Somehow I harbored no resentment toward the bird, perhaps because it had been wronged by groundless association with evil. I now enjoy hearing the call of this gnome of the night. At high school age I had a great deal of fun with screech owls because I had discovered that one could arouse their ire by mocking them, especially when they had young. I would go out after supper, stretch out on the lawn and whistle an imitation of a screech owl's call. Soon one would appear on a lower branch of a tree where I could see it silhouetted against the sky. After exchanging a few irritated calls the owl would take off and I quickly pulled my straw hat down over my face just before the owl struck it with a thud. It was great sport while it lasted, but the owls started getting out of hand by attacking without being mocked. One of my brothers was tinkering with some machinery repair one evening at dusk when a screech owl startled him by suddenly giving an eerie wail only a few inches from his face. A little later my dad was walking across the yard at dusk when a screech owl struck his hat and knocked it off his head. At this point I thought it best to stop teasing the owls and after a time they resumed normal behavior.

I have held screech owls in my hands several times and been surprised at their lightness. I doubt that their weight exceeds two ounces. I have marveled at the complete silence of their flight. One evening in the summer of 1956 I started home from the field with a pickup load of grain. As I drove past the woods something was suddenly fluttering against the side of my face. The caress was ever so gentle, but I didn't think moths were so large. The confused creature turned out to be a screech owl. I took the bird along home to show the children and when they had satisfied their curiosity I released the owl. After a moment to allow its eyes to become adjusted to the change of light it took off into the darkness as quietly as a shadow.

Our children read exciting stories and watch some of the horror shows on television but, although they may at times have nightmares, I doubt if they associate any of this with that diligent mouser and insect eater, the harmless screech owl.

. . . *Migration*

Every evening about an hour before sundown the view southward over my fields looks like a nature portrait. Hundreds, perhaps thousands, of wild ducks start flying eastward toward Albert Lea Lake after feeding in my cornfield all day. A mechanical corn picker leaves much corn in the field, even under the best picking conditions. Last fall the machine wasted far less than usual. However, I had about 30 acres left to pick when the strong wind of last November flattened the remaining crop, making harvesting difficult and wasteful. The feeding ducks concentrated in this portion of the field, so we had another demonstration of the axiom, "It's an ill wind that blows no one good."

My sheep get their exercise and all the corn they need by hunting for it in the field. But there is much more corn on the ground than my small flock can possibly utilize, so the ducks are welcome to all the corn they can find. I hope that snow stays away until my sheep and their able assistants, the ducks, complete their cleaning job because any corn left will be pure waste and, what is worse, much of it will sprout in the spring and be a serious problem in the new crop. If we had a substantial snowstorm now, the ducks on Albert Lea Lake would soon take off for some sanctuary farther south where natural or man-supplied food is available. Birds get around. Their power of flight makes them the most mobile of all earth's creatures.

I suppose that my early fascination with birds arose at least partly from the fact that they could fly. I was not very old before I realized that a bird could get from one place to another much more conveniently than I could. I found it hard work to climb to the top of a tree, while a bird got there quickly and with ease. Fences, streams and other obstructions in my path were no hindrance to birds. Furthermore, I was told that they flew long distances to escape disagreeable winter weather. They seemed so free, and who doesn't love liberty and freedom from restraint? I have learned later that their situation is not as carefree as it may have seemed. Not only can birds fly from zone to zone, but most of them must migrate or starve. Our northern winter, with snow and ice-covered ground and dormant insect life, could not support the number of birds found here in the warmer seasons. Nevertheless, migration is a lure for such earth-bound creatures as we humans. Who hasn't paused in his daily routine to watch a skein of wild geese wing their way overhead, listened to their clamor diminish in the distance and longed to follow them?

If it were possible for us to follow some of our birds to their destination we might be in for high adventure. I just finished reading a book about a small group of scientists on an expedition to Bilot Island, which is well within the Arctic Circle and far enough north to permit crossing inlets on the ice by dogteam, even into July. Of the 33 species of birds observed there, I have seen 18 here in Minnesota. Lapland longspurs, snow buntings, American pipits and golden plovers nested there in great numbers, while snow geese and Arctic terns flew on even farther north to nest. But, enough of the frigid north. At this time of year it is more pleasant to think about warm weather, even though that may be all we do about it. Some fortunate people make arrangements to follow the birds to balmier climates for at least part of the winter, but most of us accept the lot of the chickadee, stay put and take the weather as it comes. However, there is nothing to stop the rest of us from thinking about the places where some of our familiar summer birds are spending the winter.

That curious and talkative little sprite of our woodlands, the red-eyed vireo, is now conversing with the natives in the wooded upper reaches of the Amazon River in Colombia, Peru and western Brazil. The rose-breasted grosbeak, one of our most gifted woodland songsters, is wintering throughout Central

America and southward into Colombia and Ecuador. The flashy redstart is neighbor to the rose-breasted grosbeak in winter as well as summer, although its range is more extensive in both areas. Its winter range includes the islands of the Caribbean. That jubilant minstrel of our June hayfields, the bobolink, is now sporting about in and around the swampy lowlands adjoining the Paraguay River in that South American country and in the Mato Grosso region of Southern Brazil. The upland plover and many of its relatives, the shore birds, are wintering on the pampas of Argentina and southward. The killdeer may be found in winter all the way from the mideastern United States to the northern part of Venezuela and Peru. The cheerful meadow lark is quite satisfied to stay on this side of the Gulf of Mexico.

I am not sure I would like to follow some of our birds from Bilot Island to Patagonia, or into all of the out-of-the-way places they inhabit during the course of the year, but it would be nice to cut loose for awhile and spend some of the winter in the balmier parts of the United States. Not only do birds beckon me southward and westward, but birding people add their inducement as well. Screen Tour lecturer Howard Cleaves has suggested Brownsville, Texas, in the very southern tip of that state. Brownsville has often had the highest Christmas bird count in the nation. In 1951 they counted 172 species in an 8-hour period. That's thirty more species than we here in Minnesota can find on our spring bird count at the high tide of migration in May. Our winter count is usually about twenty species. I recently had a card from a birding friend in New Jersey. She and her husband had just returned from a two-week vacation in Arizona, and she highly recommended a winter visit to that part of the country. These suggestions are very tempting, but somehow I seem to stay put and wait for the birds to return.

...*The winter lunch counter*

March, 1959

A great many people put out food for birds. Some of the most ardent bird-feeding enthusiasts maintain feeding stations throughout the year. But most of us are content to supply food only during the winter months when nature sets such a scanty table in this northern latitude. Providing food to supplement the natural bill of fare often means the difference between seeing birds and not seeing them at this season. Most of the birds that stay for the winter will respond to human hospitality, so one may often see more birds by keeping an eye on the bird feeder than by taking a winter field trip.

Insectivorous birds such as woodpeckers, nuthatches, chickadees, kinglets, creepers and jays can be attracted to winter feeders by supplying fatty substances like suet, meat scraps, nuts, peanut butter, sunflower seed or even pancakes and doughnuts. Juncos, evening grosbeaks and of course the irrepressible English sparrow are seed eaters and will respond to a handout of any kind of seeds, chick feed, mill screenings, bread crumbs, etc. Besides helping to nourish the birds through the difficult season, the practice of feeding them provides us with a great deal of enjoyment in seeing them at close range where we can readily identify them and study the behavior of the various species. Who hasn't chuckled at the activity around a bird feeder as their feathered guests feast and snitch morsels to hide away in ever so secret places? I have seen chickadees working in relays to carry away great quantities of suet and hide it in bark crevices of trees about my yard. Of course, there is no assurance that the birds will later find what they have so carefully hidden. There is much pilfering since birds have keen eyesight — and consider finders keepers. A piece of suet is no harder for a foraging bird to find than an insect egg or a cocoon. The finder may only move the suet to another hiding place, and this process may continue for some time before some bird finally eats it.

It didn't take long for word to get around among my birds the other day that I had replenished the feeder in our juniper tree with fresh beef suet. Apparently the last of the previous suet supply was not very appetizing because there had been few callers. With the new supply, however, there was soon a breadline of several species establishing their respective peck order. As one might expect, the chickadees were the first to arrive at the feast. There were half a dozen of them and all seemed hungry, but only one at a time worked at the suet. Apparently there is priority even among chickadees, depending upon their individual aggressiveness. When a female downy woodpecker arrived, all the chickadees scattered respectfully, but stayed nearby and fidgeted impatiently while downy enjoyed her meal. Perched so low on the feeder that her tail was extended forward and braced up against the bottom of the feeder, the downy ate heartily until there was a sudden flash of wings as a male white-breasted nuthatch descended on the feeder. Downy quickly yielded her place to the new guest. The nuthatch not only could perch with his head downward, but seemed to prefer that position while feeding. Chickadees took turns on the ground under the feeder, picking at morsels of suet that dropped. After satisfying his appetite the nuthatch seemed to enjoy keeping the downy and the chickadees waiting while he squatted atop the feeder. He darted swiftly away, however, when a hairy woodpecker came to feed. The hairy woodpecker in turn was wary of the bluejays that came too close. I have no red-bellied woodpeckers at the feeder this year, but I noticed last year that the hairy woodpeckers, and even the domineering blue jays, respected this bird's priority at the feeder. The peck order may not always follow this exact pattern. Sometimes a downy woodpecker will stand its ground and keep a nuthatch waiting at the feeder. Although no actual combat takes place, there is order among birds at the winter lunch counter.

. . . Gray-cheeked thrush

April, 1959

How well I remember my first look at a gray-cheeked thrush! It is always a thrill to see a new bird but, in this case, the experience was rather unusual. Early one May morning back in 1948 I was crossing the yard to begin my morning chores. May is a wonderfully satisfying time of the year for a birdwatcher because of the rising tide of migrating birds returning to their summer nesting range. Their songs are welcome and inspiring after their long absence. On this particular morning the air was ringing with bird songs from the fields, woods and fence-rows. From overhead came the high-pitched musical twitter of horned larks and the liquid, flute-like whistle of the upland plover. The bird that caught my attention, however, was not singing at all. Hopping about on the ground a few feet ahead of me was a drab, silent bird, a little larger than a sparrow. Its form and behavior were so much like those of a robin that I felt sure it belonged to the thrush family — a sort of sports model robin in modest plumage. I was so absorbed in studying the distinguishing features of this new bird that, for a while, I failed to notice another bird of the same kind a few feet farther on. As I looked around I was astonished to see literally hundreds of these same birds rather evenly spaced only a few feet apart over the entire yard.

Most passerine (or perching) birds migrate at night and stop to feed and rest during the day, dropping down at the nearest likely spot wherever they happen to be when daylight comes. One doesn't ordinarily think of thrushes migrating in flocks like blackbirds, shorebirds, longspurs and sparrows, but there was no other explanation for this deluge of thrushes. The chores took on a little extra speed that morning because I was eager to get at my bird books to look up the identity and a little of the life history of this new thrush.

Bird students of today have a great advantage over the early day students such as Nuttall, Wilson and Audubon, who had no convenient bird guides with descriptive text and colored illustrations for identifying the various species. Since their time, a great many professional ornithologists (and amateurs alike) have probed into the private lives of birds until today one can turn to books galore covering every phase of bird life and find answers to questions regarding any species. We don't have all the answers, of course, and I don't suppose we ever shall. Nevertheless, there is a vast literature on birds, teeming with information.

The gray-cheeked thrush is one of the five species of eastern North American birds that bear the name thrush. All of these are so nearly alike in form, size, behavior and general coloration that in poor light, as in woodland shadows, they can be confusing. The wood thrush, hermit thrush and veery (or Wilson's) thrush, however, all have the same rufous or rusty color in the plumage of their upper parts and can easily be distinguished from the other two species when seen in good light. With a little care they can be recognized also in woodland light conditions. The gray-cheeked thrush and the olive-backed thrush both have uniformly dull, gray-brown backs with a slight olive-green tinge. It is hard to tell the difference between these two species unless one happens to see them both together, but there are minor differences. The olive-backed thrush has a buffy eye ring and buffy colored cheeks and breast. The gray-cheeked thrush, as its name indicates, has distinctly gray cheeks and no eye ring. I have seen both of these thrushes together, in good light and at close range. The gray-cheeked is definitely a plainer gray.

Though drab in color and retiring in disposition, the gray-cheeked thrush does have some interesting ways. It migrates rapidly. Typically, birds move northward by keeping pace with advancing spring. Not so, the gray-cheeked thrush. Even though it has farther to go than many of the other birds, it remains in its winter home — northwestern South America — until many other species are well on their way, then overtakes and even passes them enroute.

Its breeding range extends farther north than that of any other American thrush. We ordinarily think of thrushes, with their spotted breast and dreamy eyes, as being inhabitants of shadowy woodlands — and the gray-cheeked thrush does indeed nest in such places. But it also breaks thrush tradition by nesting far beyond the timber line onto the open tundra clear to the Arctic coast. Several birds found only east of the 100th meridian in the United States fan out westward toward, and even into, Alaska. The gray-cheeked thrush goes even farther west. Crossing Bering Strait, it penetrates the Iron Curtain into bleak northeastern Siberia. The gray-cheeked thrushes nesting in Siberia could just as well fly to southern Asia to spend the winter. Instead, they fly eastward over 100 degrees longitude before turning southward to travel down the Mississippi River flyway to their winter home in the wooded mountains of Colombia, Ecuador, Peru and Venezuela.

As a songster the gray-cheeked thrush ranks below the wood thrush and the hermit thrush. Some think that even the veery and the olive-backed thrush outrank it in vocal ability, but it must be remembered that the gray-cheeked thrush does not sing its best song until it reaches its nesting ground. I have never heard this thrush utter any sound, and perhaps that explains why it escaped my observation until that morning when I practically had to wade through a gathering of them to get to my barn.

. . . The birding fraternity

May, 1959

It is human nature to become weary with repetition. Whatever we may be doing to earn our daily bread, we tire of the monotony of recurring tasks. The effect is cumulative, so we periodically seek diversion. Something we can do purely for the joy we find in doing it. A great many people find enjoyment in the out-of-doors, though their recreation may take different forms.

The hunting group is large. Their demand for gear and equipment has created a vast industry. The cash outlay cannot be justified on the basis of the commercial value of the game actually bagged. But there are other values. Hunting offers such a good excuse for getting out-of-doors to tramp carefree over God's green earth.

Fishing is another hobby with a vast following, and again a great industry is required to meet the demands of the angler, who may drive hundreds of miles and consider his trip worthwhile even though he may land but a single fish. He could have bought such a fish at the supermarket for a few cents per pound, but there would have been no recreation in that. Who can measure the cash value of the scenery, the anticipation of the catch, the feel of the boat in the water, the thrill of the strike, the uncertainty of success, the tug at the line, the triumph of landing even one fish and the enjoyment of telling others about the ones that got away?

Another, and rapidly growing, group of outdoor people is the birding fraternity. Some of these manage to stow away considerable cash in gear and equipment, but it isn't really necessary. Like many a bird enthusiast I started with no other equipment than eyes, ears and a burning curiosity. I have since acquired binoculars, bird guides and the enjoyment of fellowship with other birders. There is no closed season for birding because birders are not predatory. They live and let live. There are times, however, when they take to the countryside as though it were opening day. In this part of the country the latter half of May, and particularly the third weekend, is the most inviting.

For several years I have met with members of the Minnesota Ornithologists Union when they have gathered in a favorite birding spot for their annual spring bird-counting field trip. We gather as early as possible on Saturday, bird for the rest of the day and meet for dinner and a program in the evening. We stay overnight and bird again on Sunday until noon when we have lunch and make up the composite list of bird species identified. Then we head for home on Sunday afternoon.

At Frontenac, Minnesota, some years ago I was with a small group searching for the rare prothonotary warbler. The fact that it was Sunday morning never entered my mind until one of the birders, a middle-aged lady clad in faded field jacket, visored cap, slacks and galoshes, asked me point-blank if I thought it was wrong to bird on Sunday. After I recovered from the surprise I told her that I didn't think it was right to make a practice of skipping church services to go looking for birds, but since the Lord chose to send so many kinds of birds through our area in such a short time — which is our only chance during the year to see and hear them at their springtime best — I took it as an invitation for birders to look for, listen to and enjoy the beauty of this portion of His handiwork. She seemed pleased with my reply, and said she agreed with me.

As I drove into Whitewater State Park last May I was met by half a dozen familiar birding friends. When I first saw the group their binoculars were turned toward the top of a tree beside the driveway. After a cheery greeting and a good birder's handshake all around, I asked the group what they were so intent on seeing. One replied that they had heard a blue-winged warbler and were trying to locate it. I quickly parked my car and joined them because the blue-winged warbler is something special. In addition to being somewhat rare, it is one of those unusual species in the bird world that interbreed with another species. It sometimes mates with the golden-winged warbler to produce two types of hybrid warblers known as Brewster's warbler and Lawrence's warbler.

When the one hundred or more birders converged on the dining hall at noon there was great excitement because one of the professionals had spotted a Kentucky warbler. There had been only two previous sight records of this bird in Minnesota. Several birders, upon hearing the news, had gone to the area indicated and found the bird. I had been through the area, but could report nothing more sensational than the song of an oven-bird in the distance.

There was no need for an alarm clock the next morning. How can a birder sleep when cardinals, Baltimore orioles, rose-breasted grosbeaks, wood thrushes and vireos announce day-break by blending their songs with the drumming of ruffed grouse in such an enchanting place as the wooded ravine in Whitewater State Park? One needs to be up and about long before breakfast to hear the chorus, listen for unfamiliar songs and try to spot the songsters. The first birdwatcher I met that morning was a lady from Duluth. She had seen the Kentucky warbler on Saturday and told me that its song resembled that of the ovenbird. With this clue, I went directly to the area where the elusive warbler had been seen, listened for my presumed ovenbird song and, with binoculars, saw the Kentucky warbler perched on a dry twig near the top of a red oak tree — black sideburns, yellow spectacles and all, exactly as illustrated in Peterson's *Bird Guide.*

. . .The birding month of May

If all the birds were constantly with us we might tire of them and accept them as commonplace. But when they are absent for part of the year we enjoy seeing them return. Only a small percentage of them stay with us for the summer, but we have the opportunity of seeing the many others because we happen to be in the path they travel in their migration. Sometimes our fields, woodlands and dooryards are suddenly teeming with birds, then just as suddenly they are gone. Some birds are as predictable as sunrise while others often surprise us. We need to be alert at this season lest some of them slip by us unnoticed.

May is the month of the birdwatcher's greatest delight. Birds have, of course, been showing up ever since the first horned lark twittered in January. A few of the hardiest seedeaters appeared in February. March brought more of them as well as a parade of waterfowl. April found our hawks, most of our shore birds and a sprinkling of insect-eaters. But in May insect life is really astir and the pageant is on in all its glamour. The trees and shrubbery are full of feathered busybodies in full regalia, living off the land as they journey through, announcing their presence with song. One can hardly step outside the door in May without being greeted by a new arrival.

While checking the oil in my tractor one day I heard a familiar bubbling call and glanced skyward to see a pair of upland plovers, absent since last July. When I stopped my tractor to clean a wad of cornstalks from my plow the first Savannah sparrow sang for me its peculiar song, one which seems to shift gears in the middle. A flurry of small birds alighted on the plowing and teetered their tails like chickens perched on a wiggly wire. They were the first American pipits of the season. This has been a good pipit year. I usually see a few of these birds in their spring migration every year — perhaps a dozen, but sometimes only one or two. But on May 11th and 12th this year I saw hundreds in my fields. These sparrow-sized birds are closely related to the true larks and are birds of the open fields. They are easily identified because of their tail-bobbing. We see pipits only during migration because they nest farther north and winter in the southern United States.

While sorting out the daily mail one day, I turned to throw an assortment of boxholder pleas into the waste basket and saw, through my den window, a hermit thrush. In about three hops he disappeared under the juniper tree. But his rusty tail had identified him. On May 7th I was greeted by eight new birds. In my den, at noon again, I looked out to see an olive-backed thrush. In a moment, that bird was gone and a gray-cheeked thrush was looking at me from under the juniper tree. Olive-backed and gray-cheeked thrushes often migrate together. I went out to check my soggy field for possible corn planting and a hoarse "creak" betrayed the presence of a yellow-headed black-bird perched in the top of a green ash tree in my windbreak. The yellow-heads are more numerous this year. From my woods a quarter mile away the first rose-breasted grosbeak sang pleasantly. A tiny, persistent singer was searching the foliage of a bur oak tree near our house. These fellows look so much alike in the top of a tree that I hurried after my binoculars. The blue-gray head, yellow throat and conspicuous eye-ring labeled it as a Nashville warbler. Just then, a distinct "spear-a-fish" from overhead announced the first black tern. Around chore time I heard harsh, low-pitched twittering overhead and looked up to see hundreds of bank swallows criss-crossing the sky. Someone's sand pit was due for a mass invasion.

Each spring I see birds that I have never seen before. While plowing cornstalk ground on April 25th I saw a Nelson's sparrow, one of the sharp-tailed sparrows found inland. It may seem strange to say that I recognized a bird I was seeing for the first time, but an experience at Frontenac in May 1957 may explain that. An enthusiastic teen age birder had seen a sparrow and was seeking a professional ornithologist's aid in determining whether it was a Nelson's or a Le Conte's sparrow. Since I was not familiar with either sparrow, I went along with the group in search of the mysterious bird. The lad took us out from the campus to a farmer's rye field where the bird had been seen. Enroute, I absorbed enough information from the ornithologist's description of the differences between the two species to recognize both of them.

. . . A spring bird count

September, 1959

On Memorial Day weekend seven members of the Albert Lea Audubon Society motored to Itasca State Park for the spring bird counting field trip of the Minnesota Ornithologists Union. It was rather late in the season for composing the longest possible list of birds. The early migrants — especially the shore birds — were absent. But despite this (and the rainy weather) we did see many birds, including some new and interesting ones. This was the first time my wife and I had seen this historic and scenic area, which is comprised of 32,000 acres of gently rolling hills covered with virgin coniferous forests and dotted with more than 150 lakes as well as numerous ponds and marshes, most of which are made accessible by roads and footpaths. As soon as we turned off the highway at the sign directing us to Itasca State Park it was easy to understand why this sanctuary is so widely known as one of the top beauty spots of Minnesota. Towering red pines banked the winding, blacktop road leading to Douglas Lodge. There were also giant white pines, balsam fir, white birch, white cedar, tamarack, sugar maple, both white and black spruce and, of course, jack pine. We saw woodchucks, red squirrels, chipmunks, coons and white-tailed deer. The sharp, ringing call of the ovenbird sounded from the forest floor. Several species of warblers and other birds sang among the trees and underbrush. The colorful parula warblers were as numerous as chickadees and a flock of pine siskins flitted about in the treetops.

I thought about those whose wisdom and influence led to the setting aside of this area as a state park, thus preserving it for posterity, unblemished by the greed of commercialization. I thought of Henry Schoolcraft, who spent a whole summer with

Indian guides canoeing and portaging to reach Lake Itasca, and of us who journeyed there in a pleasant afternoon drive.

In the parking area by Douglas Lodge several birders were gathered near one of the cars. I joined the group to see what held their attention. A young farm boy from Sebeka, Minnesota was holding a saw-whet owl perched on his finger. The tiny owl, about the size of a cedar waxwing, was quite attractive in its immature plumage of chocolate brown with black face and white eyebrow line. When I expressed satisfaction at being able to add the saw-whet owl as a new bird on my life list, a birding friend from Duluth remarked, with a wry smile, that it didn't count since this was a captive bird. I maintained, however, that it was not captive since it was able and free to fly. The fact that it was so absurdly tame was no fault of mine.

Fifty square miles is a large place to go looking for birds. Several guided auto trips were planned for Saturday afternoon but, since a number of us were at the park early, one of the professionals took us for an interesting bird-walk along the La Salle Trail east of Lake Itasca. He called our attention to the songs of several birds, including that of the black-throated green warbler, which he said sounded like the first six notes of "The Lullaby of Broadway." It rained constantly, so we had to shield our binoculars to keep raindrops from getting on the lenses and distorting our vision. The birds were cooperative, however, and the time till noon seemed all too short.

After dining in style at Douglas Lodge the hundred or more birders divided into several groups and started on auto trips to various parts of the park. My wife and I chose to accompany our morning group again, this time by Mary Lake and Chambers Creek. Across the west wing of Lake Itasca we spotted a bald eagle's nest and saw the two eagles soaring. On the far shore of Elk Lake we saw an osprey and its nest. Warblers were cooperative during the early part of our trip but later on rain plagued us again to the extent that some of us got separated from the group and returned to Douglas Lodge.

When the birders gathered for the evening meal there was great excitement about a pair of arctic three-toed woodpeckers that one of the groups had seen on the Lakes Trail east of Mary Lake. Many of the birders, including myself, had never seen this bird and were eager to see it before leaving for home. We were assured that these birds were very cooperative (show-offs, in fact), so the only problem was locating the tree in which they were nesting. Directions for finding it were legion.

On Sunday morning most of the birders went in a single auto caravan, very leisurely following the road completely around Lake Itasca. At one stop we heard the song of the rare golden-winged warbler, a new bird for me if I could see it. The insect-like noises, "bee-bzz-bzz-bzz," were only a few feet away, but before I could spot the bird among the foliage, our guide shouted, "There he goes." All I saw was a tiny speck flying away over the marsh, so that bird is not yet on my list. Our next stop was in a solid stand of giant red pines, where the botanists in the group had a heyday among the orchids on the forest floor, while I listened to the wind in the treetops far overhead and wondered how tall and how old these monarchs were.

After the noon meal on Sunday the group dispersed for home but, just before leaving for Duluth, a birder from that city escorted the Albert Lea people to the nesting tree of the arctic three-toed woodpeckers. Aside from keeping silent the birds put on a good show for us. They were about the size of red-headed woodpeckers. Their backs were solid black. Their under parts were white, with flanks distinctly barred. The male had a yellow crown. And, of course, their feet had only three toes rather than four, as do other woodpeckers' feet.

. . . Be alert!

October, 1959

A good birder has to be an opportunist. He must be constantly alert for the presence of birds and must take advantage
of every chance to observe them, whatever the activity of the
moment may be. A birdwatcher is usually pictured as a person
dressed in field clothes, cautiously prowling through woodland,
field or marsh with a pair of binoculars in one hand and a bird
guide in the other. But I often have better luck spotting birds as
I go about my daily work. I was walking across the yard the
other day when a shadow crossed my path. Expecting to see a
gull, I glanced skyward and was surprised to see an osprey.
While milking the cows one morning several years ago I heard a
strange bird song in a tree just outside the barn. Stepping
outside for a moment to satisfy my curiosity, I saw my first
cerulean warbler. While checking my west line electric fence
one fall in preparation for turning the cattle to graze on a new
field I heard a stir among the leaves on the ground in a plum
thicket. I paused for a moment and was thrilled to see an
eastern towhee hop into full view. The birds I have seen while
driving the tractor would make a long list indeed.

A few days ago I added another vantage point. While at the
top of a ladder painting my corn crib I found myself near a
hornet's nest, where a couple of their warriors had me under
surveillance. It was the shady side of the crib and the mosquitoes
were showing less consideration for me than for the hornets. Did
you ever try chasing mosquitoes with a saturated paint brush in
your hand? As if this wasn't enough distraction, a pig started
rubbing itself against my ladder and I grabbed at the wall for
support while shouting at the pig. Just then I heard the rattled

call of a kingfisher and somehow managed to turn and catch a glimpse of the bird in flight before the corn crib roof shielded it from view.

Although it may seem like the height of lethargy, I also do considerable birding in bed, listening to the daybreak songs of birds — especially in the spring. One night I was awakened suddenly without realizing what had disturbed me. Everything was quiet for a moment, then came a low-pitched, throaty hoot that all but shook the window panes. A great horned owl was evidently perched in a tree just outside our house. It was pleasant to wake up on Sunday, August 30th to the sound of rain, so welcome after the long dry spell this summer. What made this morning extra special, however, was the song of a quail. At first I wasn't sure. Sound is decidedly muffled by the insulated walls of our new house. But as the call was repeated I arose and listened at the bedroom window. There was no mistaking the cheerful, clearly enunciated whistle, "poor-bob-white." Somewhere in my next door neighbor's soybean field, just across the road from our house, was a quail, evidently happy despite the local thunder shower. Where this individual bird came from and where it went I do not know. But for a while that morning its call brought back a flood of memories of a time when quails were common in this area. They are seldom seen or even heard here now. I heard one at Frontenac in 1952. A couple of years later I followed one by its call up the auxiliary road alongside our farm, across to our windbreak, past our house to the fence along the highway, then west till its whistles were lost in the distance. The last time I had the good fortune to see a brood of bobwhites was in the early thirties. While eating breakfast one morning I glanced out the kitchen window to see a watchful mother quail crossing our lawn less than fifty feet from our house. Close behind her in single file were about a dozen tiny, downy chicks. Hurrying after the anxious mother, and sometimes stumbling in the grass, the little fellows soon reached the protective cover of a clump of lilacs and disappeared.

Bobwhites are small, plump, chicken-like game birds a little larger than meadow larks. They are gallinaceous (or ground dwelling) birds. Foraging for food on foot and scratching for it like chickens, they habitually follow sheltered trails such as fence rows and seldom venture far into the open. They were originally southern birds. The northern limit of their range varied. But as land was cleared for farming, with consequent waste grain, weeds and insects associated with crop production, bobwhites extended their range northward as far as Minnesota and Ontario. Their numbers were greatest in this area during the time of small fields, rail fences and interspersed woodlands. The coming of barbed wire fences, large cleared fields and scant cover, together with unwise overshooting, spelled the doom of bobwhites in the North. They are still found and quite extensively hunted in the South. But the hardy northern strain has been destroyed. We must now be satisfied with the call of an occasional stray bird to remind us of something wonderful that is gone.

. . . Harris's sparrow

A person may become interested in birds at any age. It may be a continuation of a natural childhood curiosity about all living creatures. Often the spark of interest is first kindled by the sight of an unusual bird.

One of my aunts — a widow in her eighties who lives in Lake Mills, Iowa — has found her days a bit more enjoyable since being initiated into the fascinating pursuit of birdwatching. I like to think that in a small indirect way I have helped her discover this new avenue of delight. At our family reunion two years ago my cousin and I were visiting when the conversation turned to hobbies. He talked enthusiastically about the enjoyment he found in taking a fishing trip with friends to northern Minnesota each summer. Not only was he thrilled by the experience of catching fish, but he found great enjoyment in the smell of pine trees, the sound of running water, the scenery, and chance encounters with unfamiliar wildlife. When I told him my hobby was birdwatching he interrupted to suggest that if I had been along on his last fishing excursion I might have identified a strange bird his group had seen — a large, hawklike bird with a featherless head that reminded them of a turkey. He was delighted and a little surprised to find that I was familiar with this bird, the turkey vulture, and listened intently while I launched into a discourse on the enjoyment of birding, not only on organized field trips, but also during daily home activities.

When I met my cousin again this summer he told me that he had bought a bird bath and had set it up on his mother's lawn. Both he and his mother had been amazed at the great number and variety of birds that had been attracted to the bird bath during the spring and summer. His mother was spending much time at a window from which she could see the birds as they came to drink and bathe. A daughter, who lives in Chicago, heard about her mother's new interest and sent her a copy of a bird guide with which she can identify the birds she sees. Now my aunt has become a full-fledged birdwatcher. The bird bath has been moved close to the house where birds may be observed at close range. Apparently the birds do not resent the new location for they come in equal numbers. I have not checked with these folks to see how many of the fall migrants have been attracted. But even at this season birds love to bathe and, although water hasn't been a scarcity this fall, it wouldn't surprise me to hear that the bird bath is still a popular stopping place.

Speaking of fall migrants, have you noticed the abundance of Harris's sparrows this fall? These large sparrows are easily recognized in spring plumage by their conspicuous black crown, face and bib. Their fall plumage is toned down some and the immatures may even be confused with white-throats. But the alarm note is the same as in the spring. Their migration in this area is unpredictable. Some years they are not seen at all and in other years they come through in great numbers.

1948 was a memorable year for two reasons — the building of our new house and the spring migration of Harris's sparrows. While working on the foundation forms for our new home we would always hear a great hubbub in the trees on our lawn every evening about quitting time. The nearby juniper tree was the chosen sleeping quarters for dozens of Harris's sparrows, who kept complaining as long as we worked. As soon as we laid our tools aside the birds quieted down for the night. Since that experience it has been no great task for me to recognize the presence of Harris's sparrows. Although most of this fall's multitude is farther south by now, there are still a few stragglers. As I came by the hen house the other morning there was a flurry of wings in the brush under the plum trees. A lone sparrow took up a position on the topmost branch of the tallest plum tree and started scolding, "wink! wink! wink!" The throat was white, the black markings subdued and the cheeks buffy-brown. But, after hearing that "wink," there was no mistaking the species. The bird was still scolding when I reached the house, so I asked my wife if she wanted to see and hear a Harris's sparrow. She came to the door and the bird obligingly stayed in the same place and continued scolding.

...Birding from a tractor seat

December, 1959

On November 10th my wife and I motored to Austin for the Audubon Screen Tour program, "Ranch of the Purple Flowers," filmed and presented by naturalist Robert C. Hermes. When one cannot travel to other parts of the world to observe wildlife first hand the next best thing is to listen to someone who has been there in person. I an sure that all the other Albert Lea people who were in the audience that evening would agree with us that the program was well worth the trip. The 2000 feet of film was taken on a ranch in the Orinoco Basin of southern Venezuela. Despite being within ten degrees of the equator the area was of such high elevation that it was described by the narrator as a land of perpetual spring. Mr Hermes expressed surprise at encountering so few familiar birds because Venezuela is considered a winter home for many of our summer resident birds. He did have a close-up of a great blue heron and a rough-and-tumble fight between two male mockingbirds who had been lured into the scrap by a mockingbird voice from a tape recorder. He also gave the area a homey touch by saying that the plains were swarming with dickcissels. The audience was thrilled with the many colorful tropical birds and the strange-looking mammals native to the area. I shall never forget the acrobatic antics of the red howler monkeys or that bouncing bulk of oddly-shaped animation, the giant anteater, in retreat. I have seen scarlet macaws in captivity. But the action picture of a flock of them in pheasant-like flight was far more beautiful.

Mr. Hermes had been in Albert Lea on an Audubon Screen Tour appearance back in 1953, so I stopped after the program for a few words with him. I was surprised to find that, without prompting, he still remembered me. As he extended his hand in greeting, he said, "Your name escapes me at the moment, but you are from Albert Lea and you write." Then, with a smile, he added, "You wrote about birding from a tractor seat." He wanted to know if I had seen any new birds from that vantage point. We talked about birds until the custodian gave obvious hints that he wished to lock up the building and call it a day. Mr. Hermes had read an article I had written when he stayed at our house on his Screen Tour visit to Albert Lea. Now, after six years, he had understandably forgotten my name, but "Birding From a Tractor Seat" still stuck in his mind.

My original paper, "Birding From a Tractor Seat," was written in response to a request for a five-minute paper on the program at the 1952 Frontenac meeting of the Minnesota Ornithologists Union. It was my first experience in this role and, knowing that the audience would include both professional ornithologists and seasoned birders, I sought to avoid goofing by sticking to the familiar. I certainly didn't anticipate how tenaciously the title of this minor program contribution would stick in the minds of those who heard it. People still refer to it at M.O.U. gatherings. Last December I met a commercial writer who happened to be at that 1952 Frontenac meeting. I remembered him because he approached me after the program to ask if I had ever done any newspaper writing. I had forgotten his name, but he remembered mine, and my paper, "Birding From a Tractor Seat."

To the average birder I suppose a tractor seat does seem like a strange place from which to observe birds. But for a farmer it is an ideal vantage point. There is constant opportunity. Birds also show much less fear when approached in this way. On November 8th several members of the Albert Lea Audubon Society came abirding to my woods, hoping to get a glimpse of the red-tailed hawks and great horned owls that reside there. We saw several species of small woodland birds but no hawks or owls, even though I had seen both the hawk and owl a day or two before the field trip. I anticipated this result, and told the group beforehand that all I would guarantee was a look at the woods.

During the following week I saw my red-tailed hawk once and the great horned owl three times while driving to and from the field on my tractor.

One spring day a couple of years ago a local pastor, who has become an enthusiastic birder, stopped by and came out to the field to talk to me. During our conversation he mentioned that he had never seen a Brewer's blackbird. I looked about me but could not spot any, so I asked him to step onto the tractor for one trip across the field and back. Before we were half-way across the field we saw several Brewer's blackbirds at close range. Western kingbird, Nelson's sparrow, Lapland longspur, American pipit, red-shafted flicker, golden plover, black-bellied plover, Wilson's snipe and many many others were first seen by me while in the field driving my tractor.

This fall will be long remembered for its excessive moisture during corn and soybean harvest. It was necessary for me to use a tractor to help loaded corn trucks out of the field and we made some unsightly tracks in the process. On one of these trips to the field one morning a Wilson's snipe took off with its peculiar zigzag flight from a water-filled track in my cow yard. *Audubon Magazine* recently had a section devoted to attracting birds. Perhaps I should suggest for this section a water-filled tractor track to attract Wilson's snipe.

. . .The long life of a white oak

January, 1960

Trees are so closely associated with birds that perhaps a bird-watcher may be pardoned for writing on that theme, especially since trees play such an important role at this festive season. Without the traditional Christmas tree, yuletide would be woefully incomplete. And how about the yule log? The yule log, being an English custom, has never been a part of Christmas festivity at our house. But a plentiful supply of firewood for heating the home has always seemed necessary for the fullest enjoyment of Christmas. With this in mind I recently hired a man with a power saw to cut a number of fallen trees into furnace-length chunks. Since then I have been busy splitting, carrying, hauling and stowing away wood in my furnace room.

I have been particularly interested in one of these trees, a large white oak that I have known for nearly forty years. I saw it first in 1920 when I went along with my brothers and some neighbor boys on a rabbit hunt. The tree was then sufficiently decayed at the base to let one of the lucky rabbits use it as a secure hiding place. I remember marveling at the size of the tree. "Great oaks from little acorns grow," Mother used to say. But, having lived all my life on the prairie, I had never seen an acorn until I was fourteen years old.

Some time last summer this tree, having died a natural death, fell to the ground. What a crash that must have been! I wonder how many wild creatures were frightened by the noise. The great horned owls must at least have turned to look in that direction. Perhaps the red-tailed hawk nestlings wondered what kind of a world they were getting into. I have often wondered, as I walked through the woods, how long some of these monarchs have been standing. Pausing to catch my breath while working with the wood one day, I started prying into the private life of this tree by counting the annual rings in one of the lower cross sections. Some rings were wider than others, indicating good and bad years. The outer rings were very narrow and indistinct. Growth had been slight in the last few years. But to my surprise I counted more than 225 rings. Evidently this tree was several years old at the time of the American Revolution. What a life story that tree could tell us if it could speak!

Did some French squirrel hide a French acorn under some fertile Louisiana leafmold and fail to find it the next winter, or was it a French blue jay that did the planting? At any rate, the tree lived through much of the desperate struggle between three European nations for the possession of the North American continent. The sapling was large enough for deer to polish their antlers on when Evangeline and 6000 of her kin were so rudely abducted from their homes in Acadia. When France finally withdrew from America in 1762 the Louisiana territory west of the Mississippi was ceded to Spain in payment for losses suffered as an ally of France in the war with England, so the tree became part of Spanish territory for 38 years. In 1800 Napoleon was in power and put pressure on Spain to return Louisiana to France, so by secret treaty the fleur-de-lis was again the tree's national emblem. Three years later, however, it came under the Stars and Stripes when Napoleon, in need of money and fearful that Louisiana territory might be lost to England, sold it to the United States for $15,000,000. How much Uncle Sam paid for this tree would be hard to calculate, but the cost of my ten-acre woods came to about thirty cents.

After the Civil War the Northwest was thrown open to settlement, encouraged by the Homestead Act and railroad interests. The first private owner of the tree was a man named Taylor. But shortly afterwards it came into the possession of Bill Horning, Union veteran and Indian fighter. Bill claimed, so the story goes, that he killed the American Indian Chief Hole-in-The-Day, who had been causing trouble among the settlers to the north. His regiment had caught up with the Indian near Little Falls. But he was getting away from them by running while the soldiers were reloading their muskets. Under the captain's orders all guns were discharged in volleys. Bill tired of these tactics and aimed but did not fire. When the Indian leaped from behind his tree after the volley, Bill fired alone and hit the Indian in the back. He got a terrible scolding from his captain for disobeying orders, but Chief Hole-in-The-Day was no more.

I have wandered far from the subject of birds. But a tree is a living breathing thing — a gift from God and a friend of man, bird and beast. How many *coureurs de bois* have rested in this tree's shade? How many moose and bison have tramped in the vicinity? How many warblers have searched for insects among its leaves? How many nuthatches and brown creepers have looked for insect eggs and pupae in its bark crevices during all those winters? And what caused the scar at its base through which bacteria and fungi entered to start the decay that eventually caused its death? I know only that my muscles ache a little after carrying the entire tree, piece by piece, out of the woods and loading it into my pickup truck, unloading it again and stacking it up in my basement. I have the assurance, however, that our house will be warm during this Christmas season, thanks to an acorn that sprouted before George Washington was born.

. . . Red-bellied woodpecker

March, 1960

At our last Audubon Screen Tour program a woman asked me to identify a strange bird that some of her friends had seen at their suet feeder. Identifying birds from oral description is usually difficult. In this case it was not, because the red-bellied woodpecker is so conspicuously marked. Furthermore, I had a vivid recollection of my first acquaintance with this bird. It is not strange, however, that many people in this area are unfamiliar with the red-bellied woodpecker because it is so shy and retiring, besides being relatively scarce. Only when winter hunger drives it to suet feeders can it be readily seen at close range.

At one of our first meetings of the Albert Lea Audubon Society, one member had arranged for the Minnesota Museum of Natural History to send us a number of laboratory bird skins for an identification contest. I should have felt very proud after having correctly identified thirteen out of the fourteen species. But my ego was deflated because I did not know the largest and most brightly plumaged bird in the lot. Except for recognizing it as a member of the woodpecker family I had no knowledge of the bird at all. What sort of phantom was this? The bird measured ten inches in length. Its back was a finely striped zebra pattern. The scarlet cap extended from the beak over the top of the head and down the back of the neck to the shoulders where it cut off squarely. The face and underparts were light gray except for a reddish tinge on the belly feathers. At that time I had no bird guide or other bird book in which I might have seen a pictured likeness of the red-bellied woodpecker. Nevertheless, it was a strange experience for me to find that a bird so distinctly marked and native to this area should have completely escaped my notice, even though rare. I would not have minded the tardiness of the discovery if my first encounter had been a chance look at the live bird. Indeed, this would have been as thrilling an experience as the first glimpse of other birds I have learned to know. The shocking part was to see it first as a lifeless laboratory bird skin. Having studied the plumage markings in detail, I now felt that I would easily recognize the red-bellied woodpecker if I ever saw one. Of course, I did not know the bird's habits or its call. These I would have to learn first hand.

In May of 1951 the members of the Albert Lea Audubon Society were invited to a local doctor's farm near Spring Valley for breakfast and a field trip. After exploring the rugged terrain for some time a group of us had stopped to rest on a sunny hillside near the creek when I heard a muffled bird call in the distance. It sounded a little off key for a red-headed woodpecker, but no other bird call in my vocabulary resembled it, so I added the red-headed woodpecker to my list. One skeptical member wanted to know how I could be sure of the species without actually seeing the bird. I felt a twinge of conscience at his question and should have taken the hint to go in search of the bird. But I decided not to because the breakfast deadline was near. Later, during our business meeting, my bird list somehow was pushed off the table and fell to the ground. My skeptical friend saw and retrieved it and, before putting it back on the table, added opposite red-headed woodpecker the notation: "(only heard)." Later in the day two other birders returned from a ramble through the woods to announce that they had seen a red-bellied woodpecker. They had heard its call and had followed it until they could get a good look at the bird through their binoculars. They said its call sounded something like that of a red-headed woodpecker. Again, this bird, the red-bellied woodpecker, had humiliated me! But I remembered the call.

I was in my woods some years later when I heard a loud "churr-churr-churr." I stopped splitting wood and looked in the direction from which the call came. The call was repeated several times. But I did not see the bird until it flew to another tree. In the bare-boughed winter woods it was not hard, even without binoculars, to make out the plumage markings of the elusive bird, the first live red-bellied woodpecker I had seen. Later that winter a male red-bellied woodpecker, which I assumed was the same individual, came nearly every day to the suet feeder outside my den window where it ate great quantities of suet. After that winter, when I saw and heard it so often, I have not considered the red-bellied woodpecker a stranger. But I still have some of its calls to learn. The bird books say it has several. I now find the "churr-churr-churr" quite easy to distinguish from the "queer-queer" of the red-headed wood-pecker. On sight, it is easy to recognize. The sexes look alike, except that the female is scarlet only on the nape.

I often hear the question, "Why is this bird called the red-bellied woodpecker?" I agree that it is not well named, since the red feathers on its abdomen are not as bright as those on its head. Besides, it is almost impossible to see these feathers in the field because of the way a woodpecker perches. A better name might have been red-crowned.

...*Water thrush*

April, 1960

Of the fifty or more species of warblers to be found north of the Mexican border, one of the most interesting is the water thrush. It seems strange to associate such a leisurely procedure as walking with such incessantly active little creatures as the warblers, but the water thrush is a pedestrian extraordinary. Not only does it walk on the ground but, as it proceeds, it constantly teeters the back part of its body up and down in the same comical manner as the spotted sandpiper. Since there doesn't seem to be any rhythm to the performance it is all the more amusing.

Because of the bird's fondness for the banks of running streams and because its plumage pattern — dark above and spotted below — resembles that of the true thrushes, this warbler is appropriately called a water thrush. It isn't the kind of bird that comes to see you. You must search for it in the right habitat at the right season. I saw my first one in May, 1952 while birding with members of the Minnesota Ornithologists Union at Frontenac. I was with a group headed for a cattail slough a short ways up the highway to see what we could spot in the way of shore birds when we came upon several cars parked beside the road. At an M.O.U. gathering that sort of thing denotes something of special interest, so we stopped to investigate. Following the trail of deep footprints through the swampy woods we soon heard voices and found a dozen or more birders with binoculars trained on the shoreline of a Mississippi River backwater. When I asked one of them what was holding everyone's rapt attention he replied, "We're watching a water thrush." With his help I finally spotted the little bird walking along the water's edge, sometimes on the ground, sometimes on a fallen branch lying in the water and sometimes wading in the shallow water. The bird was well camouflaged. Even though it was continually on the move with its peculiar gait, it wasn't easy to keep it always in view among the trees, shadows and debris.

I was fortunate to make the acquaintance of the water thrush under such circumstances. I certainly would not have spotted it by myself because the bird made no sound at all. There are other tail-bobbing birds, even among the warblers. Each has its own particular style. The palm warbler, busily searching for insect larvae amongst the foliage of trees and shrubs, bobs its tail whenever it pauses long enough to do so. The ovenbird, another ground-walking warbler, proceeds through its dense woodland habitat with deliberate, comic dignity. Someone has described it as a farmer with a hammer handle protruding from his hip pocket, pacing off the distance between fence posts. American pipits, perched on the plowing near my tractor, bob their tails like a chicken on a wiggly wire. The dipper (or water ouzel) of our western states bobs quite differently. Instead of tilting its tail upwards first and then down, it squats down first and then bobs up in a neat curtsy. Is such a behavior a release of nervous energy, like our habit of fumbling with coins in our pocket when there is no change to make, and scratching our heads when there is no itch in our scalp? Or did the Creator deign thus to make birdwatching a more interesting hobby? Presently, a tap on my shoulder disturbed my reverie and reminded me of my original destination, the cattail slough.

The next water thrush I saw was at Whitewater State Park in May, 1958. Someone spotted the bird and a group quickly gathered to see it. I ventured to call it a northern water thrush, but there were those who thought it was a Louisiana. In the poor light I couldn't be sure but, before I had expressed any doubt, a professional ornithologist who was present said it was definitely a northern.

Last May several members of the Albert Lea Audubon Society took a field trip, starting at a mink farm northwest of the city. The walk along a railroad track through a marsh was particularly rewarding. The whinny of the sora rails, accompanied by the songs of red-winged blackbirds, marsh wrens, swamp sparrows, yellowthroats and many others, took me back in memory to my boyhood days on our Iowa prairie farm. The highlight of the trip for me, however, was the song of a northern water thrush. We had left the railroad track and were making our way through a dense growth of stinging nettle along a nearby creek. Last season's dry stalks towered above our heads. Perhaps the going was too tough for some. At any rate, when someone suggested that it was about time to return for lunch the whole group started crashing through the weeds like the Swedes at the Battle of Copenhagen. Just then, I heard a strange bird song. I called to the group. I had never heard the song of a water thrush before, but suspected that this might be it since it came from a spot where a little irregularity in the creek bottom caused a rippling sound in the water. I stole closer. Imagine my joy to discover a northern water thrush walking along the edge of the stream! The bird sang once more, but disappeared before I could point it out to my fellow birders.

. . . *Bird song*

At this time of the year birds, with their gift of song, lend enchantment to the countryside and entice one to search for a glimpse of them in their most attractive attire. The few birds that have remained with us all winter have, for the most part, been rather quiet. How strange spring would be if silence were the rule! When winter's snow is gone the landscape may at first appear depressing. But all we need to send our spirits soaring is the song of some familiar bird, just returned from the south. I suppose the robin has brought springtime cheer to more people than any other American bird because it is so distinctly marked and because it comes to everyone's dooryard singing so lustily that people cannot avoid noticing it, however lax their interest in birds may be. There are many other harbingers of spring for those who have learned their songs — the friendly warble of the first bluebird, the flute-like greeting of the western meadow lark, the whistled melody of the song sparrow, the clamor of wild geese, the plaintive call of the killdeer and many others that come in ever increasing numbers until the high tide (in this latitude, about May 20th) when one may count more than a hundred species in a single day.

For the ardent birdwatcher, bird songs mean more than a reminder of more pleasant weather. The more one has learned about the life history of a particular bird the more will be included in the mental picture one gets whenever that bird's song is heard. The more experiences one has had with the bird the more episodes there will be to recall — with special significance attached to those bird songs which have puzzled one the longest. To ascertain the identity of a bird whose song has long been a mystery is indeed a rewarding experience.

As a youngster I was fascinated each spring by a mysterious, musical yodel, "whee-oodle-ee, whee-oodle-ee, whee-oodle-ee." I imagined that the singer was some kind of water-loving bird because the sound always came from the direction of a neighbor's bulrush slough. Not until the spring of 1931 was this mystery solved — and, believe it or not, from the tractor seat. I had not heard that captivating sound for years. But as I was discing a field next to my then undrained pasture, I suddenly heard the yodel loud and clear. I turned quickly and saw a greater yellowlegs come in for a landing in a slough a few rods away. When, on rare occasions, I hear that yodel these days I see again those long, bright, yellow legs fully extended as the bird alighted in the slough thirty years ago. When, on May field trips, I see a yellowlegs wading about in shallow water I think of the musical yodel that filled me with wonder so long ago.

Another boyhood mystery was the bubbling, liquid whistle of the upland plover. That mystery had to wait another decade for solution. After a twenty-five year intermission, the call sounded clearly from somewhere over my pasture just as I was getting the cows into the barn for milking one early May evening in 1940. I stood transfixed in the doorway, listening to the long-lost song until the cows had finished their feed and had started moving about in the barn, no doubt wondering what had happened to me. Since then I have learned to know these plovers well. I have seen their nests, handled the eggs, had my hand within six inches of a brooding plover, caught the young chicks on several occasions and often seen these graceful birds walking about in my fields, sometimes within a rod of my tractor.

No bird song has kept me guessing as long as the leisurely, gentle strain of the warbling vireo. It was one of the first bird songs that I remember hearing, yet I did not have it positively associated with the right bird until a few years ago, when I acquired a set of bird song recordings prepared by Cornell University. This small, inconspicuously-colored bird, whose peculiar voice wandered up and down the musical scale, led me on many a fruitless boyhood search. One of my tedious daily chores in those days was to pump water by hand and carry it to the calves that were kept in a separate pasture, which included a portion of our box-elder windbreak. I used to think these calves drank more water than they needed just to see me work. When I complained of weariness Mother suggested short rest periods, which I utilized by going from tree to tree, hopefully searching for the bird that sang so beautifully, but that always stayed hidden in the tops of the densely-leaved box-elders. Whenever I chance to hear this pleasant song I think of those calves with their distended stomachs.

A few years ago I was changing a sickle in my mower in the shade of an oak tree in my yard when I heard the familiar, rippling melody just overhead. Glancing up, I saw a warbler-sized bird perched on a twig and peering up at the under side of a leaf. That pose reminded me of the pictures I had seen of vireos and, judging by its song, I concluded that my mysterious bird must be a warbling vireo. For some time I had been considering the purchase of a set of bird song recordings. I now promptly sent my order. When the package arrived I first played the record which included the song of the warbling vireo. It was gratifying to hear the phonograph recording verify my hunch as to the bird's identity.

. . . Nests

May brings the greatest number of birds to this latitude and, for that reason, is the favorite time for field trips by birders in this area. By the third week of May one may, with patient, diligent search of the various habitats, spot over 100 — even up to 150 — species in a single day. Many birds in spring plumage are very colorful and, since they nest farther north, can be seen here only for a few days at this particular time of the year. When members of the Minnesota Ornithologists Union gathered here to count birds in 1956 the composite list was 141 species. This year when they met here again the weather was very unfavorable, but the bird count was still high — 126 species. During the height of migration there is also the possibility of seeing rare migrants. This year the group was highly pleased when some members spotted a Florida galanule in a small marshy area where the M. & St. L. track intersects Highway 13 west of town.

As the season advances, the number of birds one may see drops rapidly. By June most birds have reached their summer range and are occupied with such activities as nest-building, egg-laying, incubating and care of their young. Field trips may have lost some glamour since observations will be limited to summer resident species. But there are some advantages. One of the constant complaints of birdwatchers is that their quarry is so elusive. In May this is certainly true. But by June home ties have been established and the parent birds are more or less anchored to a limited area. June is the best time for observing the family life of birds, their skill in concealing their nests, their concern for their young, their methods of luring enemies away from their nest, their methods of feeding their young, the great variation in tidiness of nests, etc. Bird song reaches its greatest vigor and beauty during the nest-building and incubating season. Many species are rather silent during migration, yet sing beautifully at nesting time. Go to Nerstrand Woods near Northfield in June and listen to the songs of the hermit thrush, wood thrush and ovenbird.

It is interesting to observe what the various species consider a nest. Nests vary from nothing at all, as with the nighthawk, through all degrees of construction to the intricately-woven and tenaciously-suspended swinging nest of the Baltimore oriole. A mourning dove's nest in our windbreak is so flimsily built that the two white eggs can be plainly seen through the nest from beneath. Many bird nests are quite similar in construction and are therefore difficult to identify unless seen while still being occupied. Locating them is a problem challenging even expert ornithologists. Since my birding is purely a hobby, and necessarily haphazard, I seldom take time to search for nests. But I discover many by chance.

One of the pleasant duties I had as a lad was fetching the cows for the evening milking. The path I took across the pasture varied according to where the cows happened to be grazing at the time. On one of these trips a meadow lark startled me by flying up from underfoot. I suspected the presence of a nest and searched the area until I got to a position from which I could see the eggs under the canopy of dry grass. At that age I naturally thought I was the first person to make such a discovery. The cows went home much faster that evening, spurred on by my eagerness to tell Mother what I had seen. To my surprise, she knew all about meadow lark nests, including the color and the number of eggs. Puzzled, I asked where she had seen such a nest. "Oh!" she replied, "When I was a little girl I herded cows on the prairie every day before there were such things as pasture fences near our home."

During my barefoot days there were dozens of grackle nests in our windbreak. These birds nested in colonies in the box elders and Scotch pines. I would climb up to look into every nest, methodically counting eggs and seeing the young birds in every stage of development. There was always a great hubbub as all the grackles gathered to scold me each time I started to climb a tree. The volume and tempo of the racket increased as I neared the nest. It was fun and, incidently, good exercise to pry into the grackle's secrets. But my tree-climbing zeal all but ceased with the advent of summer footwear. The pair of grackles that nested near our garage a few years ago reared their family in peace until one of the fledglings, as yet unable to fly, fluttered along the ground ahead of me one day, bringing back a flood of early birding memories. I caught the bird and put it on a branch of the nearest oak tree out of cats' reach, accompanied by the familiar screaming of the juveniles and the vehement scolding of the parent birds.

...Migrant shrike

After a day spent with neighbors raking the cemetery and sawing wood at the Pickerel Lake Methodist Church last April I rode home with a neighbor couple. Near the northwest corner of my farm I was pleased to see a migrant shrike perched on the telephone wire where I had seen it perching so often last summer. When I called attention to the bird my neighbor's wife asked how I could tell what kind of bird it was so quickly. When one is familiar with a bird it doesn't take long to grasp the clues to its identity. The shrike's position on the telephone wire narrowed the field down to about a dozen species one might call wire sitters. The profile of a shrike, with its proportionately large head, is as easily recognized among birds as is a bullhead among fish. A glimpse of the light gray upper parts and the black wings and face mask is all that is necessary to be certain.

I rather expected to see a shrike there again this spring because, like most birds, they usually return to the same territory occupied the previous season — often nesting in the same tree or shrub. I did not take time to hunt for a nest last summer but, since I saw a shrike hunting so consistently on this portion of the farm, I assumed there was a nest somewhere nearby, perhaps in the shrubbery along a neighboring farm's west line fence. So far, I haven't seen a shrike's nest, which I understand is a bulky affair of twigs, grass and various other material well hidden in a dense tangle of shrubs or trees.

Shrikes are not numerous, at least in this part of the country. They prefer open farming country with a few scattered trees and some fence row thickets in which to nest. Although they sometimes hover like a sparrow hawk before dropping down

upon their prey, they do most of their hunting from elevated perches, from which they fly swiftly and directly to their prey. They may perch in a tree, preferably one with a dead exposed branch from which they can get a clear view of the countryside. But they are much more often seen perching on a telephone wire or highline. They feed chiefly on large insects such as grasshoppers, crickets, caterpillars, cutworms, beetles, moths, etc. But they also take mice, frogs, snakes, lizards and, occasionally, birds. A shrike's bill is hooked. But the bird lacks the strong talons characteristic of birds of prey. It therefore wedges the larger prey into a crotch or impales it on a thorn or a fence wire barb to hold it securely while tearing it to pieces for swallowing.

The first shrike I ever saw was perched on the highest point of the hay loader one June morning in 1922 when I drove out to the field for a load of hay. As I prepared to hitch the loader to the wagon I noticed a meadow mouse impaled on a tine of the hay loader boom. I wondered how it got there, since it could not conceivably have been pierced by accident. The next morning the shrike was again perched on the hay loader, and another mouse was impaled in the same way. This happened so often during the haying season that I concluded the bird must be responsible, although I never caught him in the act of either catching mice or impaling them. It seemed strange that the mice were not at least partially eaten. Perhaps the shrike found the hunting so good after the hay was cut that it captured more mice than its appetite required. Since that time I have often seen a shrike capture a mouse in the field. Unlike a grackle, which pecks or jabs a mouse to death, a shrike seizes its victim by the neck with its strong beak and beats it viciously against the ground. For so small a bird (smaller than a brown thrasher), a shrike is a fierce assailant. Some years ago I saw a newly fledged sparrow take off on its first flight from a henhouse window toward an oak tree in our yard, chirping gleefully as it flew. Suddenly a shrike appeared and met the fledgling head on so fiercely that a lot of loose feathers marked the spot of impact, while the victim, uttering a few muffled screams, was carried swiftly into another tree by the shrike.

The shrike usually seen in these parts is the migrant shrike, a subspecies of the true loggerhead shrike (or butcher bird) characteristic of southeastern United States — especially along the Atlantic coast. Another species, the northern shrike, inhabits regions farther north and may sometimes be seen here during the winter. In areas where loggerheads are common they have unfortunately, on some occasions, aroused the ire of canary bird fanciers. When a loggerhead appears at a canary's cage that is hung outdoors, the canary, rather than staying in the center of the cage where it would be safe, attempts to escape by struggling against the cage with its head stuck out between the bars, whereupon the shrike snips off its head. These incidents have been overemphasized and have brought undue prejudice against shrikes. I hope this account doesn't strike terror into the hearts of Albert Lea area canary owners. Our migrant shrikes are well-behaved fellows that inhabit areas where canaries are unlikely to be. I welcome the shrike as an interesting bird and as an asset to my agricultural endeavor. I am sure he can find enough food here to keep him away from canary heads.

...*Upland plover*

September, 1960

On June 15th I found an upland plover's nest in my oat field. I was applying 2-4-D, a selective spray for the control of broad-leaved weeds. On one trip across the field an upland plover flushed from directly under the sprayer boom. Suspecting the presence of a nest I stopped to look and had no difficulty finding the little depression in the ground lined with a little grass and containing four eggs. This is the second time I have been fortunate enough to find an upland plover's nest. I discovered the first one in June, 1948 while plowing a field of rye. Again, I was impressed by the size of the eggs. It seems incredible that a bird only a little larger than a meadow lark actually lays eggs that are larger than ring-necked pheasant eggs. Shore birds, to which group the upland plover belongs, characteristically lay large eggs. The young — large and precocial when hatched — develop rapidly and are ready for their long southward journey earlier than are most other birds.

As this plover left her nest she made no sound of protest. At the far side of the field I saw what may have been a reason why wise nature bade the plover to hold its tongue. A mother red fox was out hunting for food for herself and her family. As I watched, she pounced upon some luckless creature in the grass. With her head turned in the opposite direction and intent upon her quarry, the fox, I am sure, was not aware of the plover's takeoff. Had the plover voiced consternation, however, the fox most certainly would have sensed the situation and, like myself, looked for a nest. I did not pause long at the nest lest I make its location conspicuous. I enjoy seeing the fox and her two playful young. But I was not about to help her find an upland plover's nest.

Every time I see or hear an upland plover I am reminded of the sad history of the species. Natural enemies were not responsible for the plover's undoing. Every summer countless thousands populated the western prairies. When land was developed for agriculture many species suffered from the change of habitat. But the upland plover adapted itself well, nesting in grain fields, hayfields and pastures and finding elevated perches on fence posts instead of boulders and bleaching buffalo skulls. When timbered areas in northeastern United States were cleared for farming, upland plovers, finding the cleared areas suitable habitat, moved eastward and rendered yeoman service by devouring great quantities of insects harmful to agricultural crops.

Then, alas, in the 80's and 90's came the orgy of market hunting that all but exterminated our shore birds. Taking advantage of the upland plover's unusual lack of suspicion when approached in any other way than on foot, hunters armed with shot guns rode horseback or in wagons into concentrated flocks of plovers and blazed away. Birds by the barrelful were shipped to markets in New York City and Boston where city hordes feasted on broiled plover.

When plover flocks began thinning there were voices of concern, and then of protest — voices that eventually reached and impressed legislative and executive ears. At long last came migratory bird laws, but not before the upland plovers had almost vanished. I never heard a single upland plover's call from about 1915 until 1940. With complete protection on its breeding grounds, it is now increasing in numbers. Since 1940 I have had these birds on my farm every summer. The recovery is slow, however, because there is a potential of only four young a year per pair, because of a long hazardous migration route and because hunting still continues on its wintering grounds. An Albert Lea friend, who for some years was with a meat packing company in Buenos Aires, Argentina, told me that one just cannot talk conservation to hunters on the pampas. In his words: "They shoot at anything with wings." But who are we to point an accusing finger? After all, it was not on the pampas of

Argentina but here on its breeding grounds that the upland plover was so thoughtlessly persecuted.

Besides their economic value as insect destroyers, upland plovers, with their beauty of song and winsome ways, lend animated enchantment to our countryside. Their flight song is one of the most beautiful sounds in nature — a sound that has special significance for me because it is one of the mysterious bird calls of my early boyhood. A particularly appealing behavior trait is the upland plover's habit, when alighting, of holding its wings extended upwards over its back for a moment before folding them carefully. How can one ponder the plight of the upland plover without becoming an ardent wildlife conservationist?

. . . *Heading south*

October, 1960

The extra hustle and bustle you may have noticed among the birds lately is accounted for by moving days. It is time that most of our song birds were on their way to their winter homes. With the added hazards accompanying migration, birds are naturally more alert and restless than usual. For all of those hatched this year it is the first trip away from home, and how they find their way through strange territory is still an unsolved mystery. At this season birds may be seen far from their normal habitat. The bird flying over the cornfield is just as likely to be a kingfisher as a red-winged blackbird. The little fellow flitting along the furrow ahead of the tractor is just as likely to be a palm warbler as a vesper sparrow. Flickers may be seen hunting ants in a plowed field and ospreys may be seen flying over farming country far from water.

Our permanent residents take notice of the influx of travelers. The female redstart searching for insects in the plum trees is surrounded by gossiping house sparrows. The blue jays that have been staying around our yard all summer are holding a protest meeting down in the windbreak. The protests grow loud and furious when the visitor happens to be a sharp-shinned hawk like the one I saw taking off from among the ash trees this morning. At the Duluth hawk watch one fall a professional ornithologist observed that one could be almost certain to see a sharp-shinned hawk following a flight of blue jays. I did not attend the Duluth hawk count this fall but have seen a few hawks passing through here, including a peregrine, a broad-winged hawk, an osprey, a pigeon hawk and several sharp-shins.

The lilac bush is alive today with ruby-crowned kinglets

flipping their wings. Brown thrashers and catbirds dash excitedly from one cover to another. On my way to town a few days ago I saw a gathering of about fifty pied-billed grebes on the slough across the highway from Pickerel Lake. The wood pewees that went through some time ago were cooperative enough to utter an occasional snatch of song by which they were easily recognized.

One day, as I drove into my garage, I heard a one-syllable bird call coming from within the building. The call was vaguely familiar, but I was not certain of the bird until I stepped out of the car and saw the bird perched on a rafter brace near the peak. The least flycatcher resembles the alder flycatcher so closely that they are not distinguishable by sight. Their songs, however, are quite different. The song of the alder is a spirited "we-be-o" while that of the least is an abrupt "chebec". The call I heard in the garage was neither of these. It was a mere "squit", which would not have helped me identify the bird had it not been for an experience I had while attending the meeting of the Wilson Ornithological Society at Duluth in June of 1957.

On the first evening a small group of us went birding along the skyline drive, and en route, were invited by a Duluth resident to her home to see the planting and other bird attractions in her yard. While there, I heard this strange call — "squit" — repeatedly. Using binoculars, I tried to locate the bird responsible. There was a least flycatcher or two among the trees. But I had known this bird for so long by its "chebec" song that I dismissed it and continued searching for a mysterious bird. In our group were a doctor and his wife from Ontario, Canada. The doctor was also searching the trees with binoculars, and I assumed that he was searching for the same bird I was. Presently, he went to his car after a telescope and tripod. After a great deal of maneuvering with the equipment he asked his hostess if she knew she had a least flycatcher nesting in her yard. She was unaware of any such nest, so he asked her to look through the telescope, which he had aimed at a spot high up on the trunk of a white birch. We all took turns looking through the telescope and saw, protruding above a sliver of bark, the head and tail of a bird that our Canadian friend said was a least flycatcher which he had watched with binoculars until it had returned to the nest, thus revealing the location. I was still hearing the "squit" call, so I asked him about it. "That is the male bird," he replied. "And that is a call the least flycatchers use when alarmed or annoyed." He went on to explain that the "squit" call had alerted him to the possibility of a nest being nearby. And I learned something new about a familiar bird.

Among the migrants this fall was a birder's counterpart of the "fish that got away." From the windbreak some days ago came the call of a bird that I have been trying to get a good look at for several years, so far unsuccessfully. Once, I caught a glimpse of the bird. Just enough to know that in size and profile it resembles a grosbeak. A friend suggested that it might be a black-headed grosbeak, a western bird that is sometimes seen here. But, to me, it is still "the bird that got away."

...Bird hazards

The other day I received a letter from a school boy who lives on Route 2 at Hollandale. He has a problem. One day at school he found a bird with a broken leg, a broken wing and its tail feathers missing. He is very much interested in caring for this bird until it recovers. He has been feeding it bird seeds and water but wants to know if there is anything more he can do for it, and what I think about the situation. I am glad that he has taken the trouble to search through bird books to identify the bird as a black-billed cuckoo. It shows interest on his part and also helps me in advising him because birds differ greatly in their food habits. Seed-eating birds are easy to provide for. But, since the cuckoo is an insect-eating bird, it is a real problem because finding insects in sufficient quantities gets to be a real chore, especially with winter coming. I suggested that he look for meal worms, which inhabit places where ground grain is stored, and colonies of tent caterpillars that may be found, especially, on walnut trees. As a substitute for insect food, I suggested boiled eggs crumbled.

I will be much interested in hearing how my young friend makes out in his undertaking. One hears of so much interest directed at the killing of wildlife that it is a relief to hear from someone who is interested in helping one of the lesser fellow creatures with which we share the earth. I hope he succeeds, but it is a real problem because so much depends upon the bird's cooperation. Nature's way would be to let such a bird become the victim of some predator. A bird deprived of its power of flight is a helpless creature that would otherwise starve to death before its wing could heal.

Birds encounter many hazards, especially during migration. Besides the necessity for constant alertness lest they fall prey to some natural enemy, they often collide with objects in their path of flight. My car stalled on the way home from town one evening and, when I stepped out to have a look at the motor, I saw a mourning dove strike a telephone wire and hurtle — lifeless — to the ground while the wire hummed like a guitar string. On their bus trip to Whitewater State Park on October 9th, members of the Albert Lea Audubon Society saw some pheasants take off from a field nearby and fly across the road over the bus. One of them struck a highline wire and fell to the ground. We did not stop to investigate, but the bird hit with such force that it was very likely killed on impact. A friend told me that one evening, after he had relaxed in his favorite chair to watch television, something struck his house with such force that a large framed picture on the wall was seen to wiggle. The program was forgotten while he searched with a flashlight to find a dead and badly mangled pheasant. On my way home from country school one bygone day I saw a young prairie chicken that had flown into a barbed wire so solidly that a barb had punctured its throat. It had swung around so that its neck was looped around the wire and there it hung, lifeless. This spring a robin, newly arrived at our house, had somehow broken a wing. We did not undertake to nurse it back to health, so it went nature's way. But the loss to the species was not serious, as evidenced by the thousands of robins I have observed migrating this fall.

Sometimes birds in flight meet with mass destruction. The Empire State Building in New York City gets into the news occasionally when thousands of birds collide with it in a single night. Lighthouses are an old hazard to migrating birds. More recently, television towers with their many brace wires have at times caused great bird destruction.

At times, weather conditions combine to cause mass destruction of migrants. During the night of March 13, 1904, more than five million Lapland longspurs perished in a 1,500 square mile area around Worthington, Minnesota. Although the temperature that night was above the freezing mark, the longspurs, in mass migration, encountered a storm of heavy, wet snow. After struggling against the weather for several hours until thoroughly soaked and utterly exhausted, they hurtled downward wherever their strength gave out. People up late that night saw birds falling out of the sky and thudding against roofs, streets and sidewalks. Most of the birds when examined were dead with broken necks, legs, wings and skulls, ruptured lungs, etc. Those still living were in a dazed stupor and could be picked up without any effort being made to escape.

One may wonder how any species can survive such mass destruction. But, since nature has a way of replenishing losses that she causes, longspurs still congregate to winter on Iowa farms and return each spring to their nesting grounds in the arctic.

...*Fall migration*

There was no need to look at a calendar this fall to know that November was here. On the topmost branch of a plum tree, surrounded by a dozen boisterous house sparrows, perched a sprightly little sparrow with a neat brown cap, a notched tail and a dark stickpin dot on its breast. Its familiar call notes, "tseet — tseet," first attracted my attention. As if to make sure that I took notice, the newcomer surprised me with a few snatches of springtime song. Yes, the first tree sparrow was back from its summer sojourn in the arctic. November was here.

One day, after greasing the corn picker, I started fieldward and was just rounding the windbreak when I saw another November reminder. A large hawk soaring overhead bore tell-tale sooty smudges under the wings at the wrist joint which identified it as another arctic summer resident, the American rough-legged hawk. He was perhaps checking my cornfield for rabbit population and deciding whether or not to take up winter residence here.

While plowing a field of cornstalks south of my ten-acre woods, I saw a good demonstration of what happens to the wind when it strikes a grove of trees. About fifty feet above the edge of the woods and facing the wind with wings extended was a red-tailed hawk, suspended as motionless as a kite. The wind striking the woods was deflected upwards and the hawk was riding the updraft in effortless poise.

On the same day, as I neared the south end of my farm, I had the very pleasant experience of encountering a large flock of migrating Lapland longspurs. At first I thought they were horned larks, which are summer residents here and are frequently encountered during field work. However, when the number of birds flying up from the ground as my tractor proceeded grew into the hundreds I saw that, although some of the birds were horned larks, most of them were the longspurs, the same species that I mentioned as the victims of the great disaster around Worthington, Minnesota in March of 1904. Unlike birds that take flight from the ground in unison, the longspurs take flight individually. There are birds constantly leaving the ground and alighting again. As they accomplish this characteristic bounding lark flight they utter a constant, sociable twitter. In spring plumage the male Lapland longspurs are beautiful birds with distinct white, black and chestnut markings about their head, neck and throat. In fall plumage they are plain and sparrow-colored.

While plowing grain stubble on the last day of September I saw in the distance seven objects flying in formation. My first thought was of aircraft. But the progress was not steady enough for that, so I decided they must be large birds. Their flight was like that of hawks. But I knew that hawks do not fly in formation. Imagine my surprise when the birds came close enough so I could see that they were turkey vultures! I had seen turkey vultures before, but always at a distance and only one at a time. This was the first time I had seen a flock of them and the first time I had seen any on my own farm. After circling directly over the tractor they circled over the woods twice and then descended there to roost for the night. There is nothing appealing about these carrion-eating scavengers in a perching pose. But a flock of them in flight is beautiful to see. When I mentioned this experience to a friend from the East who stopped in to see us one day this fall, he said that he had once seen a flock of turkey vultures circle over a baseball field while a game was in progress. He added that he had remarked to a companion in jest that one of the ball teams must have been "pretty rotten."

There have been an unusually great number of migrating robins this fall. They came in two waves. The first wave came through in the last days of August and the first days of September. The last and much larger wave came through about the middle of October. I had been seeing a great many robins about the yard and even out in the fields for several days. One morning on my way to the field I saw what at first appeared to be a flock of blackbirds stretching from my woods northwestward far past the limits of my farm. There was something about the greater distance between individual birds, however, that caught my attention. As I came nearer I could see that they were all robins. There were thousands of them! They had apparently spent the night in my woods. The gray dogwood berries that were abundant this fall were stripped nearly completely from the bushes surrounding the woods. I asked John Moyer, our last Audubon Screen Tour lecturer, if he had noticed an unusual number of robins this fall. He replied that he had not noticed an unusual number, but had recently talked with a bird bander who had trapped and banded over 300 of them this fall.

The story is quite different with another member of the thrush family, the eastern bluebird. There have been no bluebirds nesting in any of my nesting boxes this summer. I have heard an occasional warble overhead this fall, but this is nothing compared to the abundance of bluebirds in this area in 1949 and 1950. It seems that, despite efforts to help them, they find difficulty maintaining their numbers. I hope these beautiful birds get a break so we may always have them with us.

. . .*Cooper's hawk*

A while back, an unannounced but welcome Thanksgiving guest stopped at our place for a bounteous meal of hen pheasant to sustain him on his journey. Now before you call the game warden, let me explain that our guest was a Cooper's hawk. I believe the warden will agree that, for a Cooper's hawk, hen pheasant is perfectly legal fare.

As I approached the west line fence with my tractor and plow, this hawk perched nonchalantly on a fence post until I was **within four or five rods, then took off in typical accipiter flight** — three wingbeats and a short sail, three more wingbeats and another short sail. It flew only a short distance before perching conspicuously on another post. This is unusual behavior. One does not often get such a close range view of the Cooper's hawk, which is habitually so secretive in its activities. When I neared the fence on my next round the hawk was again perched on its original post and seemed as reluctant to leave as before. I now suspected that the raptor was feeding on something nearby, but could not see evidence of the prey. On the third round, however, I saw from a distance where the hawk left the ground to assume his position on the post. As I turned at the end of the field I watched for and saw, nestled in the grass next to the woven fence, a hen pheasant, minus its head and a good deal of flesh about its neck and shoulders. The hawk continued feeding between my interruptions for about two hours, during which time it consumed nearly a third of the pheasant. After the hawk had left I stopped to examine the remains and, since there was still body heat, I concluded that the prey had been taken alive. Whether or not the pheasant was sick or crippled at the time of capture, I of course, could not tell.

Cooper's hawk is the species often called "chicken hawk." Occasionally — and I mean OCCASIONALLY — one will turn criminal and seek food the lazy way by returning time after time to the same poultry yard. I vividly recall the first and only time I have seen a hawk take a chicken. I was just a youngster at the time, but already fascinated by birds. Mother had been complaining about a chicken hawk for some days and often stepped outside to scan the sky when there was any disturbance among the chickens. One day while she was doing dishes I happened to be in the kitchen when suddenly all the roosters gave the alarm call at once. "The hawk!" shouted Mother as she dashed out the door, frantically waving the dishtowel and screaming. Bursting with curiosity, I ran out the door after her in time to see a crow-sized bird shoot like a meteor down through the box elders, snatch a fist-sized chick from a frantic cluck hen and disappear through the cottonwoods with the chick clutched in its talons. It was a dramatic moment. I marveled at the speed and the skill of the hawk dashing headlong among the trees, and at the precision of the capture, without a pause in its flight. With Mother in tears and pandemonium reigning among the chickens, I wondered why the Creator had turned such a bird loose in the world. Through the years I have tried to find the answer to that question. Certainly the Cooper's hawk is here for some purpose.

In bird literature I find that there has been much controversy about birds of prey. Despite the fact that intensive food habit studies by biologists in recent years have dispelled many of the myths and half-truths about these birds, prejudice still persists, especially against the accipiters, or bird hawks. Sportsmen and farmers generally consider them as enemies of game and poultry. For a time, after my childhood experience, I too was prejudiced but, through observation and the study of research on the subject, I have long since concluded that accipiters are valuable birds. I do not, of course, condone chicken stealing by hawks, but let me emphasize that these incidents are rare and that the melodrama associated with the loss of a chicken to a hawk throws the importance of the incident out of perspective and can allow one's imagination to run wild. There is much less excitement, for example, when a chicken is killed by a car or by disease. But the loss is just as important.

How does one justify the Cooper's hawk diet, consisting of up to 90% birds? It does prey to some extent upon game birds, especially the young after hay is cut and grain is harvested, thus reducing protective cover. But by far the largest part of its prey consists of smaller birds. What then is the role of accipiters in the balance of nature? The explanation generally accepted by biologists is that hawks naturally take first the prey that is most easily captured. Hence, they eliminate the weak, sick, crippled, slow and unwise individuals, thereby actually improving the species on which they prey. It has also been established that predation only harvests a surplus that otherwise would be lost in some other way. This fall, for example, so much cornstalk ground has been plowed that I am sure many pheasants will starve to death. Thus, available food will be the limiting factor in pheasant survival numbers. I do not begrudge my Thanksgiving Day hawk visitor its honestly earned meal.

. . . A pet Baltimore oriole

February, 1961

Wherever there is a gathering of Minnesota birders one is almost certain to find a woman whose husband is a district judge at Glenwood. An enthusiastic birder, she is a past secretary of the Minnesota Ornithologists Union, a bird bander and always brimful of interesting news about birding experiences.

When my wife and I arrived at the Museum of Natural History in Minneapolis for the winter meeting of the M.O.U. we met this woman at the registration desk. After we had exchanged greetings she began telling us about a Baltimore oriole that she had been foster mother to during the past summer. At her request, I am writing of her experience, even though it may not be seasonal to write about a Baltimore oriole in January. After all, why should a bird column always be seasonal? Next May there will be plenty of other birds to write about and just now they are rather scarce around here.

There is nothing very unusual about a tame bird. We may find them in almost any neighborhood every summer. The story is much the same in each case. A young bird, perhaps a robin or blue jay, tumbles out of its nest prematurely. Some good samaritan rescues it, feeds and cares for it until it can fend for itself. During the process the bird becomes so accustomed to humans that, for a time at least, it will come when called.

A pet Baltimore oriole, however, is rarely encountered because the young of this species spend their helpless days in the safest of all bird nests, a woven pouch six inches deep, constricted at the top and tenaciously suspended from the outer end of a limber branch high up in a tall tree. Attached as it usually is to a drooping branch, it may sway about considerably in a strong wind. But I find it hard to imagine a young bird falling out of a nest like this. Nature must have pulled a boner last summer by permitting a certain pair of orioles to attach their nest to a rather upright branch of a tree in this lady's yard. When she stepped outside one morning after a violent wind and rain storm last June she found two helpless nestling orioles on the ground under the tree, apparently catapulted from their nest during the night. They were soaking wet, hungry and crying their hearts out. Well versed in the needs of nestling birds, she took them into the house where they were soon warm and dry, then fed them boiled egg yolk with a tweezers and water with a medicine dropper.

The adult orioles were naturally much concerned about the plight of their offspring, and my friend tried to cooperate with them by putting one of the nestlings outdoors on a branch where the parent birds could find and feed it. She was successful in getting them to take over the feeding and care of one of the nestlings but was stuck with the other one for the rest of the summer, perhaps because she rather enjoyed caring for the bird and had waited a little too long before putting it outside.

The young oriole turned out to be more of a pet than she had anticipated. There was no difficulty at all in getting it to come when called. In fact, the real problem was to get rid of it. The bird was free to go outdoors, but liked to be in the house so well that it would alight on the head or shoulder of anyone entering the house. This naturally called for some explanation at times. After all, when a person enters someone's house as a guest he doesn't expect to have a Baltimore oriole plunk down on his head or shoulder and start pleading for a handout.

She was particularly amused when telling about the day her housework kept her busy until long after the oriole's usual feeding time. When she at last took time to call it in, the bird did not respond. She saw it perching silently, apparently pouting like a spoiled child because it had been neglected. She called and coaxed without success. Finally, her patience exhausted, she turned to enter the house. Just before the door slammed behind her, the oriole plopped down on her shoulder.

During the summer she had wondered if her pet oriole, having known only human care, would migrate southward at the proper time or stay on through the winter. Instinct, however, was stronger than habit because when the other orioles left her pet also disappeared. One naturally wonders how this strangely reared oriole is faring since leaving its Glenwood home. If it is with others of its kind it is probably somewhere between Mexico and Colombia. What will happen if and when it chooses to alight on some Latin American's head or shoulder as he enters his house? Will its confidence in humans lead to its capture or destruction and, if so, will the captor or destructor take enough interest in the aluminum band on its leg to send the band number to the United States Fish and Wildlife Service so that my friend will learn of her pet's fate? If it survives all the hazards of the migratory journey it will be interesting to know if it will return again to my friend's home next May. And, since we are speculating, will it build a safer nest than its parents did?

... *Migration theories*

Two other Albert Leans and I were discussing the homing instinct of birds the other day while I was at a local farm service store to arrange for some custom grinding. It all started with the question: "How do homing pigeons find their way home?" We didn't arrive at a completely satisfactory answer because this homing instinct, or direction-finding ability, of birds is something that has puzzled bird students throughout history, and still has ornithologists stumped.

As far as pigeons are concerned, it has been pretty well established that untrained individuals have no inherited homing ability, presumably because they are not migratory birds. The reason we think about pigeons first in connection with homing is perhaps because man, for convenience, uses pigeons more often than other species for racing and carrying messages. The so-called homing pigeons are common pigeons that are specially trained for racing. Their ability to find the home loft accurately and quickly is developed by long training and practice. Even so, some individuals have acquired remarkable ability to fly directly to their home loft from distant, unfamiliar territory, regardless of the direction of the home loft.

The perspective orientation which we find in migratory birds differs from the homing ability of pigeons in that there is no human influence. Instead of one home loft there are two points toward which the individual bird is drawn, depending upon the season. In the spring it is drawn toward its nesting area. In the fall it is just as strongly drawn toward its wintering area. These points may be thousands of miles apart and over long stretches of open sea. By attaching numbered bands on birds' legs so they can be identified it has been determined that birds of many species return year after year to the very same location in which they were hatched and, equally interesting, to the very same thicket in which they spent the previous winter.

Many theories have been advanced in attempting to explain migration fully. Some bird students try to explain it very simply by saying that a bird's view presents a much wider area from horizon to horizon than a view from the ground. Therefore, natural pathways such as river valleys, mountain ranges and shorelines can be readily followed. This might very well help daytime migrants. But most birds migrate during the night. Many migratory birds fly great distances over the open, unmarked sea. How about the birds that find their way unerringly through the densest fog?

The argument is advanced that young birds learn the migratory route by following adults that have made the journey before. This is, no doubt, true with species like geese, that migrate as families or groups of families. And swallows, which congregate before migrating in great flocks which include all ages. But how about the species, notably the shore birds, in which the adults and young do not migrate at the same time? Golden plovers, for example, nest on the arctic tundra. When the young are about six weeks old the parents leave them to shift for themselves and strike out for the Labrador coast where they feed on the abundant aquatic life along the shore for a time, then take off southward over the Atlantic Ocean to the Bahama Islands and on through Venezuela and Brazil. Later in the fall the young plovers, entirely on their own, take the same route over completely unfamiliar territory to join the adults on the Argentine pampas 8,000 miles away where they spend the winter.

One theory suggests that the birds orient themselves by the sun but doesn't explain how this works after sunset. It has been suggested that night migrants orient themselves by certain stars. This theory doesn't explain how the stars could help on a cloudy night. One theory has it — and this is getting deep — that birds respond to forces related to the rotation of the earth and that their north and south journeys are guided by the variation of these forces. Another theory connects bird orientation with the earth's magnetic field. Still other theories claim response to infrared radiation, radio waves, etc. Confusing, isn't it?

After all the speculation concerning this mysterious phase of bird migration, the question still remains: How do the birds find their way? Certainly not by random searching. For us, who hardly dare leave our home town without a road map, it is hard to comprehend in a lower form of life an attribute so far superior to our own. But it is obvious that birds have been endowed by the Creator with a sense of direction far more accurate than ours, just as they have been endowed with far superior mobility.

. . . *Pine siskin*

April, 1961

On February 12th several members of the Albert Lea Audubon Society went on a field trip to Hayek's Island in Pickerel Lake. The ice on the lake was slushy, the raw southeast wind was chilly enough to make some noses run and the only birds that showed up were two black-capped chickadees. I enjoyed the trip, however, because — strange as it may seem — I had never been to the island before, though I have lived within sight of it for more than forty years. After our ramble we were invited by one couple to gather at their house for lunch. As we approached our destination I was much impressed with the many arborvitae (or white cedar) trees in the neighborhood. I assumed that this was what gave Cedar Avenue its name, and our host assured me that this was correct.

Shortly after we arrived there was a sudden flurry of excitement in the kitchen and I was called to come and look at a bird. On the ground a few feet from the kitchen window was a small, brown-streaked bird picking at something that I took to be an arborvitae cone. Little brown birds are not the easiest birds to identify. To paraphrase Abraham Lincoln, whose birthday it was, God must have loved little brown birds because he made so many of them. Someone wondered if it was one of the sparrows. But the bill was not heavy enough. Someone else wondered if it might be a redpoll. Immature redpolls do not have the red forehead like the adults of this species. The bird's uniformly streaked appearance above and below, the narrow, pointed bill and the conspicuous wing bars reminded me of the pine siskins I had seen in the treetops at Itasca State Park. I had seen pine siskins only twice, neither time at close range. During the hawk watch at Duluth in September 1953 I happened to be standing near a professional ornithologist when I became aware of an approaching chorus of strange, talkative bird music. I looked up and saw several dozen small birds, which the ornithologist indicated were pine siskins. At the M.O.U. spring field trip in Itasca State Park in May 1959 I heard the same cheerful song as flock after flock of pine siskins swarmed about the tops of the tall spruce trees near Douglas Lodge. The birds were so active and wary that it was difficult to get a good look at them with binoculars. But I got a fair idea of their plumage pattern.

It seemed strange to see such a quiet, solitary, unconcerned pine siskin as the one we were now watching at close range. But the longer I watched it, the more certain I was of its identity. There was a scramble for bird guides, which everyone seemed to have left at home as being unnecessary on a midwinter field trip. One birder saved the day, however, by dashing out to his car after a copy of Richard Pough's *Audubon Bird Guide* and satisfying everyone that the bird in question was indeed a pine siskin. Pine siskins are about as rare in this area as muskies in Albert Lea's Fountain Lake. Our field trip had turned out to be a red letter day, even though our composite list numbered but two species.

Since the day of our field trip this couple has seen flocks of several pine siskins about their yard so, apparently, this is a siskin winter for this area. If you are curious about how a pine siskin looks, it might be well to keep a watchful eye on your conifers, especially arborvitae. It may be years before siskins show up here again since they are very erratic, unpredictable wanderers. This is true also of many other northern forest finches, including redpolls, crossbills, purple finches and evening grosbeaks. Pine siskins eat many insects when they are avail able. During the winter they subsist on conifer seeds and are especially fond of the seeds of arborvitae, which no doubt explains their partiality for Cedar Avenue in Albert Lea.

But we are now on the threshold of April and are looking for the return of familiar birds from the south. Prairie horned larks, of course, are already here in abundance. I saw the first one on February 5th. I wonder how many of their nests have been destroyed by snow. Horned larks start nesting so early that the first nests are often destroyed by heavy March snow. They don't give up without a struggle, however. Birds have been found brooding eggs at the bottom of a deep hole in the snow.

On March 8th my feeder cattle waited patiently while I shoveled foot deep snow out of their feed bunk. Amid the whirling snow four horned larks circled overhead. I wondered where these ground-perching birds could possibly alight, with the ground so deeply covered with the white stuff. As I watched them they suddenly descended to alight on a tiny spot of bare ground in my cowyard. Their musical twitter was so loud that it attracted the attention of some of the cattle. No sooner had the hardy birds folded their wings than half a dozen of the Herefords watching them suddenly started prancing through the deep snow, tails in the air, straight towards them, frightening them away. I now have bird-watching cattle!

... *Remember baking soda bird cards?*

May, 1961

A few birds stay with us throughout the entire year. A few others are with us only during the winter months. Many species spend only the summer here. But a far greater number spend the winter farther south, so our only chance to see them is during the time they pass through in spring and fall. To catch a glimpse of one of these transients as it happens to cross our path in its migratory journey brings a thrill to those of us who enjoy birds as a hobby. But the mere observation tells us little about the bird's life history. As we approach the season when bird migration reaches its greatest height, how many of us stop to think of the debt we owe to professional ornithologists?

It stands to reason that the more we know about a bird the more that bird will mean to us when we see it. To help us acquire this knowledge there has accumulated through the years, and especially during the last few decades, a vast, reliable storehouse of information about every known species. Thanks to the pains-taking research of professional ornithologists we need only open a book to find almost any information we may seek. There are text books, research reports, area studies and experience narratives galore. There are also concise, pocket-sized bird guides with colored portraits of each species, together with a description of distinguishing field marks, voice, habits, nests, summer and winter range, etc. The preparation of these ex-tremely helpful guides has required years of diligent work by such distinguished ornithologists as Roger Tory Peterson and Richard H. Pough, with the help of a great many expert bird students. Experts and amateurs alike use these bird guides for quick reference in field identification.

In the early nineteen hundreds, Church & Co. of New York City used to enclose a small bird card in each package of Arm & Hammer brand baking soda. On one side was the colored portrait of a bird and on the other side was a brief but authentic life story of that particular species, ending with the admonition: "For the good of all, do not destroy the birds." These cards were the first bits of bird literature I knew. I studied and treasured them. Suddenly, without any explanation, the cards were discontinued. When Tom Hadley of Detroit, Michigan, was in Albert Lea on an Audubon Screen Tour appearance I mentioned my experience with these cards to him as we were visiting. He smiled, and said that he too had been disappointed when they were discontinued. He then told me how he had, by chance, learned why they were discontinued. After presenting one of his Audubon Screen Tour programs, during which he had mentioned his experience with the baking soda bird cards, an elderly gentleman had come up to talk to him. It developed that he had been connected with Church & Co. at the time the cards were being distributed. The practice, he said, was stopped because officials checking on pure food law violations claimed that chemicals in some of the paints used in making the portraits were considered impurities that might contaminate the baking soda. The company was thus left with an unusable quantity of the cards on hand. He now had them at his house and offered to give them to Mr. Hadley, thinking he might distribute them to children in his audiences. Mr Hadley went to the gentleman's house, expecting to get a few hundred cards. He was astonished to find several boxes, measuring about a cubic yard. These, being tightly packed cards, were so heavy he could hardly lift them. For a time he carried a supply for distribution but because of the equipment he carried and other problems connected with Screen Tour presentations, he finally had to drop them. "If you are ever in Detroit," he bantered, "stop at our house and I'll give you a box."

Although I still have my collection of baking soda bird cards, and occasionally reminisce with them, my bird literature has now increased to a three foot shelf authored by more than twenty ornithologists. Despite this array, however, the birds still hold many secrets. But there is a great deal of satisfaction in looking up all the verified knowledge that I am unable to learn from direct observation.

The big weekend is coming up on May 20th when M.O.U. birders will converge on Whitewater State Park to fraternize and get a good look at all the birds possible. I know that a good birding friend from Minneapolis is dreaming of a warbler wave because I had a postal card from him stating that he is just back from a stay with his brother in Florida. He is going to take time off from writing his third book on Minnesota Swedish folklore to be at Whitewater, and hopes to see me there. So, come May 20th, I'll take my binoculars, my dog-eared copy of Peterson's *Guide to the Birds* and wend my way thither. While there, I also hope to learn the step by step procedure in the successful climb of the bird that entered Minnesota politics. The common loon is now, officially, the state bird of Minnesota. It takes its place beside the red pine — our state tree — and the showy lady's-slipper — our state flower.

... *Birding at home*

June, 1961

It would have been fun to join the members of the Minneapolis Bird Club for their annual weekend of birding at Frontenac on May 13th and 14th. But, with my corn planting incomplete, I felt that I could not spare an ideal planting day away from my fields. I am sure that the birding at Frontenac was good because the weather was excellent. Birdwise, I did fairly well at home. Without any special effort, and with no interruption in my work, I spotted twelve newly arrived species on Saturday — which isn't a bad total for one day.

The first bird that I saw when I stepped out of the house in the morning was a little green heron looking over our windbreak for a possible nesting site. This was quite possibly the same individual bird that has been nesting here for the past two seasons. On my way to the barn I heard both the yellow warbler and the chestnut-sided warbler. The cornfield beckoned and the beef cattle were awaiting their breakfast, so I did not pause to get a look at these beautifully marked warblers. But their songs are by now as familiar as that of the house wren. This was not always so. There was another song, which I took to be that of either the Tennessee warbler or the blackpoll warbler. Their songs are somewhat similar and I need a little more practice to be sure of the difference.

On my way to the field with the tractor I saw two Savannah sparrows perched on the fence along my cowlane. At less than fifteen feet it was easy to see their yellowish, triangular face pattern. When the M.O.U. birders were at my farm in May of 1956, they had to be satisfied with seeing Savannah sparrows at a distance of about twenty rods. Birds apparently consider a tractor operator a part of the machine and do not associate the machine with danger. At any rate, a tractor seat is a good vantage point from which to see field birds at close range. While pouring seed corn into the planter hoppers I heard the whispered insect-like trill of the grasshopper sparrow in my alfalfa field. From my ten-acre woods came the welcome song of the rose-breasted grosbeak, accompanied by the songs of the chipping sparrow, the least flycatcher, the gossipy catbird and the yellowthroat. To make the newcomers an even dozen, a nighthawk flew about over the woods towards evening.

Sunday morning the trees about our yard were alive with faint lisps, chirps, and whisperings. Little forms flitted among the branches but in the hustle to get ready for church there was no time for birding. While walking up the sidewalk toward First Lutheran Church I heard the unmistakable song of a Blackburnian warbler in the tree tops. This beautifully-colored warbler, with its fiery throat-lining sharply visible as it sings, has a variety of songs. But this individual was singing exactly the same series of rapid, high-pitched, wiry trills as the first one I saw along the shrubbery on the south shore of Albert Lea Lake in May of 1949.

After returning from church services, I thought there would be time before dinner to take a look at my wheat field. There was a fairly large area near the highway that was too wet at seeding time to get into with the grain drill, so I had seeded it by hand and had tried to cover the seed with the harrow. Now, when the grain was up, I was curious to see if the hand-seeded part looked presentable. On the chance of seeing some new birds I took my binoculars along on my shortcut through the windbreak. Near the ash heap I encountered a miniature warbler wave. The chokecherry and elderberry shrubbery was alive with tiny birds, most of them blackpoll and palm warblers. A blackpoll searched for tasty morsels less than ten feet away. A palm warbler, bobbing its tail pump-handle fashion, was perched on a discarded tin can. The trees seemed full of these brown-capped tail bobbers. Among the darting forms was one with a rather loud song. I had difficulty getting my binoculars trained on the restless fellow but, after glancing in every direction and following the bird by its song, I finally got a good look at it in clear sunlight. The plain gray upper parts, bright yellow underparts, yellow spectacles and black, festooned necklace marked it unmistakably as a mature male Canada warbler. What gems these tiny birds are in spring plumage! A larger thrush-like bird flew up from the ground to perch near the top of the tree. Its evenly brown back and sparse dotting underneath identified it as a veery. Then, while still standing in the same place, I saw what I have wanted to see for a long time. A little warbler — green as a traffic light — plunked down on a chokecherry twig less than ten feet away. With its back towards me, it stretched upward to reach something on another twig and as it picked at the insect — or whatever it was — the bird lowered the end of its beak, thus erecting the feathers on the top of its head to reveal some orange coloring. Never before have I had such a good view of a male orange-crowned warbler in typical plumage, and at such close range. Binoculars weren't even necessary.

But I had started out to have a look at my wheat field. My dog, no doubt bored with my interrupted trip, had gone back to the house. I hurried to the wheat field and on to inspect the barley before returning through the windbreak. And — you guessed it — I was late for dinner.

The composite list of the M.O.U. birders at Whitewater State Park on May 20th was 126 species. A week later we would have done well to spot half that many. The third week in May brings a host of new arrivals from the south, including most of the warblers and other insect-eating northern nesters. But with June and homemaking so near, these late migrants depart en masse as suddenly as they came, leaving us with only the summer residents. The sudden lull is like a Monday morning when the youngsters have all departed for school after a noisy weekend.

The trip to Whitewater was very rewarding. I spotted 94 species, including 21 species of warblers. I have seen more species than this on a spring field trip, but never this many warblers. Not only did we see many species of warblers, but other species were also numerous. Blackburnian and chestnut-sided warblers were very abundant, not only in the trees and shrubbery, but also feeding on the ground. Even such rarely seen species as the blue-winged and black-throated green warblers were plentiful. I also got a good look at a golden-winged warbler, a new one on my life list. On the road to the tree nursery I climbed the bluff in search of a bird making a buzzing sound, only to discover that it was a blue-winged which we had seen before. During a warbler wave it pays to investigate every sound because these warbler songs are not easy to distinguish. Some members of the group stopped to admire a plum tree in full bloom. I stopped too because I heard a high, thin "seet seet seet" somewhere amongst those blossoms. When I yelled "Cape May," the group closed in to have a look. I had not seen a Cape May warbler since 1957 when I saw one at Estherville, Iowa.

The days since the M.O.U. Whitewater trip have been hectic ones here on the farm, but not too hectic for me to notice the birds around me. I am seldom alone while working in my fields. While preparing my corn ground I could not help being impressed by how thoroughly my fields were being scrutinized every day by the birds feeding there. Besides the species that live and nest there, many birds from surrounding woodland and marshes gather to join the field bird fraternity in their diligent search for insects and insect larvae, especially in the area where the soil is being stirred by whatever farm implement I happen to be using. It has been good to see so many eager helpers with this difficult job of raising crops. It has been a joy also to see these birds near enough to identify some of the insects they are catching. With nestlings to feed, Brewer's blackbirds, redwings and grackles were making repeated trips nestward with beaks filled with worms. Even the detested starlings and English sparrows got into the act. The cowbirds, of course, do not feed their nestlings but, despite their social standing, they are good field workers. Originally they followed bison herds to feed on the insects disturbed by the grazing animals. Later on they followed domestic cattle. Now they follow tractor-drawn implements for the same purpose.

Every time I put up a bluebird house it is promptly occupied by a pair of tree swallows. I now have quite a colony of these valuable birds skimming over my fields every day all summer. The other evening, after sundown, I watched a pair skillfully maneuvering to catch flying insects and making such hurried trips to their nesting box that I wondered how they avoided meeting head on in the entrance.

I am a little disappointed with the red-tailed hawks nesting in my woods this summer. They are so secretive in their feeding habits that I hardly know they are here. They are paying for their shyness by losing the mice that my implements disturb to the crows. The crows are too wise to try nesting in my woods — where both red-tailed hawks and great horned owls live — but they have been visiting my fields nearly every day all spring and have proved to be excellent mousers. I often see robins, flickers, red-headed woodpeckers, kingbirds and even blue jays in my fields. Near the woods I often see crested flycatchers and indigo buntings feeding on the cultivated field. With the black soil as a background the indigo bunting's plumage displays its utmost brilliance. There are surprises, too. On May 27th I saw a western kingbird while planting corn. Only twice before have I seen this beautiful bird and, in both cases, in the field while planting corn. The bird is the same size as the eastern kingbird but has a light gray head, dark back, coal black tail and lemon yellow breast.

The most industrious fieldworkers this spring have been the bronzed grackles, probably the ones nesting in my windbreak. Some people resent grackles. To hear them talk one might think that grackles have no virtues. I have heard them called ugly. I disagree. I have seen neckties that looked much worse.

...Defending the young

When I stopped in at a local farmer's supply store one day, the owner told me about a bird commotion in their yard one evening. By prior arrangement some small kittens had been brought over and while these were being introduced to their new surroundings a blue jay flew in and, to use my friend's words, "let out a squawk." Next a brown thrasher came to raise his voice in protest. Then a grackle dashed in to start scolding. In a short time it seemed that all the birds in the neighborhood had gathered to join in the excitement.

Many of our perching birds use this aggressive method of defending their young. Scenes like this are common during the family-rearing season, especially when the young birds start leaving their nests. Inexperienced in flight, they flutter awkwardly for short distances, often getting nearer the ground with each try. Sometimes they fall to the ground where they squat like toads while uttering their hunger calls by which their parents can find and feed them. Their calls also attract predators to which they fall easy prey during the brief time they require to become skilled in flight. During this critical period of their offspring's life, parent birds naturally become intensely alert for enemies. Anything suggesting possible danger will trigger an alarm call which is readily recognized, even by other species. Birds within hearing quickly gather to scold, assume threatening poses, and even feign bodily attack. The intensity of the hubbub will vary with the degree of danger. Any distress call from a young bird will spark an uproar. Calls become piercing while angry birds rush at the intruder. I have seen squirrels and even cats driven to frantic flight by infuriated robins and grackles.

Speaking of aggressive defense reminds me of the African geese that my sister used to raise while we lived on our Iowa farm. Geese, being water birds, naturally seek water puddles after a rain. One Sunday we had turned our twelve work horses out to pasture with the cattle. The nose flys were bad, and they finally pestered the horses into a stampede. Homeward they came at a dead gallop, heading straight for the cowyard gate where all the geese with their small goslings were gathered in a water puddle. The proud gander, with head aloft, sounded a warning honk that could be heard for miles. For a moment it looked as if the goslings would be trampled to death in a flash. Goslings are like children. When they are having fun they hate to leave. Anyway, there was no time for them to waddle away. With necks outstretched and pointing toward the oncoming horses, the geese suddenly took to the air and flew directly at the horses' heads with screams and beating wings. The startled horses slid to a stop, then wheeled about and charged off just as frantically in another direction while the geese gathered their small fry and escorted them to safer puddles. Although this example involved domestic birds, those who have also observed the home life of wild geese find them very aggressive defenders of their young.

Effective as this belligerent method of defense may often be, there are other more subtle, and sometimes equally effective, ways used by many birds in guarding their young. Some of these methods deal with the enemy only indirectly. Gallinaceous (or ground-dwelling) birds, when sensing danger, often lure their young to a safer location by various movements and calls and by the pretense of feeding. More noticeable perhaps is the warning call of the parent bird, which immediately causes the young to stop all movement and remain silent until the all clear signal is given. This method, combined as it is with protective coloration, is very effective. I have often searched for young pheasants after hearing the hen give a warning call but have seldom found any chicks, unless one was forced to move to avoid being stepped on.

Howard Cleaves, who has been in Albert Lea several times to present Audubon wildlife films, was telling me on one of his visits that an ornithologist whom he knew had demonstrated how well established this instinct is, even in chicks that have not yet hatched. A microphone was placed inside an incubator containing eggs that were so near hatching that the chicks could be heard peeping within the shell. The sound was carried by wire to the classroom and amplified so those in the room could hear the sounds made by the unhatched chicks. A hen was then prompted to give the danger signal, whereupon all the peeping suddenly stopped.

Still another method of defending young is the familiar distraction display so popular with shore birds and many other species. Who hasn't seen the broken wing act of the killdeer and the mourning dove? As a youngster I chased many a fluttering mourning dove before I learned that the act was deliberate and was designed to lure me away from the nest and nestlings.

Some birds use different methods of defense with different enemies. They may scold and threaten humans, yet try to lure small animals away from their nest and young. Species, and even individual pairs within species, may vary in their intensity of defense. A kingbird will attack a hawk or crow, or even alight on the larger bird's back to inflict injury. On the other extreme, some of the herons will sit by, apparently unconcerned, while a coon devours their eggs or young. How can one explain the latter behavior? There are many questions concerning the defense behavior of birds that are as yet unanswered. I think the subject of parental care remains one of the most interesting phases of bird study.

...The "peeps"

Have you been to a lake shore, a stream or a pond this fall to see the "peeps"? This term is used by birding people in referring to several species of small, sparrow-sized sandpipers. Such a term is understandably convenient because the various species of these little shore birds are so much alike — especially in fall plumage — that they even puzzle the experts. It is seldom possible to get close enough to the sandpipers to see them distinctly. Their color — gray above and white below — blends so well with the shoreline background that it is difficult enough spotting the bird, let alone observing the minor differences that make positive identification possible. Even with binoculars, how can one tell at a hundred yards whether the base of the lower mandible is yellowish, or whether the tips of the folded wings extend slightly past the tip of the tail? In spring plumage, which runs more to brownish above, there are more observable differences between the species. But in the fall even the spotted sandpiper has lost its pretty polka dot underparts and appears like the other "peeps," gray above and white below. Fortunately, for purposes of identification, these familiar "peet-weet" birds retain their comical, tail teetering habit and can easily be recognized as spotted sandpipers — even when they are not spotted.

In this area any gathering of "peeps," in spring or fall, is almost certain to include both semipalmated and least sandpipers. Occasionally there may also be Baird's sandpipers, western sandpipers and white-rumped sandpipers, all in the same gathering. The western sandpiper resembles the semipalmated sandpiper so closely that the two were not recognized as separate species until a century ago. At the Whitewater State Park meeting of the M.O.U. in May of 1960, I joined a group of birders that seemed puzzled about some bird they were watching. On a mudflat about 300 yards away were a few sandpipers in a group. Some thought that one of them was a western. A professional ornithologist from Duluth reminded them that to be certain of identity one must have the bird in hand. When we gathered for Sunday dinner — our last get-together — there was still argument about whether or not the bird was a western. I was both surprised and embarrased when I heard a lady clinch her argument with a fellow birder by stating rather loudly, "If Mr. Flugum says it's a western, that's good enough for me!" She had evidently heard me say that, since the bird appeared a little different from the semipalmated sandpipers, it might be a western. Professional ornithologists are understandably rather critical about sight records involving such fine field distinctions. The western sandpiper was not entered on our composite list.

At the Audubon Nature Center near Greenwich, Connecticut, in 1953, one of the men attending the delegates' session was certain that he had spotted a Baird's sandpiper on the beach. This is the species with the wing tips extending slightly past the tip of the tail. When the camp director was critical of this sight record the man became so annoyed that, during the following night, he spoke out very distinctly about it while asleep.

Many members of the sandpiper group are larger than sparrow-size. They vary in size from the least sandpiper, which measures six inches, to the long-billed curlew, measuring over twenty inches. The largest sandpipers I have seen are the willet and the Hudsonian godwit, both measuring fifteen inches. While combining oats on July 29th this year I saw six shore birds approaching in a compact group. Maneuvering in unison, they flew rapidly southward in a zigzag pattern. As they passed directly overhead, less than fifty feet above me, I recognized them as pectoral sandpipers. This species is easily recognized by the sharp line of separation between the dark upper breast and the white underparts.

Sandpipers start their southward journey early. Some of them start showing up in northern United States in early July. They are great travelers. Most of them nest in the arctic regions, arriving there in May. Family rearing with them is a whirlwind affair. Their precocial young are left to fend for themselves, and migrate southward later. How they find their way — many of them as far south as Argentina and southward — is a migratory mystery.

In this area August is a good time to look for southward bound sandpipers. Mudflats along the edge of any water are a favorite gathering place. The heavy rains in early August this year raised the water and covered these mudflats, so the sandpipers, if present, are likely to be hidden by vegetation. Although the positive identification of the various species of small sandpipers is a painstaking and time consuming task, one can improve on it bit by bit. And, of course, when one tires of it he can always use the inclusive term "unidentified peeps."

...Fall migration

Just as the tide of northward migration reaches its height in May, so the peak of southward movements comes in October. Although there are more birds in the fall migration following the nesting season than there were in the spring, the fall migration is less spectacular because, for the most part, their conspicuous plumage and bursting courtship song is lacking. Shore birds lead the southward exodus, many of them taking off in July. August finds the swallow clans gathering in preparation for the journey. September marks the height of hawk migration. Outside on a cool October night one can listen to the faint lisps coming from far overhead where myriads of warblers and other small passerines are using their voices to maintain their distances in formation while flying blind. Of course, one can get into an argument as to whether or not birds can see and find their way at night. But why should we assume that a bird flying in the dark can see any better than a chicken searching for its roost at dusk?

Hawks are daytime migrants. They need to pause only occasionally to catch prey for food. All swallows migrate in daylight because they gather their food as they fly. Most birds, however, must spend the daylight hours in search of food and for rest, and must therefore migrate at night. This fall I have been aware of many small voices in the trees, shrubbery and weedy fence rows, but haven't always taken time to trace the source. While on an errand that took me past a plum tree behind the hen house one day, I chanced to see what I took to be a Wilson's warbler. Minus their bright plumage and springtime song the warblers are a confusing lot. The warbling vireo that I heard in Pine City on August 28th was an exception. He came close enough for me to see without binoculars. But I would not have been aware of his presence had it not been for his out of season song.

At this season one may expect to see birds out of their natural habitat. While feeding my beef cattle on September 9th I saw 15 lesser yellowlegs take to the air, displaying their white tails and trailing their yellow feet. On September 14th I saw two more, as well as a solitary sandpiper in my cowyard which — in the kind of weather we have been having — has been as good as any lake side mudflat for attracting shore birds.

Migration is a hazardous time for birds. Night migrants often collide with man-made structures such as tall buildings, radio and television broadcasting towers, airport lights, etc. There have also been several cases where thousands of birds have been killed on a single night in this way. Daytime window collisions are also common. While my wife was busy on the telephone one day she heard some object strike one of the workroom windows with such force she thought it strange the glass did not break. Some time later, our daughter brought in a small dead bird that she had found on the ground near the window. I saw at once that it was a red-eyed vireo. One eye was crushed by the impact. Although the red-eyed vireo is thought to be one of the most numerous woodland birds of North America, it is seldom seen by anyone but experienced birders, who recognize the song and trace it to its source. I remember what a frustrating time I had in first making the acquaintance of this bird.

In case you wondered, a few paragraphs back, how I happened to be in Pine City on August 28th, perhaps I should explain that our whole family was enroute home from Duluth and had stopped in the park at Pine City to eat lunch. It was the last weekend that our three college-aged children would all be home, and none of them had been farther north than the Twin Cities. So, on August 26th, we all took off for Duluth, our scenic inland port. Birdwise, the trip was not too rewarding, although we did see many nighthawks on the way and the bird feeder outside our Duluth host's kitchen window was actively patronized by a number of pine siskins, purple finches, rose-breasted grosbeaks, blue jays, and even a cowbird. We drove out to Park Point where we saw the herring and ring-billed gulls, a few semipalmated sandpipers, killdeer, and common tern. There were two foreign boats in the harbor, one from England and one from Norway. We crossed over the sandbar to put our fingers and feet into Lake Superior and watch the breakers roll in.

We stopped at Hawk Hill on the skyline drive to show the children where we watch for hawks. We were three weeks early for the big flights, but we did see two broadwings and a sharp-shin. After a swing up the north shore to Two Harbors we returned to our host's back yard for a picnic. She had been busy on the telephone. Twenty people came to enjoy a steak bar-becue. It was pleasant indeed to renew acquaintances with the Duluth birding people.

...*Plowing companions*

November, 1961

I was out plowing on one of those miserable days when the rain was coming down in a borderline drizzle — not enough to send a fellow home from the field, yet too much to let him stay there. While I was debating whether or not to stop plowing, a lone ring-billed gull came to join me in my discomfort. Flying slowly into the wind he set his wings for a long, graceful glide downward. Checking his speed with a couple of wingbeats and a spread tail, he lowered his landing gear and alighted on the wet plowing. Folding his wings carefully and drawing in his neck, he appeared as comfortable as a gull can get in such weather. Presently another ringbill came to join him, then another and another, until there were 38 gulls in a compact group, all perched on the ground facing the wind and all identically posed. Although the drizzle continued as I reached the end of the field, my farm work was pressing and I decided to plow another round. As I came near the resting gulls one of them fluffed out its plumage and vigorously shook the moisture from its feathers. It then took to the air and, as it did so, it seemed to be carrying something with its feet, a strange thing for a gull to do since its webbed feet are not designed for that. When more of the gulls took flight they also seemed to be carrying something. But by this time I was close enough to see that what they were carrying was dirt sticking to the under side of their feet. When a gull flies it normally folds its webbed feet so the toes come together and holds its legs straight back so its feet are held against the under side of its tail feathers. These gulls were a strange sight as they flew away with their legs hanging straight down and their webbed feet fully extended. Whether their feet were too heavy to lift comfortably or whether they could not fold their dirt-laden feet, I could not determine. Perhaps they just did not want to get their tail feathers dirty. By this time the rain was beginning to soak through my clothing and I went home, leaving the gulls to solve their own problem.

Although ringbills often follow my plow in both spring and fall, I haven't seen a herring gull among their flocks for several years. It has also been several years since Franklin's gulls have visited my fields. On September 23, however, a flock of about a hundred of these graceful "prairie pigeons" came to hawk insects overhead and gather larvae from freshly turned furrows. While watching these beautiful gulls I get the impression that they really enjoy flying as they wheel and turn, glide downward or set their wings to catch the breeze and are lifted skyward without a wingbeat. Franklin's gulls range widely in the fall and consume great quantities of egg-laying grasshoppers, thus effectively reducing the next season's population of these pests. Unlike the other gulls, Franklin's nest in deep water inland sloughs and reed-grown lakes. However, drainage operations in recent years have made these areas less numerous than they once were. I wonder which adds up to the greater value: the crops raised on the drained land or the additional crops sacrificed in the surrounding area by the absence of thousands of pest-destroying gulls feeding among growing farm crops.

On September 22nd I disturbed a great many migrating sparrows as I finished plowing a field about sundown. Small sparrows were constantly flying up from the grain stubble as the tractor approached them. They flew low with a very rapid wingbeat and dropped back in the stubble. Apparently they had decided to roost among the stubble for the night. As the unplowed strip became narrower the sparrows became more concentrated. When at last the strip was only a few feet wide they reluctantly took off for the nearby corn field. I saw many of them at close range as they were being disturbed. They had streaked breasts and a light stripe through the center of the crown. Judging by their size, plumage markings and flight pattern, I took them to be immature grasshopper sparrows.

During the first two weeks of October there have been hundreds of robins about our yard, in the fields and in our woods. These are probably northern robins migrating through this area. As I started for the field one morning in the third week of October last year I saw a great concentration of robins in flight. The flock extended from our ten-acre woods westward as far as I could see. There must have been several thousand birds in this flock. They had lunched well in the woods because there were only a few gray dogwood berries left. The day before, the bushes had been loaded with fruit.

On Sunday morning, October 15th, I saw the first fox sparrow. The next morning there were a few juncos about the yard. On the field to the south there was a gathering of horned larks and a small flock of Lapland longspurs. There have been several pied-billed grebes in the slough across the highway from Pickerel Lake all fall but, with the opening of duck hunting season, all have left. The few shots fired in the area must have hurried them on their southward way. In this sunny weather I am waiting, apparently in vain, for the friendly, contented warble of a bluebird. Are they really going to disappear entirely?

...Canadian visitors

December, 1961

For several mornings during the early part of November I was pleasantly awakened at daybreak by the tremulous call of a screech owl outside my bedroom window. It amuses me now to think of how the screech owl's song used to frighten me as a youngster. To me, it was the embodiment of all the fierce, nocturnal creatures depicted in the hair-raising yarns that appeared in that old weekly magazine *The Youth's Companion.* The conveniences of indoor plumbing were slow in coming to rural homes in our neighborhood, and it was standard practice at our house for small fry to make a trip outdoors before bedtime. On these trips in the dark I always went in high gear. But when a screech owl's eerie wail broke the stillness, I shifted into overdrive. Through the years I have become very well acquainted with this small predator, one of the least appreciated of all birds. I enjoy hearing its odd song. As I listened to it the other morning, a blue jay interrupted the reverie with a loud scream as much as to say, "Oh, shut up!" The owl must have interpreted the blue jay's call in the same way I did because it stopped vocalizing.

The chill, blustery weather that ushered in the month of November this year brought with it some guests from the Canadian northland. Whenever I neared my woods with my corn picker a flurry of small birds would arise from the corn field and disappear among the trees. Some of them were juncos flashing their white outer tail feathers. But most of them belonged to another species of which I was not certain until one of them obligingly perched momentarily on a fence wire where I could get a look at its jaunty rust-colored cap, white wing bars and notched tail. The bird was facing away from me, so I could not see the small, stickpin dot on its breast. But I had seen enough to assure me that it was a tree sparrow. Don't ask me why they call them tree sparrows. Every bird must have a common name and tree sparrow serves it as well as any. At least it is easier to say than *Spizella arborea*, its Latin name. These sparrows nest at the arctic timber line, where a pine tree may take half a century to reach a height of two feet. Some of them may winter in this area, if your yard is not tidy and a few spears of pigeon grass are allowed to protrude above the snow during the winter. Most of them go a little farther south. Iowa harbors many of them through the winter. After we built our house in 1948 there was considerable raw soil exposed where pigeon grass flourished in spite of our efforts. The pay-off came the following winter when we could look out a window on any snow-covered day and see tree sparrows feasting on the seeds of this objectionable lawn grass.

Bittersweet berries are not very palatable food, but they will do in a pinch. There are some bittersweet vines along my west line fence and, while picking corn on November 13th, I noticed two robins helping themselves to some of the colorful fruit. Bumming their way southward at this late season, they were probably hungry enough to accept bittersweet berries in lieu of earthworms. Bittersweet seed is indigestible. So in due time there may be new bittersweet vines, perhaps along someone else's line fence. How else did the bittersweet vines get started along my fence? They certainly were not planted there by human hands.

When I stepped outside my hog house one morning to get a bale of straw I heard a bird call nearby, "churd-churd." That could only mean one bird — a red-bellied woodpecker. There were no trees in the direction from which the sound came, and woodpeckers usually stick pretty close to trees. Flickers are often seen on the ground, but I was not aware that this species had a similar habit. Had the bird turned ventriloquist, so its voice would seem to come from a false direction? Presently, I heard the sound again. Then I spotted the bird peek-a-booing at me from the opposite side of a hog yard post. It must have sensed being seen because it immediately took off for my neighbor's windbreak, where I had heard the call of a red-bellied woodpecker earlier this fall. There are cottonwoods in that windbreak, and woodpeckers like cottonwoods.

This has been a banner year for kinglets. This fall's migration brought an abundance of the ruby-crowned variety. One Sunday morning the juniper tree outside my den window was literally alive with the short-tailed, wing-flipping tiny mites. Golden crowned kinglets have not always been so abundant. But on almost every day I have heard one about our yard. The high-pitched, lisping, three-note call, "see-see-see," is easily recognized.

On the morning of November 15th my wife and I had a pleasant surprise. Out under our lilac bush, about thirty feet from our house, was a big, beautiful pheasant rooster acting as nonchalant as you please, despite the dog on the porch and the two faces inside the kitchen window. Several people have asked and been permitted to hunt on our farm during pheasant season, but I haven't noticed any trophies displayed. I told the latest hunters that they were welcome to any roosters they could get but that my roosters were smart. That was Sunday afternoon. Then on Wednesday morning this grand rooster presents himself at our house as much as to say, "They didn't get me." As I leaned closer to the window to get a better look he took off with a roar of wings, so I guess he was sound in every way.

...*The cardinal*

The National Audubon Society's Christmas greeting card pictures a male and female cardinal perched on a snow-laden tree. The painting, by the eminent bird artist Don R. Eckelberry, is very lifelike. The pose and plumage color is authentic. Which is more than can be said for most of the bird pictures that appear on Christmas cards. Perhaps a bird enthusiast may be pardoned for being a bit critical of bird portraits that cannot be traced to any living species. The cardinal, like our other colorful, crested dandy, the blue jay, retains its bright plumage throughout the year. However, its splendor shows up to best advantage against a background of snow.

A comparative newcomer to this area, the cardinal is a very abundant bird in the old South along with the celebrated mockingbird and the Carolina wren. I shall never forget the abundance of these birds in Montgomery, Alabama, in early April of 1944. What was a Minnesota farmer doing in Dixie at that time? The wedding of a sister-in-law to an Air Force lieutenant stationed at Maxwell Field accounted for the two day whirlwind trip to the southern metropolis. Although I heard my first mockingbird song before I was ten miles beyond the Alabama border and saw several of these birds during my short stay, the mockingbirds were not yet in full song. However, the male cardinals — two or three for every city block — were proclaiming their territorial rights with fervor. At home I had, on rare occasions, heard a cardinal sing. But such profusion of song was a new and captivating experience. The rich, loud, clear and pleasantly musical whistles "whoit whoit whoit whoit" or "what-cheer what-cheer" and the rapidly slurred "whurty,

whurty, whurty" from far away and nearby, burst on my ears constantly from before daybreak until dark.

Half a century ago the cardinal was rarely seen west of the Mississippi River or north of Illinois, but it has gradually been extending its range northward and westward until today it is a common sight in Minnesota along the Mississippi and even north of the Twin Cities and up along the St. Croix. It is a perfectly hardy bird and, where it becomes established, it usually stays. Although the species is non-migratory, individuals will wander extensively. For the last several years cardinals have nested in Albert Lea and in other parts of Freeborn County.

The richly clad birds are certainly a flashy and welcome addition to our winter bird population, which is too often limited to that dependable trio, the black-capped chickadee, downy woodpecker and white-breasted nuthatch. More and more people in this area can now look out their windows and often see a duplicate of the picture on the Audubon Christmas card, especially if they keep a bird feeder supplied with sunflower, melon or squash seed, of which cardinals are so fond. A good job of providing these colorful finches with a dependable supply of winter food may induce wanderers to become permanent residents. I suspected the presence of a cardinal nest near our place last summer because I frequently heard the distinct cardinal call note, "wist-wist," and I could spot the male bird at a considerable distance. On several occasions, too, I saw the female, whose call note is the same.

The sudden arrival of wintry weather on the night of December 8th put a damper on the Albert Lea Audubon Society's field trip scheduled for the following Sunday afternoon at a farm near Austin. This farmer has been reporting some unusual birds. He reported a pileated woodpecker earlier this fall, and at the December 5th Christmas party he reported seeing a bald eagle. If one could have been sure of seeing these two species it would have been worthwhile to battle the snow and wind to get there. As it turned out, I thought the birding prospects looked pretty bleak, so I stayed indoors most of the day. During the morning chores I spotted one nuthatch, two chickadees and a male cardinal. As I came by my corncrib I saw hundreds of English sparrows huddled together feasting on the corn that I had scooped out on the feeding floor for the pigs. I also heard a flock of boisterous English sparrows clear from Phoenix, Arizona, that day. The sparrows were evidently near the microphone during an open air insurance commercial on my television set.

Folks around Rockledge, Florida, and Brownsville, Texas, will probably run their Christmas bird counts to over 200 species again this year. But we will have to be satisfied with twenty or twenty-five. The only official Christmas bird count conducted by the Albert Lea Audubon Society was on December 30th, 1956, when five of our members spent the day searching various habitats for miles around, and saw only twenty-one species. However, the list included such interesting species as black duck, tree sparrow, red-bellied woodpecker, goldfinch, cedar waxwing and golden-crowned kinglet.

With snow and low temperatures, holiday lights and the bright colors of tinsel and wrapping paper, it's beginning to look a lot like Christmas in the city and country alike. By the time you read this it will be Christmas, so I want to take this opportunity to thank all who have expressed their appreciation of this column, and to wish all of you a very Merry Christmas and a Happy New Year. To top it off I hope all of you may see cardinals perched in a snow-laden tree sometime during the holiday season.

...Bohemian waxwing

February, 1962

When I stopped in an Albert Lea electrical supplies store one day the owner hailed me to say that he had been pleasantly surprised recently by rare visitors from the far north. He had looked out a window of his home to see a flock of waxwings feeding on berries still remaining on some shrubs in the yard. The appearance of cedar waxwings — though unpredictable — is not unusual in this area. But something about these birds aroused his curiosity. When he checked with his bird books he found that the visitors were Bohemian waxwings. The birds of this species are a little larger than cedar waxwings and their plumage is more grayish. A white wing patch and yellow wing edging also distinguish it from the smaller species. The most reliable mark for identification, however, is the rich brown color of the under-tail coverts, which differs from the white undertail coverts of the cedar waxwing.

I should like to have been present when those birds were at his home. I am not sure of ever having seen Bohemian waxwings. The flock of crested, silky-plumaged birds that sent me into a fit of excitement on that bleak mid-winter day back in my pre-school days by suddenly swarming into our crab apple trees to feed voraciously on the frozen fruit might have been either Bohemian or cedar waxwings. I have no way of being certain now. At the time I was far too jubilant about discovering a strange bird to notice whether the undertail coverts were white or brown.

Bohemian waxwings range throughout the far northern coniferous forests of Europe, Asia and North America. The name Bohemian does not mean that the birds are native to Bohemia, but refers rather to the birds' nomadic wandering habits. Information about their nesting habits is incomplete and difficult to get since breeding areas are in the wilderness beyond human habitations. The birds are known to form loose colonies while nesting in favorable areas, but may not return to the same area in following years. Bohemian waxwings, like cedar waxwings, depend upon wild fruits for most of their food. This may explain to some extent their unpredictable nesting habits, as the regional abundance of wild fruit may vary considerably from year to year.

In addition to their fruit diet these mysterious birds do eat insects in season. Insects are certainly available during the summer. Several members of the Albert Lea Audubon Society were made more aware of this on Sunday, January 14th, when they journeyed by bus to the Minnesota Museum of Natural History to hear a lecture on an arctic expedition. One member of the expedition, according to the speaker, killed 63 mosquitoes with one slap.

Bohemian waxwings remain together in flocks of varying size and in winter are attracted by such fruits as mountain ash, hawthorn, crab apples, rose hips, juniper berries, viburnums and other fruits that persist through the winter. Large winter flocks appear quite frequently but unpredictably in settled areas of Canada and Europe. Visiting flocks are much less frequent in the United States.

Although a rather silent bird during its winter travels, the Bohemian waxwing does have a song described by some as a hissed "zree," and by others as a chatter. But whether it is a song or just a sound, I should like to hear the voice of a Bohemian waxwing and add it to my bird song vocabulary.

Bird songs and call notes are a great help in spotting birds. We can detect the presence of birds much more readily by sound than by sight. We can hear birds all around us, whereas we can see only those that are directly ahead of us or within our field of view, and then only if there is nothing to obstruct our view or no plumage camouflage to distort our vision. Upon hearing a bird's voice, one has only to trace the sound to its source to get a look at the bird in question. Most of the cedar waxwings that I see would go unnoticed were it not for their faint utterances that I have learned to recognize. The same is true of most other birds, especially the small ones. It isn't even necessary to recognize a bird by its song. One can follow a strange song until there is an opportunity to identify the bird by sight.

Some years ago a friend of mine came to get me one morning at milking time and whisked me off to where he had spotted a flock of purple finches. It wasn't until an hour and a half later that I got back to finish the milking. But, with my friend's help, I had seen my first purple finches. Such a bird chase might happen again if my store owner friend happens to see more Bohemian waxwings.

...*Townsend's solitaire*

March, 1962

When I think of the Townsend's solitaire I get a mental picture of remote wilderness areas in the high mountains of the West with cool, splashing streams and spruce-covered canyons far off the beaten path. I have long wished that some day I might see and hear this shy bird that avoids civilization and loves to nest in lonely, shadowy places and render its enchanting song in the solitude of seldom-trod mountain recesses. I certainly did not expect to see this mountain songster perching in a box elder tree near my garage, less than fifty feet from where I stopped to stare in disbelief at the slim, long-tailed, gray bird with a conspicuous light patch in the middle of its darker wing. At first I thought it was a mockingbird, and wondered what that celebrated southerner was doing in my yard in February. Then I noticed the rounded, thrush-like head, the short beak and large, placid eye, accentuated by the white ring around it. This was no mockingbird.

After a couple of minutes the bird flew leisurely to the topmost branch of a walnut tree north of our house. I wanted to get a better look at the bird to make certain of that eye ring, so I dashed into the house for my binoculars. My wife looked startled, and made some remark about the speed with which I managed to kick off my rubbers and get through the door with an egg pail in hand. She understood completely, however, when she heard me say something about a bird. From my den window I watched the strange bird for several minutes before it took off. After looking through all the literature on the solitaire that my bookshelf provided, I concluded that — fantastic as it may seem — my visitor was indeed a Townsend's solitaire. And I added another bird to my life list.

Only a week earlier I had been discussing the Townsend's solitaire with two members of the Minneapolis Bird Club. There had been reports of a Townsend's solitaire having been seen by someone in Minneapolis. Someone in Albert Lea had also recently reported seeing one. A friend living near Estherville, Iowa, had reported seeing one earlier this winter. I had told my Minneapolis birding friends that I would like to talk with these persons before accepting their reports as authentic. After my experience on February 14th, however, I am inclined to accept those observations, and wonder whether my fellow birders will now cast skeptical glances in my direction. Are we having a minor invasion of these western birds this winter, or do some of these sight records concern the same individual bird wandering about?

During the winter Townsend's solitaires move to lower mountain slopes and those in the northern part of their nesting range migrate southward. Some individuals wander erratically, far east of their range.

For a long time the classification of this bird was an ornithological puzzle. But it is now known to belong to the thrush family. It is widely distributed in the mountainous regions of the West. In the southern part of its summer range it nests at elevations between 7,000 and 12,000 feet. Farther north it nests at much lower altitudes. Apparently, temperature is a determining factor in its choice of nesting location. Usually nesting on or near the ground, the solitaire often favors steep, rocky, fir-covered slopes, where it builds a nest of finely shredded grass with a base or platform of twigs and pine needles. The nest is generally so placed as to have some form of overhanging shelter. Immature birds have spotted plumage, so characteristic of the thrush family.

Food of the solitaire is about one-third insects and two-thirds wild fruit. It sometimes catches insects on the wing with a snap of its beak, like a flycatcher. Sometimes it catches insects on the ground, like a shrike. When gathering berries the bird hovers with beating wings, like a hummingbird. The most appealing of this interesting bird's attributes, however, is its superior gift of song. Starting low, and apparently far away, it gains in intensity and volume until it fills the air. It is said to have a swing to it that goes well with the expanse of mountain heights. My visiting solitaire uttered not a sound. Perhaps a song at this season was too much to expect. But I can still harbor the hope of visiting this minstrel of the solitudes in its distant lofty haunts and listening to its spell of enchantment.

. . . Early fascination, boundless curiosity

April, 1962

With spring at hand it is time to be alert for sounds of familiar birds returning from their winter sojourn. The prairie horned larks have been with us since early in February. Which species will be next to show up? Will it be the red-winged blackbird, the killdeer, meadow lark, robin, or song sparrow? Will we hear a snatch of spring song from the tree sparrow before it departs for the arctic timberline, or will it be the trill of the slate-colored junco?

In my pre-school years on our Iowa prairie farm it was the booming call of prairie chickens that first broke the winter silence. How pleasant it was to awaken to that stirring sound. Next came the great flocks of red-winged blackbirds and grackles to usher in the spring with pomp and gusto. From a window I once watched the approach of a living black cloud, stretching across the sky from as far as I could see. A few birds in the lead dropped down to alight in our bare-boughed windbreak. Then the whole flock cascaded into the grove like a black waterfall. The trees took on the look of suddenly having sprouted black leaves, and presently there burst upon my ears a deafening chorus of blackbird voices. The delightful music continued full blast until a sudden noise — like the barking of a dog or the slamming of a door — startled the impassioned vocalists, whereupon all singing stopped instantly, as though directed by a conductor's baton. After an instant of silence there was a thunderous swoosh as those thousands of wings all beat the air at once, and the blackbirds were off for a neighboring windbreak to pour forth their fervent song again.

From earliest recollections I have had a boundless curiosity about birds. Perhaps the enchantment of the prairie chicken's booming and the thundering blackbird chorus sparked this early interest. There were other sounds too. Strange sounds that remained mysterious for years. The captivating flight song of the upland plover, the yodel of the greater yellowlegs, the whinny of the sora rail and the tantalizing refrain of the warbling vireo. I suppose that my early fascination with birds arose also — at least partly — from the fact that they could fly. I was not very old before I realized that a bird could get from one place to another much more swiftly and conveniently than I could. Fences, streams and other obstructions in my path were no hindrance to birds. Furthermore, I was told they flew great distances to escape disagreeable winter weather. I marveled at their wonderful power of flight and envied them their freedom.

Our home must have been attractive to birds because I knew of twenty species nesting in our windbreak and about the farmstead. There were also more than twenty additional species living on other parts of the farm. For many of these birds I improvised names, because at that time I had no other bird literature than the little bird cards that came in baking soda packages. It was high adventure to look into every bird nest I found, whether it meant climbing a tree or finding a ground nest by chance.

Several years later, at the prompting of my freshman English teacher, Miss Faye Hamilton, I had the thrilling experience of discovering eight bird books in the Albert Lea High School library. I devoured those volumes and gloried in portraits, life histories and names of birds I had known so well from early boyhood. There were also a great many other birds that I had not seen. I listed them all and copied the classification tables for further study.

Through the years I have, for my own enjoyment, remained keenly aware of the presence of birds. It doesn't take much of a chirp to attract my attention regardless of what I happen to be doing. In my haphazard way I have now acquired a considerable life list of the birds of this area. New birds are getting scarce.

1962 started out very well, birdwise, with the Bohemian waxwing in January and the Townsend's solitaire in February. It doesn't often happen that I chalk up two new birds before spring.

The other day I was looking over a check list of Iowa birds, which included all species reliably reported in the last twenty years. Of the 279 species listed, there were 36 that I had never seen. Of the 286 species listed in a pamphlet published by the Minnesota Museum of Natural History, 41 have escaped my notice. It is not too surprising that I have missed seeing such extreme rarities as the gyrfalcon, swallow-tailed kite, avocet, western grebe, great gray owl, Audubon's and hooded warblers. What bothers me is that my unseen list also includes such inexcusable ones as the Lincoln sparrow, orchard oriole and Philadelphia vireo. While talking to Dr. O. S. Pettingill on one of his visits to Albert Lea on an Audubon Screen Tour appearance, I ventured the thought that perhaps I had actually seen Lincoln sparrows and had mistaken them for song sparrows. "Oh, no," he replied. "You would recognize the Lincoln sparrow. Look for the lead-colored back." That was two years ago, and the Lincoln sparrow still eludes me. On several M.O.U. field trips someone in the group has seen an orchard oriole, but never when I was at hand. Last year at Whitewater State Park I talked with some birders who had been watching an orchard oriole just before I met them. We searched for a while without any luck. Then my group went on to another area. Later, the same birders said they had seen the elusive bird again shortly after I left. How partial can a bird be?

... *Blizzard companions*

June, 1962

This year the weather played an April fool prank on a lot of people in this area and also a number of feathered friends. March left us as peacefully as "a lamb." But the freak blizzard that greeted us early on the morning of April 1 piled snowdrifts two feet deep in several places on our yard. Although the north wind was still howling at noon, there was a small spot on the south side of our house where the snow had thawed to expose a few square yards of bare ground. Any spot of bare ground in a snow-covered landscape attracts birds, especially if they are hungry. And what bird wouldn't be hungry by noon on a day like this?

When I looked out our kitchen window after dinner I saw a concentration of birds representing ten species, including winter residents, summer residents and transients. All were intent on searching for food — each in its own way — and were getting along peacefully. Most numerous in the party were the English sparrows that have been helping themselves to plenty of food in my corncrib and granary all winter. Perhaps they were seeking variety of menu, or just the company of seasonal newcomers. Next in number were the slate-colored juncos, industriously scratching for hidden seeds. Two male bronzed grackles were busy turning over last fall's leaves. Seizing a leaf with their beak, they would fling it vigorously aside and search for any chance morsel that might have been hidden beneath. The three starlings walking rapidly about did not turn any leaves but searched the ground intently for exposed tidbits. A robin hopped about in chesty dignity and occasionally cocked its head, then jabbed its beak into the ground in hopes of finding an earthworm. It did not find any while I was watching.

In the group was a lone tree sparrow that had not yet left for its summer home on the arctic timberline. A song sparrow that for several days had been singing from his chosen territory along a weedy fencerow down past the hog yard joined the group in the snowless area near our back porch. A male cardinal that has been our frequent visitor this winter came, perhaps out of a curiosity to see what was going on. At first he perched in the lilac bush, but soon dropped down to join the food searchers on the ground. The hardest searcher of all was a fox sparrow, richly clad with rusty-brown back and tail and heavily streaked breast. Jumping up to kick back with both feet at once, he would send the leaves flying, sometimes as much as two feet. These fellows are usually so shy when migrating through that I have to be satisfied with seeing an occasional flash of rusty plumage among the weeds or hearing a snatch of song that I have learned to recognize as that of a fox sparrow. I think theirs is the sweetest-sounding of all the sparrow songs I know. This spring, for some reason, fox sparrows have been more numerous and less shy, even coming close to our house to scratch for food. Although they have still been very alert, we have been able to see them at close range by looking through our windows.

For a while I thought that this completed the list of species. But then I noticed a stranger at the far edge of the bare spot. He seemed to be watching rather than taking part. Soon, however, the bird took wing and alighted near the porch. At this close range I had no trouble in recognizing him as a hermit thrush. This gifted singer — sometimes referred to as American nightingale — does not vocalize during migration. My thoughts went back to the time that I heard one sing in Nerstrand Woods. While my thoughts were wandering, the little thrush suddenly drove its beak into the ground to seize an earthworm. It was a small one to be sure, but it stretched out to about four inches before it let go its hold on the ground. The worm's sudden release set the thrush back on its tail. But the bird seemed to relish the meal.

I, for one, could have managed quite well without this April snow. But since it had to come I am glad that it served to concentrate these birds outside my window. However, I cannot help wondering about the welfare of the two bluebirds I saw on the highline on March 27th.

Today — April 18 — promises to be a pleasant spring day — and it's about time. When April 20 is so near, we farmers get anxious to be in the fields. There are no fox sparrows or tree sparrows outside my den window. Their migration schedule has taken them farther north. Under the juniper tree, however, is the first white-throated sparrow of the season. On the trunk of the juniper is another bird that probably doesn't suspect that I am watching him. The elusive yellow-bellied sapsucker is picking at the bark and hitching himself down the trunk in reverse. Yesterday I saw a fly. And that means that swallows will soon be back. With the ice clearing from our lakes the terns will be back to spear minnows. Yes! Bird arrivals will be crowding each other as we approach the glorious birding month of May. I can hardly wait for May 19 and 20 when M.O.U. birders will gather at Madison in Lac Qui Parle County. This will be my first experience with birding in western Minnesota.

This article, so far, was to have appeared in last month's issue but was a casualty in competition with last minute ads, so it appears dated. Since that time I have seen enough birds to fill several columns. I might mention a few of them if the editor will grant me space.

On April 22 all the ice had disappeared from Pickerel Lake and Forster's terns, as predicted, were back to spear minnows. On April 24 I went out to check my fields for possible spring work, and encountered a flock of about 100 Lapland longspurs. On April 26 I saw seven American pipits in a field where I was discing. There was a great movement of these ground-loving tail-bobbers on May 4. They were going through by the dozens. On that day I also saw three upland plovers back from Argentina. From the hay field came the insect-like song of the first grasshopper sparrow.

May 10 brought rain and a halt in field operations, but not in bird arrivals. While working about the yard I saw nine species of warblers, a ruby-crowned kinglet and a hermit thrush. The warblers were the magnolia, chestnut-sided, black and white, blackpoll, yellow, orange-crowned, Nashville, redstart, and that rare one — the blue-winged. May 11 brought the rose-breasted grosbeak and bobolink, but no additional warblers. May 12 brought five new species: least flycatcher, easter kingbird, chimney swift, Wilson's warbler and Tennessee warbler. That night I stepped outside my house after dark and heard a warbler wave in transit. The air overhead was filled with the faint lisps of small birds flying in pitch darkness. It is thought that they maintain their formation by means of their voices. On Sunday morning, May 13, the trees and shrubbery about our yard were alive with warblers. Especially numerous were the redstarts and Tennessee warblers. But there were others too: yellowthroats, Wilson's — and that beautiful rarity — a male parula warbler. It was the second one that I had ever seen. A female bay-breasted warbler, a crested flycatcher and several olive-backed thrushes completed this Sunday's list. It has been a long time since I could count half a dozen warblers in a single tree at one time.

...*Birding in western Minnesota*

July, 1962

On Saturday morning, May 19, my wife and I motored to Madison, Minnesota, to attend the spring meeting of the Minnesota Ornithologists Union. Since the distance from Albert Lea is well over 200 miles we had originally planned to drive there on Friday afternoon in order to be on hand for any scheduled field trip early the following morning. As it turned out, however, the unfavorable weather this spring so hampered field work that for a time I wondered if we would get to Madison at all. When Friday arrived the weather was ideal for field work, so I stayed home and planted corn all day. That evening it rained quite heavily again. It was 2 o'clock Saturday morning before we started out. It was a pleasant drive. I heartily recommend this time of day for highway travel. There were a few big trucks on the road, but we saw no cars until we were very near our destination.

As we pulled into Madison, a couple of familiar-looking figures crossing the street proved to be two veteran birding acquaintances from Duluth. We asked them to hop aboard and drove the remaining few blocks to M.O.U. headquarters in the basement of Faith Lutheran Church where we met our hosts. We were handed maps of Lac Qui Parle County, on which had been marked with crayon the best birding areas and routes to follow. The most popular area we were told was Salt Lake, which was about 15 miles west of Madison on the South Dakota line. We were told that rubber footwear would be necessary at Salt Lake. We found this to be accurate advice.

On the way to Salt Lake we saw a large hawk perched on the ground at the edge of the road. It seemed quite unconcerned while we watched it from only a few car lengths away. When it finally took off someone called it a Krider's hawk, but I doubt this, since I did not see any white feathers on it. Salt Lake was a wonderful birding area. We had chosen Madison for our meeting place in order to see shore birds. And here they were in abundance and variety! I added four species to my life list — all at Salt Lake. The first thing that caught my attention was the flight song of the willet — a loud, continuous chant with a whip-poor-will-like quality, "che-wee-willet, che-wee-willet, che-wee-willet." At times the call was loud and clear. Then it became faint, though audible. The bird came close enough for me to see the plumage markings, even without using binoculars. The flashing black and white wing pattern was unmistakable. I had seen a willet once before, but this was the first time I had heard its song.

Far off along the shore and approaching us were four birders whom I knew. They appeared bent on banding shore birds. I started out to meet them and was soon surrounded by a group of avocets. I had never before seen these large, chicken-sized, black and white shore birds with pinkish neck and long upturned beak. I became so absorbed with watching them that I almost walked into one of the bander's mist nets. The hopeful banders were herding quite a collection of shore birds toward the mist nets, but the only reward for their efforts was one Savannah sparrow.

Toward the west end of the lake was a long, narrow reef crowded with shore birds. By using spotting scopes we could single out any species we were interested in and take turns observing it. Here Hudsonian godwits and marbled godwits stood side by side for our comparison. I had had a fleeting glimpse of a Hudsonian godwit at Whitewater State Park in 1959, but the marbled godwit was a new bird on my list. I had seen one ruddy turnstone at Frontenac in 1952, but at Salt Lake this species was very numerous and could be seen at close range among the sanderlings. One of the professional ornithologists present informed us that turnstones and sanderlings were often seen together and were the most universal of birds, being found in every part of the world. The dunlin (or red-backed) sandpiper was also a new bird on my list. When the ornithologist called our attention to a flock of stilt sandpipers (another new bird for me) I got a look at them through my binoculars. But I was disappointed when they took flight just before my turn at the spotting scope.

There was just enough time before the noon meal to visit the tree nursery at the edge of town where we were told there were many birds nesting. I was particularly interested to find a grackle nest and a mourning dove nest near each other in a small spruce tree. The nests were no more than 18 inches apart, yet everything was peaceful. The grackle nest contained eggs and the mourning dove nest had one egg and one unharmed nestling. Apparently the grackle is not the vicious villain it is often thought to be.

In the afternoon we went to Marsh Lake where we saw nests of the long-billed marsh wren and spied a number of American egrets. Here we encountered two very excited birders from Minneapolis who claimed to have seen the highly unusual Bahama pintail duck in a small lake north of Madison. There was much good-natured banter about this for the remainder of our stay there, especially downtown at breakfast on Sunday morning. But that will have to wait because this article is too long now.

...Birding in western Minnesota

August, 1962

Concerning our experiences at the M.O.U. field trip at Madison, Minnesota, you will remember that last month's column concluded with our meeting the two enthusiastic birders who claimed to have seen a Bahama pintail. We must have looked skeptical because they were quick to assure us that they had professional witnesses. After leaving them we spent the remainder of the afternoon meandering in a southeasterly direction, following as closely as possible the shoreline of Marsh Lake and Lac Qui Parle Lake. We stopped at the wildlife sanctuary dam to see the white pelicans that stayed close by, despite the presence of many fishermen. Our route sometimes took us away from shore into farming areas. At one point we flushed a mysterious shore bird in a pasture. We ascertained that it was not an upland plover. But the bird was not very cooperative, so we failed to make sure of its proper identity. A little later we did see several upland plovers at close range in another pasture. We stopped the car again when I caught sight of a skunk ambling along minding its own business. While we were watching it (from a safe distance) two Albert Lea friends joined us to ask what we were up to. I pointed out our four-footed friend, that by now was aware of our presence and was making all possible haste to get elsewhere, when one of the birders pointed and asked me to identify a bird that he just heard. The bird was considerate enough to sing a couple more ditties and, although the sound was not a typical song, I recognized the voice as that of a field sparrow.

After a day of strenuous birding everyone was eager for the sumptuous meal prepared by the ladies of Faith Lutheran Church. When two of our new M.O.U. officers were exchanging appreciative remarks about the delicious fried chicken, someone asked them if they realized that they were eating a bird. During the meeting that followed, one of the ornithologists was asked to comment on the Bahama pintail sighting, since he was one of the professional witnesses referred to. By now everyone had heard much about the strange observation, so there was laughter when he did not confirm the bird's identity but, rather, referred to it as an odd duck whose plumage pattern didn't exactly fit any species.

It was late when my wife and I left the group. We were weary from the long, strenuous day's activities and were getting ready for bed when we heard a loud knock at the door. We recognized the voices of the two birders who had claimed the unusual sighting. They were shouting: "We have found the picture of the Bahama pintail and want you to take a look at it." So we had another brief session before we could call it a day.

At breakfast on Sunday morning there was great excitement and the topic was, of course, the Bahama pintail. The two birders, each with a bird guide in hand, were going from one person to the next pointing to the picture and quoting from the description while one after another of the birders would get up for another look. It was hard to know who had been served and who hadn't. The waiter made his way carefully and at times seemed confused. After that session there was but one place to head for after breakfast. There must have been a similar session at another restaurant because when we reached the lake that had supposedly harbored the mysterious duck, there was already a gathering. Some of the birders had the best of optical equipment. We saw many ducks and a western grebe (a new one on my list) — but no Bahama pintail. At last, weary of the fruitless search, we headed for Salt Lake again where we observed the many species of shorebirds until noon. We then headed homeward, eating our boxed lunch on the way.

On my first day in the field after returning from Madison I was thrilled to find bluebirds occupying one of my bluebird houses. After a year of complete bluebird absence it was pleasant to see and hear them about our farm again. This pair is certainly doing their best to boost the bluebird population. They successfully reared five young in the first brood, four in the second brood and now, July 16, have three eggs for a third brood. Another pair are old fashioned enough to be nesting in a hollow post, and have fared badly in the rainy weather because there is no roof on their apartment. They started late with a clutch of five eggs. After a three inch rain I found only four eggs. Later, there were only three. But now there are three youngsters who are doing fine.

Even though it is only July, fall is on the way. I encountered a solitary sandpiper by a water puddle in my cornfield and heard the telltale "whee-oodle-ee" song of a southward bound greater yellowlegs.

...*Anting*

September, 1962

On July 4th I had the good fortune to see, for the first time, that mysterious and rarely observed bird behavior called anting. As I looked out across the yard from our kitchen window I saw a blue jay acting rather strangely. While perched on the ground at the edge of our lawn the bird was preening its wing feathers very excitedly. Each time before stroking a wing feather with its beak it picked at something on the ground. Although I had not seen this peculiar bird ritual before, I had heard and read about it. The longer I watched the blue jay the more certain I was that it was picking up ants to stroke its feathers with. So entranced was the bird with its activity that at times it would stoop down to stroke the side of its head and neck against the ground much like a cat will do with catnip.

When someone opened the door to step out onto the porch the blue jay came to its senses and took off. I went out to look at the spot where the bird had been performing and found that an ant hill had been cut into by the rotary lawn mower. The ants were in confusion on the surface, perhaps trying to repair the damage to their abode. The blue jay did not come back, but a short time later a robin came to watch the busy ants and, as if being seized by a similar spell, picked at the ground and stroked a wing feather, but left after a few gestures. The disturbed ant hill must have been quite an attraction because when I looked out the window some time later four starlings were all busily anting at the same time and getting in each other's way.

Although anting has been known since Audubon's time few people have observed it in the wild. Because anting is so rarely encountered — or at least not recognized as such — study of the strange behavior has been difficult. By using high speed flash photography ornithologists have pretty well established how birds go about anting, but have found no explanation for the ornithological puzzle of why birds engage in this strange behavior. Many theories have been advanced, including the ridiculous suggestions that birds place ants under their feathers as a source of food during migration. Some ornithologists think the performance is a delousing process, while others feel that the formic acid ejected by ants acts as a cosmetic. Another guess is that birds stroke ants against their feathers to remove some of the formic acid before the ants are eaten. Some believe it is done purely for pleasure, and this may be true because in the process birds do seem to experience a trance-like ecstasy. Whatever the reason, the performance is amusing to watch.

While goldenrod, purple asters, black-eyed Susan and horsemint adorn untrampled areas birds are busy packing their luggage for the trip south. A little extra fat and — especially for the young — conditioning of the muscles is all the luggage they need. While swathing oats I found bobolinks feeding among the grain. Over the alfalfa field were swarms of purple martins and black terns feeding on flying insects. My ten acre woods is a great gathering place in August for fruit-loving birds, and well they may lay claim to the harvest there since they have been the planters. There are grapes, chokecherries, black cherries, bittersweet, gray dogwood and black elderberries. One may see as many as a dozen catbirds at the same time as well as thrashers and oodles of robins. Flickers and red-headed woodpeckers also have a sweet tooth this month. And, of course, the fifteen bluebirds which grew up here this summer are in their glory. I see them every day, in the woods, about the farm and often up around the house.

While working late at manure hauling one evening I saw a great horned owl leaving the woods for its evening hunt. The next day an immature red-tailed hawk came out of the woods and plunged into the alfalfa. Whatever it was after must have eluded its grasp because the big buteo arose again without any prey and flew over to a post, where it remained until my tractor was within two rods, then took off for a lesiurely circle overhead. One morning as I came by the woods a doe dashed from the cornfield into the shrubbery just ahead of the tractor. While swathing wheat late one evening I came upon a fawn that stopped grazing to watch me and the machinery approaching. I knew that this doe and fawn were living in my woods long before I saw them because I often saw their tracks side by side. There was also the telltale nipping of corn leaves along their habitual path between my woods and their watering place at Upper Twin Lake.

September will be hawk migration time again and hawk-watchers will be heading for that mecca, the Duluth skyline drive, from which point an estimated 20,000 hawks were seen on one day last year. September 15 and 16 will be the big weekend gathering, with dinner downtown for gregarious birders. Won't you join us?

... *The ovenbird and other visitors*

October, 1962

A sharp-shinned hawk flying southward over our farm on September 12th reminded me of the annual hawk count at Duluth. The official M.O.U. hawk watch, originally scheduled for September 15-16, was changed to the following weekend, so a report on that project will have to wait until next month. It should be interesting to watch the hawk migration at this later time because the pattern of hawk movement starts with the smaller hawks and brings the larger species as the season advances.

Although Duluth is a favorite spot for seeing the fall hawk migration, one need not go that far to see many of the smaller wayfarers. I need only look out a window or step into the windbreak west of our home. On one of those unseasonably cold days in the latter part of August it was necessary to light the furnace to take the chill out of our house. With our type of furnace, that meant a trip to the ash pile. When I emptied the bucket of ashes a small bird flew up suddenly into a nearby tree. The startled visitor paused only a moment, but it was long enough for me to see that this was an ovenbird. The ovenbird is a ground-loving bird which spends most of its time walking about on the leaf-covered ground in a dense woodland habitat. It renders its emphatic, accented spring song from the ground. It also builds its nest on the ground. This bird gets its name from its nest. Bird namers thought the domed nest looked like a dutch oven.

When startled, this ground-dwelling member of the warbler family habitually flies up into a tree to get a look at the intruder before taking off for a safer place. While birding with a Mankato, Minnesota, friend at the Audubon Nature Center of Connecticut in August 1953, we heard a bird song that sounded something like that of an ovenbird. When we checked with the director of the Nature Center he seemed doubtful at first, since ovenbirds do not usually sing in the fall. After pondering for a moment he asked what happened to the bird when we tried to get a better look at it. When I replied that the bird flew up into a tree for a quick look at us before disappearing, he quickly agreed that the bird must indeed have been an ovenbird.

One day last spring a man stopped in to inquire about buying some hay. During our conversation he pointed westward and asked when I was going to clean out that mess. He was referring to the portion of our windbreak that is fenced to keep the sheep from grazing there. Shocked at his suggestion, I asked him why he thought I should cut down the trees and shrubbery and live on a wind-swept knoll?

"To let people see your house," he replied. He seemed to think that insulated walls would make a windbreak un-necessary. I did not follow his suggestion because, in addition to its value as a windbreak, the thicket is my private bird sanc-tuary. During spring and fall migration I never know what surprise awaits me in this readily accessible spot. It is a favorite stopping place for warblers. This spring I was greeted by that rare gem, a colorful male parula warbler. Last spring it was an orange-crowned warbler at close range. This fall there has been a run of flycatchers, least flycatchers and phoebes. In September the crested flycatcher kept coming out of the thicket to do some flycatching from the lawn fence south of our house. During the summer there are the usual birds nesting here. One summer we were favored with a pair of wood-pewees that kept us entertained with their peaceful song.

While putting a load of furnace wood into the basement the other day, a blue jay came to scold me. The rascal seemed very upset about what I was doing. But, scolding or not, I was glad to hear him and to see him so near me. So many of the fall birds are rather quiet. But leave it to the blue jay to enliven the autumn woods with its noisy calls, flashy color and clowning antics.

After the blue jay episode I heard an unmistakable song of bluebirds nearby. I looked skyward, but saw only swallows hawking insects. Soon I spied a number of bluebirds perched in the branches of the large elm on our lawn. Every little while one would fly out to catch an insect in flycatcher fashion. Skulking in the shadows and sometimes venturing out on the lawn — probably in search of the numerous crickets — was a brown thrasher quietly feeding and casting wary looks in my direction. Though quiet at this time of year the brown thrasher, richly clad in cinnamon brown, is one of the most gifted of springtime songsters. Its varied repertoire is delightful music to be awakened by at corn planting time. While checking my tomatoes one day I saw a yellow-billed cuckoo in a walnut tree, attracted no doubt by those pesky caterpillars, of which cuckoos are so fond. The call of the cuckoo was one of the mysterious sounds of my early boyhood days. In their own shy, leisurely way cuckoos are also interesting and beautiful birds.

At the time of this writing I am also not sure if I can take time off from plowing to make the trip to Duluth. This has been a most frustrating year for getting farm field work done. This fall's deluge of rain has just now seeped into the ground enough to permit plowing, so I am now out there every day with the meadow larks, vesper sparrows and a few gulls.

. . . *Autumn guests*

Almost every spring and fall the migrating gulls come to follow my plow. But never have I seen so many gulls in one flock as on September 20th. The first 300 or so dropped in to circle around the tractor, but apparently weren't very hungry, since they seldom alighted in the plowing. Soon I noticed a much larger flock hovering over a neighbor's field. Before long, all of these came over to join me. The flock now may have numbered more than 1,200 birds. The air seemed full of these graceful birds, who were circling and criss-crossing in flight, some flying with their gray backs toward me, while others turned to show their white underplumage. All were Franklin's gulls. They stayed with me for about two hours.

Throughout October the woods, fencerows and thickets were full of white-throated sparrows. At any time of day one could hear their modest "tsee" call and, whenever disturbed, their louder call note. At times also, one could catch a bit of their spring song. They were numerous in my corn fields where they were feeding on weed seeds that should not have been there, but were.

November 7th was a disagreeable day, with a cold northwest wind and stinging snow crystals. Whenever I neared the woods with my cornpicker a flurry of juncos arose from among the cornstalks and disappeared among the trees. The next day was sunny and pleasant. Flocks of red-winged blackbirds and grackles came from the southwest, where I assumed they had spent the night roosting among the cattails around Upper Twin Lake. Flying directly overhead as I was plowing, they settled in the woods until the trees looked as if they had sprouted black leaves.

I could hear their chorus of song above the noise of the tractor. Later, they collected admission for their concert by feeding on corn that the cornpicker had wasted.

As if to let me know that we were not yet relegated to the strictly winter birds, an American pipit came to spend the afternoon with me. Its fall plumage was browner than its spring attire, but its jerky flight and tail-bobbing mannerism easily betrayed its identity. This slender relative of the larks seemed to enjoy perching on the moist soil that had been turned up by my plow. Each time I came near, it flew to the opposite side of the plowed field. Toward evening the pipit took off southward. Soon after the pipit left, another small bird came to perch among the cornstalks. I came close enough to see that it was a Savannah sparrow. From the depths of the woods came the telltale "churd, churd" call of a red-bellied woodpecker. On November 8th I saw two pheasant roosters fighting. I have seen plenty of springtime pheasant fights, but this is an odd time of year for this type of behavior. Perhaps they were unhappy with the election returns.

There is much that is pleasant in November. Just think. No mosquitoes to slap and no flies buzzing around. There is beauty in the pattern of those bare-boughed trees. And the leaves are pleasant to see and walk amongst. November also finds the ripe, colorful fruits of woodland plants adding their beauty to a walk in the woods. Birds are also easier to see without the obstructing foliage.

What would autumn be like without the scream of that crested dandy, the blue jay? Now that the cardinal has made itself at home in this area, our colorful jay has a strong competitor in formal dress, crest and all. Although the cardinal's "whist" is no match for the blue jay's sharp "teah," come spring the song of the cardinal is one of the most thrilling bird songs to hear.

From my windbreak the other day came the call of that shy, elusive fellow, the yellow-bellied sapsucker. For a long time this bird had me stumped. But I know its voice now, and am aware of its presence whenever it makes a sound. While filling the tractor tank with gas one day I heard a "quank" overhead and looked up to catch a glimpse of the bird. I saw the rusty breast and the telltale dark line through the eye before the bird took off. The red-breasted nuthatch is a rare sight this far south. I would have enjoyed a more prolonged look at it but the nuthatch thought otherwise.

...*The hawk count*

December, 1962

As things turned out, I did get to the M.O.U. hawk count at Duluth. But the decision to go was not made until half an hour before bus time on September 21. Despite the ominous look of the sky, my plowing proceeded without interruption until noon. I even enjoyed the beauty of the cloud formation — as long as the scattered showers did not strike me. After the noon meal, however, there were a few moments' hesitation because the rain was becoming a little more than a drizzle. When it suddenly became a downpour there was a wild scramble to get ready. Half an hour later I was on the bus bound for Minneapolis, where I joined the Minneapolis group on a chartered bus for Duluth. There is always good fellowship when birders get together, and nowhere is there a better opportunity for it than on a chartered bus. I met several new birders.

From the standpoint of hawk sightings, the weekend was a flop. Only 29 hawks were seen during the entire two-day watch. Whatever the reason, they just weren't flying. Thanks to the presence of the Academy of Science people, Hawk Hill thronged with watchers as never before; 187 people were served at the Saturday evening banquet. It was humiliating for the Duluth people, who had postponed the M.O.U. hawk watch for a week to make it coincide with the Academy of Science meeting, especially since an estimated 10,000 hawks had been recorded on the previous weekend. There was some consolation in that two of the 29 hawks were ospreys and one a mature bald eagle, sailing slowly and majestically overhead. But, hawks or no hawks, everyone enjoyed hobnobbing with kindred souls.

The wind coming off the lake was raw and chilly. Having been to Hawk Hill on several occasions, I came prepared. I wore a warm, knee-length, fur-lined corduroy overcoat. But some were not so fortunate. As the morning wore on, one of the chilly birders nudged me and said he felt like taking a walk to warm up. A short way down the road we met a Minneapolis Bird Club couple who had been on a hike along the Lester River for several miles. They urged us to take a similar hike to enjoy the colorful foliage. We were soon distracted, however, by a strange yellow bird. There we stood. Four experienced birders with binoculars, and no bird guide for checking autumn plumage detail. The lady suggested it might be a male goldfinch in winter plumage. But it was the size of an oriole. When the bird flew to another tree she still thought it might be a goldfinch, and reminded me that size can be misleading at a distance. I countered with the observation that it did not fly like a goldfinch and that it did not say "per-chic-o-ree."

"Oh! That's right," she replied. "It didn't have undulating flight and it didn't say 'per-chic-o-ree.' " We watched the bird for several minutes. But when it took off, about all we agreed upon was that it was a very yellow bird about the size of an oriole, but that it was no oriole since it had no wing bars.

When this lady joined our group in the lobby of Hotel Arrowhead the next morning she dropped a bombshell by announcing that the bird we had seen Saturday morning was a female summer tanager. She had found the exact picture of it among some Audubon bird cards she happened to have along. When we got to Hawk Hill I asked one of the professional ornithologists about the possibility of having seen a summer tanager. He replied that it was highly unusual but was possible, since that species had been collected there. A Minneapolis birder, who is real particular about bird identity, told me that if I wanted the opinion of a real skeptic I should ask the other professional ornithologist present. Opening the bird guide to the tanager page, the ornithologist asked if I was sure the bird was not a scarlet tanager in winter plumage? When I said I was positive, he made a number of confusing suggestions, then winked at me and said he was only kidding. My Minneapolis friend let me know that he was disappointed with me for not calling him so he could get a look at the unusual bird, and I felt like a heel for not thinking of doing so, since we had been within calling distance.

The busload of birders next went up the north shore to Gooseberry Falls State Park where we found an excellent birding area. We saw a Lapland longspur walking about only a few feet away. Along the shore were a number of American pipits. The place was alive with cedar waxwings feeding on mountain ash berries. We also spotted a pine siskin, red-eyed vireos, white-crowned sparrows, myrtle warblers, golden-crowned kinglets and redstarts, as well as many of the more common birds. We reluctantly left Gooseberry Falls to head for Minnesota Point, where the only shore birds we saw were a number of black-bellied plovers. We did see a number of small birds that we hadn't seen earlier, including a fox sparrow, a brown creeper and a hermit thrush. Four o'clock came quickly and soon we were heading homeward over the new bridge between Duluth and Superior and then down the beautifully bordered Highway 35 to Minneapolis.

...*The chickadees*

January, 1963

On the National Audubon Society's Christmas greeting card, bird artist Don R. Eckelberry has pictured three black-capped chickadees perched on the stems of a Japanese barberry bush in three of the many characteristic poses that these active feathered sprites can assume. To chickadees, energetically flitting about in search of tiny bits of food — like insect eggs — it seems to make little difference whether they perch in the conventional way or hang upside down under a twig. These familiar, confiding members of the titmouse family, with their small, stubby bills and proportionally long tails, are plainly but neatly dressed in black, gray and white. What they lack in flashy color, however, they more than make up for in nimble activity and talkativeness. Who has not heard the cheerful, friendly "chick-adee-dee-dee" of these sociable birds? At times they drop the first two syllables, leaving their song a mere "dee-dee-dee-dee-dee." What can be more appealing than a family of young chickadees following their parents and begging for food? The chickadee's whistled springtime mating call, "phe-bee," is often mistaken for the song of some other bird.

Chickadees usually nest in a deserted woodpecker hole. But sometimes, if they find a thoroughly decayed tree or stub, they excavate their own nesting cavity. When they do this they carry each fragment of wood to a safe distance, so as not to leave any telltale evidence of their nesting location. During the fall and winter months chickadees form small roving bands, which may also include other small woodland birds like nuthatches, kinglets, downy woodpeckers and brown creepers. When I go into the woods to work up firewood, chickadees are quick to show

up. They seem to know that firewood is usually made from dead trees, which harbor many insects and larvae that they cannot get at without help. When the woodcutter stops to rest, the chickadees start inspecting the split wood and pieces of loose bark, where they are able to find much that is not readily seen by human eyes.

Undaunted by howling wind, bitter cold and snow, these hardy, self-confident busybodies meet their greatest hazard in sleet storms when ice coats trees and shrubs, concealing the insect eggs and pupae which make up the major portion of their winter food. Chickadees are versatile, however, and are quick to seek fatty food from any source. On one bleak winter day I watched a hungry squirrel sitting high up in a tree eating a walnut while directly under him a number of chickadees were feeding on tiny fragments of nutmeat that fell down on the crusted snow. Chickadees are probably the most readily observed of winter birds and are easily attracted to farmsteads and city dwellings by offerings of suet, pork rind, bread crumbs, doughnuts, nutmeats, peanut butter, cut squash seed, pumpkin seed, etc. Since chickadees are small they can be favored by making a feeder that will admit them but will keep out the bothersome house sparrows and greedy squirrels. A feeder like this is easily made from an ordinary fruit jar by removing the glass from the metal cover and cutting a chickadee-sized opening through the metal, leaving one side of the cut out portion intact so it can be bent outward for a perch, to make entrance easier. When the fruit jar is then mounted in a horizontal position chickadees, being trustful birds, will enter the jar to feed in peace.

Chickadees, through their continual eating of insects and larvae in summer and insect eggs and pupae in winter, are highly beneficial to man's economic interests. And they bring enjoyment to a great many people by coming readily to window feeders.

After the corn was all in the crib this fall the weather was such that I plowed most of my cornstalk ground before the ground froze. When I stopped to remove stalks that had plugged the plow I noticed that some of them had small holes through the outer shell, indicating the presence of European corn borers. I saw, also, that I was not the only one to make this discovery. There was a downy woodpecker somewhere in my cornfield every day, picking away at the cornstalks.

Mr. Roy Coy, who presented the Audubon lecture here on December 5, was an interesting man to visit with. He stayed at our house until afternoon the following day. Among many other things of interest, he told us about an old man in his home city of St. Jospeh, Missouri, who enjoyed watching birds. Apparently this man thought blue jays were mischievous enough that he could have a little fun at their expense. Taking a thread about five feet long, he would tie a peanut on one end of it and a piece of paper on the other end. When a blue jay would pick up the peanut and take off, the piece of paper would come fluttering after him while the confused bird looked back, first over one shoulder and then over the other. One time the paper end of the thread snarled around a clothesline, and the blue jay — stubbornly hanging onto the peanut — was drawn in a circle around the clothesline. When the bird let go, the peanut had momentum enough to continue around the clothesline in ever diminishing circles, while the old birdwatcher sat inside his window convulsed with laughter.

. . . Slate-colored junco

For a long-time birder some birds have strange associations. Whenever I see a slate-colored junco, for example, I am reminded of a kitchen episode that sent Mother into gales of laughter. She seldom laughed at my interest in birds. But there were times when she couldn't help doing so. Mother was a great hand at making baking powder biscuits and, for a family of eleven, that took some doing. It was interesting to watch her measuring out the baking powder. First, a tablespoon was heaped to a sharp point, then a generous additional amount was added. A can of baking powder didn't last very long. In contrast, it seemed to me that baking soda was always used too sparingly. Whenever Mother used any soda it was usually only one teaspoon, level full.

One day, while I was watching Mother preparing a biscuit batter, I offered the suggestion that she might try using baking soda instead of baking powder. That's when Mother's laughter burst. She realized, of course, that at my tender age I could not be expected to know that this change in the recipe would never do. But she also knew precisely why I had made the suggestion. Within every package of Arm and Hammer baking soda was a small card with a colored picture of a bird on one side and a story about the bird on the other side. And, for a youngster with a curiosity about birds, it took the "patience of Job" to wait for the opening of a new soda package.

I little realized at the moment what additional frustration I was in for. When at long last the next soda package was opened I was on hand when Mother took out the card, held it at arm's length to see, and remarked, "Huh! Juno!" This mispronunciation made me think that the card was about a new bird. I remember the eager anticipation with which I reached for the card and my keen disappointment in seeing that the card pictured a junco. When Mother asked me what was wrong, I told her I already had a junco card. For awhile I could not help holding the junco responsible for this frustrating coincidence.

The junco is the celebrated "Snowbird" of New England literature. Somewhere along the line the name was changed to junco — the name "junco" being taken from the Latin word *juncus,* which means seed. It isn't always clear to laymen why professional ornithologists change bird names from time to time. But I suppose there is a reason. Perhaps it is just a simple matter of majority rule.

The junco is a seed eater. In fact, it is a sparrow, even though its solid, slate-colored plumage does not in the least resemble the traditional sparrow. Juncos are cold weather birds that nest in the northern forests of fir and spruce. Some of them nest in the cooler life zones of mountainous areas farther south. The first slate-colored junco to appear at our place from the north this fall showed up on October 24th. It was well into November, however, before they appeared in considerable numbers. They came in waves. One day there might only be a few and the following morning there would be juncos everywhere — in the trees, on the ground all around the house, in the fence rows and in the fields near the woods. The birds gradually thinned out. Then, suddenly, the place was loaded with them again. At this season they feed on the ground where they find weed seeds and perhaps some fallen fruit. They fed in the fields where, despite my efforts, there are always plenty of weed seeds. They seemed to prefer staying near the woods where they could take cover when the machinery came near them.

Besides being the most numerous of our native sparrows, they are also the most confiding, especially when they feed around our dwellings. It is not unusual to see them clustered around our back porch, where they find some grain and ground feed that has been swept off the porch from the place I kick off my work rubbers. They seldom stay around our place after the arrival of heavy snow. In the spring they show up early. My records show the earliest arrivals on February 22 in 1959. But in 1961 their arrival was delayed until March 28th.

As is usually the case, there have been a number of tree sparrows among the junco flocks this fall. These active arctic visitors feed on the ground also, but are more likely than juncos to cling to tall weeds and feed among the seed heads. They are often seen jumping up from the ground to pick seeds from pigeon grass and from other plants sticking up through the snow. Today the thermometer registers far below zero and the ground is covered with drifted snow. I see no juncos. But there are still some tree sparrows around. One Sunday when we came home from church during the unseasonably warm weather of early January the tree sparrows were singing snatches of their spring song. Lately, however, their vocal offerings have been limited to an occasional "tseet."

... *Feeding winter birds*

March, 1963

At the January meeting of the Albert Lea Audubon Society several members complained about the scarcity of birds at their feeders. The weather was still mild at that time — and that may have had something to do with the reported scarcity — but there was a suspicion among some members that mosquito spraying had reduced the bird population in the city. I had been seeing most of the familiar winter birds around our farm home, but had not been providing them with any supplementary food since the weather warmed up last spring.

When the weather suddenly turned cold I tied a freshly-baked doughnut to a string and hung it near the juniper tree outside my window, but it attracted no attention whatever. Our old suet feeders were in a bad way, so I made a new one from a piece of four by four about a foot long, augering holes nearly to the center from all four sides and fastening a wire hook to one end. After filling all the holes with suet I hung the new feeder on a branch of the juniper tree so I could conveniently see the goings on from my den window.

The chickadees were the first to patronize the feeder. But the nuthatches and woodpeckers were not long in discovering the handout. On January 19th — a bitterly cold day — there were ten species of birds in or near that tree at the same time. Among the ones that fed on the suet, each had to await his turn because there was a well established peck order. The red-bellied wood-pecker had senior priority. Next in line were the male and female downy woodpeckers — one at a time — followed by the white-breasted nuthatches — one at a time. The chickadees were last in the peck order. They compensated for this lack of

rank by feeding on the waste pieces of suet that had dropped to the snow below the feeder.

We had put out some seeds and some pulp from a squash in a covered box feeder. When the nuthatches were out-ranked at the suet feeder they busied themselves by chiseling loose and carrying away squash seeds, one at a time. The busy chickadees also tried this, but could not do much with the frozen chunk. Perched on a snow-laden branch was a male cardinal, watching all the activity with apparent keen interest. There were still a few juncos and tree sparrows on the ground and, of course, the ever-present house sparrows. We were so intent on watching the small birds that for a time we did not notice a ring-necked pheasant rooster perched on a branch close to the trunk of the juniper. He had likely spent the night there and was in no hurry to leave.

But what about the unappreciated doughnut? For two weeks it hung there untouched. Then one day the nuthatches and chickadees both worked at it. I did not notice which of the two species made the first venture, but they did eat away a portion of it. The next day, however, the eaten area was covered with snow, and again the doughnut hung untouched. When I looked out from my bedroom window a few mornings later the doughnut had mysteriously disappeared. Had one of my squirrels been up for breakfast so early, or had our wayward tomcat finally spotted the treasure? There were no telltale tracks.

There are a great many kinds of bird feeders on the market, including a number of ridiculous ones. Birds respond just as readily to simple homemade feeders as to fancy expensive ones. The other day an Albert Lea lady was telling me that she had used an old wash boiler cover fastened in an inverted position in a lilac bush near the house. This made an excellent container for chick feed or any other food for birds. She also put feed on the ground and was fortunate last winter to have a horned lark feeding there. These open-country field birds seldom come to bird feeders.

On February 10th, when my wife and I were on our way to join other members of the Albert Lea Audubon Society for a field trip to the Buckeye Woods, we saw a number of horned larks on the gravel road near Conger. There were about a dozen in one flock and others individually or in groups of two or three. At Buckeye Woods the birders were numerous but the birds were few. Someone said that they had seen one chickadee, but I had not seen it. Just as we were about to leave the woods another bird took flight and disappeared among the trees. I guessed that it was a downy woodpecker, but someone else thought it was a nuthatch. We did not pursue the bird, or even lift a binocular, because it was four o'clock and time to gather at the home of our host for lunch, where we saw more birds at a feeder outside the kitchen window than on our snow-stomping trip. We were thirty-eight people for lunch, including a ten-month-old girl, who had some misgivings concerning the birders at first, but later proved to be the belle of the party.

...*Texas, Florida* ... *Trinidad?*

When Audubon Screen Tour speaker Robert C. Hermes was in Albert Lea on February 24th I had the pleasure of visiting with him for about three hours before lecture time. The subject of birds came up, quite normally, and Mr. Hermes suggested that I take a trip to Trinidad. That small island (50 x 30 miles) just off the northeast coast of Venezuela has, according to Mr. Hermes, about 740 species of birds, many of which cannot be found anywhere else in the world. During the time that Mr. Hermes was engaged in making wildlife films in Venezuela he visited Trinidad and found it a birder's paradise.

"The convenience of getting to remote areas is ideal," he explained. One citizen of Trinidad makes his living by using his car to conduct an economical passenger service between two towns at opposite ends of the island. A person can ride clear across Trinidad for 35 cents and get off or on at any point along the way. I agreed with Mr. Hermes that a trip to Trinidad would indeed be a delightful experience. But the distance and where-withal, being what they are, put the possibility of my taking such a pilgrimage into the realm of dreams.

Since the last meeting of the Albert Lea Audubon Society I have been dreaming about another birding area a little closer to home. I have enjoyed looking through a copy of Roger Tory Peterson's *Field Guide to the Birds of Texas*, graciously lent me by an Albert Lea lady. The book covers all the 542 species of Texas birds, which is almost twice the number of species to be found in Minnesota. Texas is so large and so located that it harbors both eastern and western birds, plus many species that spill over from Mexico.

In addition to all the good features of his other field guides, Mr. Peterson has included a discussion of each species within the state of Texas, so one can tell just where and when to look for any particular species. The book is a must for anyone who goes birding in Texas, where there are birds galore. But I dare say that the mileage will run much higher than it would in Trinidad.

During my boyhood days my oldest brother farmed for three years in the Texas Panhandle. It was always exciting for us youngsters to hear him tell about his Texas experiences when he came home for Christmas each year. Especially interesting were his experiences with prairie dogs, coyotes, rattlesnakes and the little owls that lived in holes in the ground. I now looked up the burrowing owl in Peterson's *Birds of Texas* and found that they breed in the Panhandle and west Texas. Ever since I first heard about the burrowing owl so long ago I have wanted to see and hear one of these open prairie predators. They can also be found in Florida, which is another place I have never been. I have a phonograph recording of the burrowing owl's call, so I should have no trouble locating the bird whenever I get to its whereabouts.

Last November the National Audubon Society's annual convention was held in Corpus Christi, Texas, a wonderful birding area, according to those who were there from Minnesota. Next November the convention will be at Miami, Florida, and I have an invitation from Mr. Hermes to come down at the time to his home at Homestead, Florida. "After all," he pleaded, "I have stayed at your house three times." However, I will very likely be busy harvesting corn again and dreaming about Florida, Texas, the burrowing owl — and possibly Trinidad.

The annual spring bird-counting field trip of the Minnesota Ornithologists Union will be in Winona, Minnesota, next May. Now there is an opportunity that I can take advantage of! That area is one of the best birding spots in Minnesota and is within easy driving distance. I hope to add some new birds to my life list and to renew my acquaintance with many familiar species.

Meanwhile, here at my farm I will be expecting to greet twenty or more winter absentees by the end of March and an additional thirty returnees by the first of May.

There is a thrill of delight accompanying the discovery of a bird one has never seen. But there is nothing to compare with the nostalgic tug of seeing or hearing a familiar bird that has been absent for awhile — the first spring robin on the lawn, the friendly, contralto notes of a bluebird, the bewitching yodel of a greater yellowlegs, the burst of blackbird song from the wind-break, the clear, varied whistle of the song sparrow, the scream of the killdeer, the loud "wick wick wick wick" of the flicker, the clamor of northbound geese and the circling of buteo hawks far overhead.

March is a good time to visit a lake to observe returning waterfowl. The ice thaws first along the shore and, since water-fowl like to be swimming, they will be confined to the narrow strip of open water along the shore where they can be seen at close range. Later in the season they will be seen swimming farther out on the lake. While there is ice some of the birds can also be seen walking about on it, where their markings can be seen to better advantage.

...The spring birds return

May, 1963

The coming of spring is so gradual that any definite starting time is only arbitrary. For farmers, I suppose, spring isn't really here until the fields are fit to work with tillage implements and, consequently, the date varies considerably from year to year. I usually have to wait until April 20th or later before venturing into the fields for spring work. However, this year I started discing on April 9th. Only once before during the thirty-three years I have farmed here have I started field work so early. In 1957 I also started discing on April 9th.

That was the year that I saw my first Lapland longspur in breeding plumage. I had seen great flocks of them in their plain, gray fall plumage, but the spring migrants had hitherto eluded me. To see migrating Lapland longspurs one must be in the fields where they perch and feed. Since this spring was again unseasonably early I naturally hoped to be in time to get a glimpse of these interesting open-country, ground-loving birds. In this I was not disappointed. On my first day in the fields I saw a flock of about thirty birds, but they were a little too far away for me to see their plumage pattern. On April 16th, however, I saw a male Lapland longspur in full springtime regalia. The bird was only a few feet from the tractor and appeared quite unafraid as I passed it. The black and chestnut plumage markings were plainly visible.

On April 16th I also saw my first American pipit of the season. I was a little surprised to see the pipit and longspur on the same day. The pipits usually wait until May before showing up. The earliest I had seen them was on April 26th in 1962. In 1955 I saw the first pipits on May 11th; in 1956 on May 16th;

1958 on May 5th and in 1960 on May 13th. The longspurs were probably the last of the birds passing through, while the lone pipit was no doubt in advance of the pipit migration.

Ordinarily, numerous Brewer's blackbirds are here by spring-work time, but on April 9th I saw only one. Their numbers have increased on succeeding days. It doesn't seem natural to be working in the fields without a number of these ardent worm-searchers tagging along.

The field mouse population is up this spring. Perhaps this is because I have been out there to see them before the predators have had time to thin them out. At any rate, I have been seeing an unusual number of the pesky rodents running about in my fields, especially when working late and using tractor lights. I often see half-grown ones, three or four at a time. I heard the great horned owls hooting in my woods one night, and was reminded that they must be living well with such an abundance of choice fare. The day shift predators have also been having a hey-day. A female sparrow hawk has been hovering over my fields every day and carrying off booty in her talons. I have not located her nesting site, but I hope it is somewhere near my fields. I can use the little falcon pair's help. Four crows, apparently a yet unbroken family from last year, have stopped by daily to harvest my mouse crop. A red-tailed hawk came to hunt mice on April 11th. I had hoped he would establish his residence here, but I haven't seen him since. So far no red-tails have laid claim to my woods this year. I will certainly miss their presence.

Fox sparrows have been scarce this spring. I heard a snatch of spring song from a fencerow one day but have not yet seen any of these birds. Last spring we were flooded with them. Such variation in bird migration makes birding all the more interesting. I suspect that the sparrows went through without stopping here. I am concerned about my bluebirds, however. I heard and saw one on April 2nd, but have not seen any since. Through correspondence with a fellow birder from Kentucky I have learned of the experience of an Iowa bluebird enthusiast who reported the presence of over 250 bluebird families on his personal bluebird house trail last summer. Considering the rarity of bluebirds in this vicinity as recently as six or seven years ago, this is an encouraging development.

I feel assured of flicker company this summer because a pair of yellow-shafted flickers have set up housekeeping in a dead poplar stub where a pair of red-headed woodpeckers held forth last year. The yellow-shafted flicker is an early bird acquaintance and brings back memories of birding experiences in my Iowa prairie farm home. It will be great to have flickers nesting so near my home again.

...*The annual May pageant*

This has been a good spring for getting field work done. Because of favorable conditions and favorable weather it has been go, go, go, dawn to dark, with scarcely a break. On May 8th, however, I had some time to listen to the birds in my woods. I didn't deliberately take time off to go birding. The brace rod on my harrow broke, which would necessitate a trip to a local welding shop. As often happens with farm machinery, a rusty bolt needed some relaxing with a blow torch before it would come unfastened and this meant I had to spend some time in the field near my ten-acre woods getting the broken harrow part free. There had been a half inch of rain during the night, so I was not wasting valuable field work time.

The woods were alive with birds that morning. I heard yellow warblers, blue-winged warblers, Tennessee warblers, redstarts, catbirds, rose-breasted grosbeaks, Baltimore orioles, least fly-catchers, blue jays, flickers, red-headed woodpeckers, a red-eyed vireo and an ovenbird. To make the morning even more pleasant I heard the warble of bluebirds. Several tree swallows were having a gabfest around one of my bluebird houses. Near the house perched a male bluebird in an attitude that left no doubt about who had taken possession of the nesting site. I hurried home after two extra nesting boxes and fastened them to nearby posts. The tree swallows promptly stopped giving the bluebirds a bad time. By the time I had finished working on my harrow both the new nesting boxes had been enthusiastically taken over by the tree swallows. By noon the fields were fit to work again. During the afternoon I enjoyed seeing dozens of American pipits going through. Groups of them perched on the ground, teetering their tails until my tractor approached them. Then they took off northward.

While planting corn on May 14th I heard bluebird voices when I stopped the planter at the end of the field near our farmstead. When I went after the fertilizer tank to replenish the planter a male bluebird took off from his perch atop the steering wheel of the fertilizer tank tractor. Two days later a pair of bluebirds were still staying around the same area while I was checking the sheep fence around the windbreak. I checked a bluebird house nearby that has been unoccupied for three years and found a neat bluebird nest in it. So I am now assured of at least two bluebird families this summer.

The secret is out. There are red-tailed hawks nesting in my woods again this year. The small fry tattled. When I got off my tractor to set the planter stake at the end of the field nearest the woods I heard the familiar sound of young hawks begging for food. How sly can red-tailed hawks be in keeping their residence a secret? I hadn't searched for a hawk nest, but had wondered about the presence of one all spring because I had not observed any hawk activity near the woods. I was glad to hear the young hawks advertising their appetite because field mice are still numerous — and a family of growing hawks can devour a great number of these rodents in a season.

There is a robin nest in the hackberry tree east of our house and another in the arborvitae north of our house. Two robins were searching for worms on our newly mowed lawn one day. One of them was finding three worms for every one the other one found. Suddenly the one finding the least worms dashed after the other one and there was a real fight. Was it a case of envy, or just a territorial boundary dispute? I came upon another robin nest in a small box elder tree in the hog yard. I long ago ceased climbing trees to look into robin nests, so it was pleasant to see this one at shoulder height where I could easily observe its four beautiful blue eggs. A couple of days later a mourning dove was startled from its nest in a small apple tree when I came too close while repairing sheep fence. I had not noticed the dove or its nest before the bird flew. And we are going to have nesting Baltimore orioles again this year in an elm tree near our house.

Eastern kingbirds are coming through. I saw the first one on May 9th. By the middle of May there were many of them along the fence rows and in the fields. I have seen as many as fifty at one time. They perch on fence posts, wires, weed stalks or on the ground while resting or looking for insects. Goldfinches are busy among our mulberry trees. The fruit is barely recognizable, but the goldfinches are already feasting on it.

While harrowing corn ground on May 15th a great number of black terns came to follow my implement. At first there was only one. But the word must have got around that the picking was good because presently there was a flock of these slate-winged birds hovering about me. It was amusing to see one of them mistake a weed sprout for a worm. Swooping down close to the tractor, the bird came within a few inches of a brightly-colored weed sprout before realizing its mistake and turning away. I notice that Forster's terns are again flying overhead with small fish in their beaks. I imagine there are young in the nests, wherever they are. I am tempted to don hip boots and go in search of tern nests, as I have yet to see one.

. . .*Spring field trip to Winona*

July, 1963

For their annual spring bird-counting field trip, members of the Minnesota Ornithologists Union gathered this year at Winona on the weekend of May 18-19 where they were guests of the Hiawatha Valley Bird Club. The Albert Lea Audubon Society was well represented, with fourteen members registered. Some of the birders had come to Winona on Friday night, but my wife and I started from Albert Lea at four o'clock Saturday morning. With perfect weather and with birds singing along the way we anticipated a weekend of excellent birding.

When we arrived at our headquarters — the Izaak Walton League cabin on Prairie Island — we were greeted by the songs of warbling vireos, yellow-throated vireos and Baltimore orioles in the treetops and by an Albert Lea couple all decked out in birding gear.

Our first venture was with a group bound for Knopp's Valley. Just as we reached this reportedly excellent birding area, heavy clouds rolled in from the north, blotting out the sunshine. And the accompanying strong wind turned Knopp's Valley into an icebox. After a birdless walk in the woods we all returned to our cars, wiping running noses and wishing we had brought along our sheepskin coats. A rose-breasted grosbeak and a ruby-throated hummingbird perched obligingly in a dead, fallen tree for all to see. As we drove slowly back to the cabin we saw an eastern meadow lark, a bobolink, several vesper sparrows, grackles, cowbirds, red-winged blackbirds and a male bluebird.

After leaving bleak Knopp's Valley we stopped at a more sheltered place, the Woodlawn Cemetery, where the birding was better. We spotted a chestnut-sided warbler, a veery, a redstart, a crested flycatcher, a brown thrasher, a red-bellied woodpecker and such familiar birds as downy woodpeckers, flickers, blue jays, goldfinches, catbirds, etc. The weather was still too cold for picnicking, so we returned to Ike's cabin to eat our boxed lunch.

Later in the afternoon the weather moderated and the sun came through as we drove leisurely through an area called East Burns Valley. Once, we were stopped by a male cardinal that insisted on staying in the middle of the road. As we were about to cross a bridge over a dry creek we saw a very nervous, tail-flipping phoebe. We got out of the car and looked under the bridge, where we found its nest. Farther on up the narrow, winding road we were pleasantly surprised to see a male scarlet tanager perched on a barbed wire fence a few rods away across a small pasture. The afternoon sunlight showed up the bird's bright plumage to the very best advantage and we stayed quite awhile to admire it. Before we left, a male indigo bunting came to add his brilliance to the picture.

The scenery was beautiful. We could see the Mississippi River far below. We drove onward until some thought we would surely get lost. A couple of other people were concerned about strange noises in their car motors, which no one else seemed to hear. When at last we turned to go back, the strange noises were accounted for. We had not realized how steeply upgrade we had been driving. The return was like driving down a roof. As we crossed a bridge on the way back we spotted a shore bird in the water. The bird turned out to be a solitary sandpiper. It and a semipalmated sandpiper were the only shore birds we saw during the entire weekend.

At banquet time on Saturday evening we were surprised to find that the composite list had reached 131 species, almost twice as many as I had seen. I regretted that I had not joined the second birding group, which was led by a Winona priest who is an ardent birder and who knows the area birds well, and knows where to find them. The other Winona birders had also been very helpful in directing and leading out-of-town birders to the best birding areas.

After a final boxed lunch and a pleasant visit with friends from Minneapolis, Duluth, and Ontario, Canada, we left for home.

...*Summer birding*

August, 1963

In my column in May I mentioned seeing a female sparrow hawk hovering over my fields every day and carrying off mice in her talons. At that time I was not aware of the little falcon's nesting site, but hoped it was somewhere near my fields since I could use the help of these efficient predators. On May 30th I stumbled onto the sparrow hawk pair's domestic activities and — of all places — right in our own farmstead. As I crossed the sheep yard on my way to look over part of my line fence, I heard a male sparrow hawk protesting my presence. I looked up just in time to see the female emerge and take off from the entrance of the weather-beaten sparrow hawk house that had remained unoccupied since I had put it up in the spring of 1952. Last fall, when I rebuilt the sheep yard fence, I even considered taking the weary nesting box down and giving up on sparrow hawk enticing as a bad job. I am glad now that I did not act on that impulse. Apparently, patience pays in attracting sparrow hawks. I hope this pair will come back as faithfully, year after year, as the pair that had nested in the dead poplar tree along the highway a few rods west of our house until the tree blew down in the early spring of 1950.

Between corn cultivating and harvest time I have been giving our house a new coat of paint and, incidentally, listening to bird songs, including those of juvenile birds begging for food. The paint brush doesn't make much noise, so even the whisper songs have been coming in clearly from the thicket near our house. Birds feel more secure from roving cats and other enemies in the ungrazed portion of our windbreak, with its dense growth of shrubbery and other woodland plants.

There is a family of young blue jays, whose pleas are a sort of whine. Young Baltimore orioles, with their "dee-dee-dee," clamor constantly for a handout. One day an oriole, apparently curious about my painting, came to perch on a branch nearby. I thought it was a mature female until it sounded forth with the "dee-dee-dee" of a juvenile. Young flickers, whose pleas sound more like the calls of mature birds, are still easily recognized by their baby talk. I think the sweetest-sounding beggars of all are the young chickadees, whose pleas are also like the calls of the mature birds, but are so obviously babyish. And young grackles and robins, though fully grown, still coax their parents for food.

There are more nesting robins at our place this year than there have been for several years. If, as ornithologists say, a singing male means the presence of a nest, then a pair of rose-breasted grosbeaks have nested somewhere near our house this summer. For several weeks now we have also been entertained by the singing of a wood pewee. Several years have passed since I have heard the pleasant song of the pewee near our house. A meadow lark, with a peculiar song all its own, has been singing lustily from the telephone pole near my mailbox all summer, so I suppose its nest is either along the road or in my neighbor's pasture across from our house.

Unknowingly, I have wrought destruction to the home of the song sparrow that sang so beautifully near my chicken house all spring. In putting up a section of line fence to keep my sheep from visiting my neighbor's property, I used a role of woven wire that I had on hand. Only after the wire was almost completely unrolled did I see the song sparrow's nest near the center. The eggs, if there were any, had been lost during the handling of the wire. At any rate, the sparrow's vocalizing suddenly stopped. I hope the disappointed pair will renest elsewhere.

The pheasant crop looks a little better this year, perhaps because there have been no really heavy rain showers in this area. I have encountered one brood of half-grown chicks, three broods of small chicks, and two hens with nests of unhatched eggs. I had trouble with one brood of small chicks while mowing the hay on my diverted acres land. It is characteristic of pheasant hens with small chicks to stay near the edge of uncut hay or grain so they can come out in the open to see better or quickly dart back into cover. Each time my mower came close, there was a wild scramble for safety, with chicks flying farther into the uncut hay. On the next round the chicks would again be in the path of the sickle. I mowed late that evening, hoping to finish the field. But when I turned at a corner and saw three chicks that had been killed by the sickle on the previous round I decided to leave the rest of the mowing until the next morning. The next day, as the remaining patch of hay got smaller, the chicks flew more often into the open. But the hen would then call them back into the standing hay. I was glad when the youngsters finally disobeyed their mother and started for the woods, showing more wisdom than the parent. I counted thirteen chicks heading for the woods. When no amount of calling would change their course, the hen joined her retreating brood.

. . . Least bittern

September, 1963

Sometimes nature plays pranks. Caribbean hurricanes which sweep up the Atlantic coast leaving a trail of property destruction sometimes deposit tropical birds as far north as the New England states and Nova Scotia. Similar accidents, on a lesser scale, often happen elsewhere. The sudden, violent windstorm that struck Albert Lea on the evening of July 18 did more than uproot trees and blow down power lines. When things quieted down, a very confused least bittern found itself on the lawn of an Albert Lea resident. I am sure the robin-sized bird — the smallest of our herons — wished to be nowhere else than in the depths of a dense cattail slough, its natural habitat.

A neighbor, who happened to be a member of our local Audubon Society, called my wife to say that she had been telephoned by the surprised hosts, who wanted to know what to do with their strange visitor. The next morning I stopped at their home to identify the bird. I offered to return it to its familiar surroundings. The bird — a mature male — had no broken bones and could walk normally. But it must have been badly bruised because it was unable to fly.

I had an errand at a publishing company that morning. I took the least bittern with me. Although I met several people on the sidewalk, no one seemed to notice that I was carrying a bird in my hand. When I stepped off the curb at Washington Avenue, however, a neighboring farmer, who had stopped his car at the intersection, spied the bird. But, knowing of my hobby, he was perhaps not too surprised. As I entered the publishing office and held my charge aloft, the bittern, caught off balance, extended more length of neck than I knew it had. All work stopped as the staff gathered to watch while I released the heron on the floor to walk about with characteristic, deliberate steps. Perhaps it was just as well that the door to the printing room was closed or the bird might have halted work there too.

Although the least bittern, with its plumage pattern of buffy-yellow, chestnut and glossy greenish-black, is the most colorful of our herons, it is perhaps the least known because of its secretive, rail-like habits. Like the much larger American bittern, birds of this miniature species attempt to conceal themselves by compressing their feathers and freezing in a position with bill pointing skyward. They prefer to escape by running rather than by taking flight. Their limber-toed feet are designed to turn readily sideways for grasping onto the upright plant stems among which they perch. They can even travel at considerable speed through marsh growth by grasping stems at every step. When startled into flight they go only a short distance before dropping down into the vegetation again.

The first time I saw a least bittern was several years ago at Bear Lake. I was — with difficulty — poling a small fishing boat through a dense growth of cattails when this queer little buffy-colored bird exploded from the vegetation just ahead of the boat, flew a few wingbeats over the cattails and dropped down again out of sight. A few years later a neighbor's son telephoned to tell me he had picked up a small, yellowish bird in their pasture while fetching the cows. From his description I guessed that his bird was a least bittern. And that was what it turned out to be. This sighting also occurred after a windy rainstorm. Perhaps the bird he found had been as rudely transported as had the one that landed on that Albert Lea lawn July 18. My neighbor's boy had no inclination to keep the bird, so I took it home to show to my family. This bird was also unable to fly. We kept it in my den, where it regained its power of flight during the night. It kept flying up in the dark, only to come fluttering and scratching down the wall. The resulting sound was not conducive to restful sleep. I released the bird the following morning. It flew with weak, butterfly-like wingbeats into the brush part of our windbreak.

The waif of the Albert Lea storm stayed with us until Sunday, July 21, when the Shady Oak Cemetery Auxiliary was having their annual picnic. The least bittern attracted much attention, and prompted many questions concerning its life history. It is not surprising that no one who saw the bird had ever seen one like it before, since they are seldom seen by anyone except those who spend a great deal of their time in marshes. After everyone had satisfied his curiosity about the little heron I took it down to the slough south of the cemetery where I released it. With slow, cautious strides it walked toward its favorite whereabouts, the tall, protective cattails, where I hope it will be able to successfully fend for itself until it regains its ability to fly. At any rate, it should fare better there than in captivity. The children who had found the bird on their lawn after the storm had been digging up earthworms and feeding them to the bird. They claimed it had eaten some of the worms. I had no such luck. The bird ignored angleworms and swallowed only one grasshopper while with us. Its natural food consists of small fish, large insects and other small animal life, all numerous in any marsh.

... *Signs of autumn*

October, 1963

When a farmer undertakes a do-it-yourself project like painting his house, the job is certain to be interrupted by routine farm work. On July 17 my grain was ready for swathing, so I laid my paint brush aside and did not pick it up again until the last week in August. By this time there were signs of autumn. Tent caterpillars were busy on a walnut tree near my house. A black-billed cuckoo, while feasting on the hairy larvae, took time to scold me with its guttural notes.

I was up on the ladder painting a window frame when something banged against the window next to the one I was working on. I turned to see a very astonished sparrow hawk retreating with humility into the concealing foliage of a box elder tree. The collision must have hurt the assailant because its flight was unsteady and its tail was spread fanwise and held almost straight downward. I have seen male robins and cardinals beat themselves against windows in defense of their territory, mistaking their mirrored image for an intruding male, but I was surprised to see a sparrow hawk collide with a window, for whatever reason.

By the last week in August there was already quite a gathering of blue-winged teal on Pickerel Lake near the highway. Scattered about the lake, too, were many pied-billed grebes. From Pickerel Lake Park, I was looking through binoculars, trying to make out a small dark object on the lake's surface. I had just decided that the object was only a piece of wood when a small, white gull alighted on it. In flight, I had thought that the bird was perhaps a Forster's tern. But viewing it through binoculars, I could see that it was a gull. Its small size, white head and the

conspicuous black spot behind the eye marked it as a Bonaparte's gull, the first I had seen.

September is the month of ripe wild fruit. Black elderberries,
chokecherries, grapes, bittersweet, gray dogwood, thorn apples
and buckthorn are now being harvested by returning birds.
Northern robins, flickers and cedar waxwings have been especially numerous this year. While visiting friends in town one
evening we parked our car at the curb under a maple tree. When
we left, our car bore evidence that berry-eating starlings had
roosted above it.

The starling's habit of gathering in great communal roosts in
cities has brought about an extra sanitation problem for many
beautiful buildings. On our way to Williams Bay, Wisconsin, to
bring our son home from his summer job, we stopped at the
state capitol building, which is reputed to be one of the most
beautiful and costly capitol buildings in the nation. After going
through the building I can agree with that claim. The morning
that we were there, however, the beauty was disfigured by the
nightly accumulation of starling litter around the pillars at the
entrance. We spent some time in the historical museum, where I
talked with the caretaker about Old Abe, the Civil War eagle,
mascot of the Eighth Wisconsin regiment of volunteers. I first
heard about this bird from my uncle Andrew Brones, who was a
Union Army veteran and who knew the bird.

While in Madison we also stopped at the zoo, where we saw,
among the menagerie, a number of flamingoes and roseate
spoonbills. On the grounds — but free as the wind — a warbling
vireo was singing its spring song. Birdwise, the Wisconsin trip
was not very rewarding. I listened in vain for the song of an
eastern meadow lark. On a sandbar in the Wisconsin River I
spotted a sandpiper, but could not be sure of the species. Rose-
breasted grosbeaks, Baltimore orioles and cardinals could be
heard from the motel at Readstown. On the way home darkness
overtook us on the detour along the picturesque, winding Beaver
Creek Valley road, but not before we had seen several great
horned owls fly across the road ahead of our car.

September 14th and 15th found us again in a group of hawk watchers at Duluth. And again, to use a vulgar expression, we were "skunked." To have attended two poor hawk-count trips in succession was discouraging for all of us. But those who had seen good flights could at least reminisce. I felt sorry for those who were there for the first time, expecting to see thousands of the predators sail by. The total count on Saturday was only 117. Sunday morning was even worse. We saw a number of smaller birds, including palm warblers, pine siskins, cedar waxwings, northern robins, white-throated sparrows and one olive-backed thrush.

Two birders from Alden, Minnesota, were among the first-timers at the hawk count. Saturday afternoon they accompanied my wife and me to Minnesota Point, where we got some excellent film footage of black-bellied plovers walking about on the park green. While we were at the fishing dock we were fortunate enough to witness a dramatic moment in the lives of birds. We heard a scream, and looked up to see a peregrine falcon attacking a duck. The duck, sensing its danger, turned to fly straight downward, hit the water with a splash, and disappeared. The thwarted falcon turned away and left the scene.

. . . Unexpected encounters

November, 1963

As I go about my farm work I sometimes see things that I somehow never encounter on a planned field trip. While plowing one of my fields during the first week in October, for example, I noticed some small sparrows that kept flying up out of the stubble as the tractor approached. They flew with rapid wing-beat for only a short distance before dropping down into the stubble, only to be disturbed again shortly. As the strip of un-plowed field became ever narrower, the sparrows became more concentrated, since they preferred the stubble to the plowed ground. After some time I came close enough to one of the little wayfarers to see its plumage markings in detail as it tried to con-ceal itself before taking off. The bird appeared quite yellowish about the face and on the breast. According to Peterson's *Bird Guide*, sharp-tailed sparrows can be identified by the ochre-yellow of the face, which completely surrounds the gray of the ear patch. But what clinched the identity of this bird as a Nelson's sharp-tailed sparrow was the distinct yellow stripes on its back, which contrasted sharply with the brown on the upper parts.

Nelson's sharp-tailed sparrows breed mainly in the inland prairie provinces of Canada. They are marsh dwellers, although during migration they may be seen in upland fields where there is some ground cover. Many sparrows of this species have, no doubt, spent some time in my fields during spring and fall migration, but on only two occasions have I come near enough to see the plumage marking sufficiently well for identification.

On the M.O.U. field trip to Winona, Minnesota, this spring I did not see a single gull. Here on the farm the sight of one or a few gulls overhead enroute from one lake to another is almost a daily occurrence. For several days in early October I had been seeing what I thought were Franklin's gulls hawking insects high overhead. Then, on October 10th, a whole flock of screaming Franklin's descended on me, circling about the tractor and feeding on earthworms and whatever morsels the plow uncovered. In the flock — that must have numbered 700 or 800 birds — was a lone herring gull, easily distinguished by its slower wingbeat, clear white head and pinkish feet. I haven't had a herring gull follow my plow for several years, but ring-billed gulls are frequently seen with the Franklin's. These gulls seemed very hungry and their findings must have been mostly earthworms because I noticed that in the morning their droppings had shown up conspicuously white on the black plowing whereas towards sundown the droppings were almost black — at least those that happened to hit the tractor and the one that struck the back of my hand were black. This was also a study in the rapid metabolism of birds.

One doesn't expect to see a great horned owl fly out in the open at high noon, but that is what I saw on October 11th. The large predator came from somewhere west of my farm and headed straight for my ten-acre woods. From its flight pattern I knew it was not a hawk. When it sailed — as it did occasionally — the wings had a decided downward curve. I thought of the jack rabbit that has been so fond of the sprouted waste grain in my stubble field all fall. When the big owl flew overhead the hare must have laid his ears down and remained motionless to avoid detection. I also wondered what might have taken place had the owl encountered the family of crows that have occasionally visited my farm this year.

How often does one see wild geese when on a field trip? During October anyone who works outdoors can see wild geese if he bothers to look in the direction from which the goose gabble comes. On October 1st I saw the first flock of snow geese. There were about twenty-five of them, flying high, but announcing their presence. The flocks are getting larger. On October 17th I saw a flock numbering well over one hundred. I haven't seen any Canada geese yet, but hope to eventually see some of those perfect V formations passing over. Perhaps some day we could entice Canada geese to nest here in Freeborn County.

Speaking of encountering wonders in my fields, October 18th was a birding highlight. I was making my first round of the day with the corn picker when a small rail took flight from almost under the machine and flew across about thirty rows of harvested corn, a distance of about 100 feet, before disappearing into standing corn. The short, rounded wings beat furiously, but the bird proceeded forward rather slowly, considering the effort expended. The bird held its head and neck extended downward at an angle, making its flight seem even more awkward. The rail looked rather yellow in flight. Although there is a species called the yellow rail, it is so rare that I'm positive the bird I saw was an immature sora, which is also quite yellow — and much more numerous. Few people have been fortunate enough to see a rail in flight, since these marsh dwellers migrate at night. In daylight hours they depend for their safety on fleetness afoot.

. . . *A stroll through the woods*

December, 1963

Before I finished picking corn this fall a flock of snow geese started coming regularly to feed on the waste corn left in the field by the mechanical picker. Every evening at about sundown twenty of them appeared, flying low and circling over an adjoining field. They circled the field cautiously for several minutes before one of them dropped out of formation to alight among the corn stalks. Then the others followed.

I often see wild ducks feeding in harvested corn fields. Occasionally, I also see wild geese doing so. But I was a little surprised one morning to see an American bittern take flight from among the corn stalks to alight again a short distance away and assume his upright camouflaging pose. I know that migrating birds may be seen out of their normal habitat, but the sight of a bittern in a corn field is a little odd.

The flurries of small birds flying up from the edge of the field into my woods as I approach with machinery vary as to species. In mid-October they were still mostly white-throated sparrows. Slate-colored juncos began showing up about October 20th. By November 1st the white-throats had disappeared and the scurrying flocks were almost always juncos. The few fox sparrows had disappeared with the last of the white-throats. One day the flock included a stranger whose back reflected green in the sunlight. It might have been a belated vireo. On windy days the red-tailed hawks quite faithfully appeared over the woods to ride the breeze.

Squirrels — both fox squirrels and grays — have been busy all fall carrying corn from my fields into the woods. The acorn crop is short this year, but even if acorns were plentiful the squirrels would enjoy swiping corn. One of the fox squirrels is a comical looking fellow because he has been in an accident of sorts and has lost all but a short stub of his tail.

While plowing one day I noticed a doe watching me from behind a screen of shrubbery at the edge of the woods. When I came near she turned and loped off leisurely, her white tail erect and flashing as she disappeared among the trees.

Today I started out looking for a rolling coulter that I had lost while plowing, and wound up taking a stroll through the woods that all these wild creatures find so inviting. There had been a light rain during the night. The sky was overcast and the down leaves were so moist I could walk without making a sound, except when I stepped on a dry fallen twig. A few steps into the woods — and completely oblivious to the cares of my daily work — I encountered a cottontail, which suddenly decided to get elsewhere in a hurry. As I stopped to untangle a blackberry cane from my jacket two stray dogs started a rumpus in the far side of the woods. They were probably interested in rabbits. But I wondered if they were the same two dogs that had been chasing my sheep the other day. I stood still for awhile, hoping to get a glimpse of them. But they must have become aware of my presence and fled because I spent more than an hour in the woods without seeing or hearing any more from them.

While thus waiting, everything was strangely quiet. But soon I noticed a movement overhead and spotted my first bird, a downy woodpecker. Soon a curious chickadee spoke up and, before long, some more of its kind came by. A larger bird in the distance turned out to be a blue jay — a silent one. I saw several of them, and they were all silent. As something flashed across my path I turned to see a white-breasted nuthatch searching up, down and around a nearby tree trunk and making a few nasal remarks. Where were the juncos? Where were the great horned owls? A cottontail, snuggled in the grass a few feet from me, made a slight move as though ready to take off, then decided that his camouflage was perfect and stayed put. A cherry sapling was stripped of its bark for about two feet. Some amorous buck had lately been polishing its antlers. I stopped to search the ground for owl pellets where splashes indicated that either hawks or owls had roosted overhead, but found none. A large white oak had broken off and fallen, probably during the July 18th windstorm. It was completely dead and well rotted. Atop the high, broken stump I saw some raccoon hair — and evidence that coons also like my corn.

On the leeward side of the woods I found the juncos — lots of them — feeding on the plowed ground and at the edge of the woods. As I stepped out of the woods I happened to look northward just at the moment that a great horned owl chose to leave the perch from where it had probably been watching me. It swooped down close to the ground and flew toward a small patch of woods on a neighboring farm. These large predators have to be elusive to live as successfully as they do in densely settled areas.

I didn't find my coulter and the bird list was not impressive, but I enjoyed the meandering anyway.

... An appreciated
winter handout

Today the view from my den window is real Christmas-like, so: Merry Christmas, everyone! The sight of a landscape covered with a mantle of white makes it seem pleasant to be indoors, and reminds me of the thousands of homes where folks provide food for winter birds to supplement nature's scanty table. Whether the motive be compassion for the birds or self enjoyment or a mixture of both makes no difference to the birds. They relish the handout. In extremely severe weather it may mean the difference between life or death for some of them. It is natural for humans to enjoy having wild creatures come near enough for close observation. One might say that bird feeding "blesseth him that gives and him that takes."

The feeding setup varies from the very simple — like throwing a handful of crumbs out onto the snow — to the very elaborate, with all manner of commercial equipment being employed. My offering is modest. I had no beef suet on hand, so I filled the suet stick with lard, which the chickadees promptly let me know was a little on the rancid side. As consolation, I put a handful of chicken feed in a glass jar with a chickadee-sized entrance. So far, the sprightly mites have paid no attention to it. Despite the threat of hoggish squirrels, I also stuck an ear of corn onto a nail in the bird feeder post for whatever birds might like whole corn. I noticed this morning that quite a number of kernels were missing from the corn ear, so I know that some creature has been there when I wasn't looking.

I decided today would be a good time to write my monthly epistle. My wife is at the church helping the ladies decorate Christmas trees. I have turned the radio off and the house is real quiet. But the birds have been interrupting me. Who can concentrate on writing with cardinals, blue jays and other flashy birds disporting themselves so nearby?

A male cardinal, in all his splendor against a background of snow, is looking for something on the ground. Perhaps he has lost a corn kernel in the snow. After some fruitless searching he pounces on the corn ear, seizes a kernel and disappears. Immediately, a blue jay flashes past my window, snatches a kernel with one peck, carries it to a branch of the juniper tree and starts to dine. It is interesting to observe how the various species go about cracking a kernel of corn. A nuthatch places the kernel in a crevice of a branch or tree trunk while chiseling it apart with its sharp beak. A cardinal can crack a corn kernel by biting it with its strong beak. The blue jay's method is the most amusing to watch. While perching on a branch or the top of a post, the bird holds its kernel securely with its feet while delivering forceful hammer blows with its beak, raising itself almost upright each time to get as much striking power as possible. While thus engaged, the bird reminds me of the stuffing arm of a hay baler. I sometimes wonder what would happen if the blue jay missed his aim and hit a toe.

While the blue jay is busy with his kernel, a female cardinal comes to get some corn and to watch the activity at the suet stick. The chickadees are feeding — though rather gingerly — on the lard. They suddenly disperse when a male and female nuthatch take turns at the suet stick. While the male nuthatch is at the stick the female alights on the ear of corn. But swoosh! A male cardinal chases her away. She then proceeds to inspect the jar containing chicken feed, hopping around it several times. The male cardinal apparently isn't hungry, but still perches possessively on the corn ear until another male cardinal challenges him, and the two chase each other about among the trees.

Now there is a male downy woodpecker at the suet stick, displaying its telltale red nape. And now a female downy is awaiting her turn. I hear a sharp "pleet," and a male hairy woodpecker flashes past my window. And is he hungry! I will have to get some more beef suet real soon if he continues to feed here — and he probably will. Before the day is over a female hairy woodpecker shows up. Perhaps "Sir Hairy" has invited her. All of these birds are the usual dependable patrons of winter feeders. But I feel that this is still quite a response for such a meager handout. I have not seen any tree sparrows yet. But then my table setting is not very attractive to them. I shall never forget how faithfully these little birds from the far north came to my window during the winter of 1948 and '49. We had just finished building our new house and there was a considerable amount of raw dirt from the basement excavation still exposed, with a good growth of pigeon grass. Several tree sparrows stayed here all winter and entertained me by jumping up to feed on the pigeon grass seed heads sticking above the snow. I am sometimes tempted to dig up some of the lawn outside my den window and plant it to pigeon grass again, with perhaps some lamb's-quarters and pigweed thrown in to add to the invitation. But my wife — and perhaps the weed inspector — would probably veto that plan.

Don't take my yard as a shining example, but a great deal can be done to feed winter birds by judicious planting of trees, shrubs, vines and flowers that retain their fruit and seeds throughout the winter.

. . . Downy woodpecker

February, 1964

One of the most faithful patrons of my suet feeder this winter is the downy woodpecker. I know there are at least two of them — a male and a female — taking advantage of the handout. I cannot be certain if there are any more since I have not seen more than one male or one female at a time, and, of course, I cannot recognize individuals. However, it doesn't seem that it would take long for such a small bird to get its daily fill of suet, so — unless the two of them have a voracious appetite — there must be more downys coming to my table. Almost any time I look out at the feeder there is a downy dining there, or awaiting its turn while a hairy woodpecker, nuthatch or blue jay is at the feeder.

As I looked out across the bleak, snow-covered fields while feeding my sheep one bitterly cold morning, I saw a small bird flying toward me from my ten-acre woods, half a mile away. From its conspicuously undulating flight I took it to be a small woodpecker, and guessed correctly that it was a downy and that it was headed straight for breakfast at my suet stick. So the secret was out as to where this particular downy was spending its nights. Having discovered an abundant, dependable supply of nourishing and easily accessible food, the adaptable downy had apparently settled down to a simple winter routine of shuttling back and forth between its cozy sleeping quarters and my suet feeder as hunger and comfort demanded.

There are enough roosting holes in dead trees and decayed stubs in that woods to serve as winter quarters for a great many woodpeckers, nuthatches, chickadees and brown creepers. No bird is more entitled to its well-insulated and protected roosting

hole than the industrious downy, which in all probability excavated most of these cavities. They were originally intended for
nesting sites. A downy woodpecker normally excavates a cavity
eight to twelve inches deep in a decayed tree, branch or stub
and, since these are often in decayed parts of a tree that is otherwise sound, they may serve as roosting or nesting holes for
several years. These holes are often taken over as nesting sites by
nuthatches, chickadees, brown creepers and other hole-nesting
birds. The woodpeckers, who are the carpenters of the bird
world, usually make a new nesting cavity each spring.

When I started farming here in 1930 there were quite a few
apple trees on the place — or, perhaps I should say, remains of
apple trees. They were all very old and in a bad way. They were
so badly decayed that any strong wind would break off large
branches or blow over entire trees. One of these trees stood on
the yard between the house and barn. It was a small tree with
only two stub branches and a few live twigs. The trunk was so
badly decayed that there was only a narrow strip of bark on one
side. It had such a thin layer of sound wood that I wondered why
it did not fall over by itself. Although it was an eyesore I let it
stand because it somehow managed to produce a half-dozen
good-tasting apples every summer. And because a downy
woodpecker nested in its decayed trunk every summer and
successfully reared a brood of young, despite the presence of a
curious   birdwatcher   and   numerous   troublesome   house
sparrows.

The sparrow-sized downy — an old acquaintance of mine —
is the smallest of our woodpeckers and also the most versatile.
Many and varied are the places where it searches for its food. It
is typically an open farming country bird, and a farmer's friend.
In addition to searching trees for cambium borers, ants and
other destructive insects, it is often found working on weed
stalks along neglected fence rows, searching for burrowing
larvae. At corn picking time I often see it working on cornstalks,
where it has learned to find European corn borers. I have also
found downys chiseling out the larvae from goldenrod galls.

However, I thought it was the height of ingenuity when I

found a downy inside my corncrib looking for European corn borers there. I became aware of its presence when I heard it picking at the sash inside a window, trying to get out. I was at a loss as to its motive for entering the crib until a short time later when I saw a downy — probably the same bird — working on a corncob on the hog feeding floor. After the downy left I inspected the cob and saw that it had been split open. A tiny cavity showed where a corn borer had been removed from the pithy center. Yes! I admire the versatile downy. May its tribe increase. And may its winters be made more pleasant by an ample supply of suet.

...*Astronomy and birds*

March, 1964

Since we are approaching the vernal equinox, how about starting this column with a bit of astronomy? After all, the relationship of the world to the sun applies to birds as well as to the rest of us.

If the earth's axis were perpendicular to the plane of the earth's orbit, days and nights would always be of equal length. The distance from the sun and the angle of the sun's axis, at any latitude, would remain the same throughout the year. There would be no change of seasons.

As it is, however, the earth, spinning through space on its journey around the sun, travels with its axis tilted. In March, the earth reaches a point in its orbit at which its north and south poles are the same distance from the sun. In the north temperate zone this is known as the vernal equinox — or the beginning of spring. It is characterized by moderate temperatures and by days and nights of equal length. In June, however, the north pole, still pointing in the same direction, tilts toward the sun. When this occurs we have summer, with its long days, short nights and high temperatures. In September, the earth reaches another point in its orbit where its axis is again at right angles to the direction of the sun. For us, this is the autumnal equinox, with days and nights again of equal length and with moderate temperatures. In December, the earth is at its winter solstice — the point at which its axis tilts farthest away from the sun. We then have short days, long nights and low temperatures.

This can be easily demonstrated. Impale an orange on a knitting needle. With the knitting needle tilted and pointing continually in the same direction, move it to the four points around a lighted candle on a table in an otherwise darkened room. By the simple geometric arrangement of tilting the earth's axis 23° 27' away from the perpendicular the all-wise Creator has instituted the cycle of seasons to which all life on earth responds, including those versatile and mobile creatures called birds.

March is a month of contrasts and surprises. Traditionally, it comes in like a lion and goes out like a lamb — or vice versa. Although the season may at times seem in the grip of winter there are unmistakable signs of spring. Buds swell, sap begins to run, and birds begin returning from their winter sojourn.

Bird migration has puzzled mankind since earliest times, and still poses many unanswered questions. But we do know that migration is synchronized with annual seasonal changes. Migration is most pronounced in temperate regions, where there are mass movements of many species away from the poles when length of day, temperature and food supply decrease. Conversely, movement toward the poles begins when these environmental factors increase. Such migratory movements are more noticeable in the north temperate zone, where there is much more land area and where more species are involved.

Ornithologists generally agree that a bird's motivation to migrate is influenced by its pituitary gland, whose activity in spring is stimulated by the increase in the length of daylight. With that age-old urge for elbow room for rearing young, migrants move northward to establish nesting territories in areas they would have found uninhabitable earlier in the year. The actual time of take-off is usually determined by some external factor such as sudden change of temperature. A warm front of moist air moving in from the Gulf of Mexico and the Caribbean often triggers a mass movement of birds northward.

Since insect life is still dormant in early spring, the first birds to venture northward are those that can subsist on weed seeds. This year I saw my first horned lark on February 1st when Audubon wildlife film lecturer Chester Lyons and I walked across an alfalfa field enroute to my woods. On February 9th I was birding with members of the Albert Lea Audubon Society when we saw a flock of tree sparrows at the edge of a woods where they had apparently been feeding among some weeds. There have been several juncos about our yard throughout February, perhaps attracted by a patch of annual weeds that neither the sheep nor I attended to last summer.

Checking my notes for previous years, I find thirty-one species arriving in March, including fourteen species of ducks. A trip to Albert Lea Lake in March after the ice near shore has thawed can be very rewarding. Ducks can be observed at close range in

the narrow strip of open water and will not be disturbed if you remain in your car. My notes show thirty species of birds showing up in April and seventy-eight species arriving in May, including eighteen species of warblers.

These are my day to day notes of birds I happen to see as I go about my farm work, without searching for them in their various habitats. It does not include some of the birds that I have seen only on field trips to other areas of the state. However, one can see from these notes that May is obviously the high tide of bird migration in this area. Many birds wait for insect life to become rather abundant before showing up. My notes drop rather abruptly by the first of June. The northward surge of birds is over.

. . . *March arrivals*

April, 1964

When I see wild geese passing northward, sweet-voiced fox sparrows scratching in the leafmold and red-tailed hawks circling over my woods, I know April is not far away.

The patrons of my suet feeder have dwindled recently. I suppose the absentees are either finding more natural food or are being attracted to a better grade of suet elsewhere. However, the other day I was amused by a blue jay that got more suet than he had bargained for. I had just replenished the feeder. Because the weather was mild the suet did not stick well. As the blue jay tugged at a bite, the whole plug came loose. However, the obviously surprised and over-burdened jay proved equal to the situation by flying off with the whole thing. With neck extending awkwardly downward, the flying jay appeared far from dignified.

On one blustery March day a hungry crow came to perch in the top of a walnut tree outside my den window. He must have been hungry to come so close to our house, attracted by so small a handout as a little beef suet. Hopping leisurely downward from branch to branch into the juniper tree and casting a covetous eye at the suet stick, the big bird seemed strangely out of place. There was no branch strong enough to support a crow near enough to the suet to permit my black visitor to feed. All he could do was sit and look frustrated. Then, spying me through the window, he burst forth with a violent protest. If I understood him correctly, he was reminding me that he was aware this was lambing time and that, even with the best of luck, it was reasonable to expect some lambs to die and that these should be made available for him to feast on. I — callous host — told him to go look for field mice as he had last summer.

Speaking of mice, I heard good news from another of my good mousers. On March 13th the male sparrow hawk was back to claim the nesting box where he and his industrious spouse reared a family of four last summer. I didn't see his mate anywhere. But he made a few calls and gyrations anyway. The pair certainly made away with plenty of mice last season, and I had been hoping that they would return to nest here again. While out in my field taking soil samples for testing, I saw the little falcon again and heard him scold me for intruding on his territory.

While April is called the month of awakening nature, the awakening — at least as far as birds are concerned — starts long before April 1st. Besides that early bird — the horned lark — some 30 species may show up before that date. The dependable red-winged blackbirds appear in flocks. This year I saw the first flock flying across the highway north of Emmons on the evening of March 12. It was too dark to see whether or not there were any grackles among them. The two species often arrive together. The next morning I saw both species about our yard. Then, of course, there is the traditional robin, often seen before it is heard. On March 14 there were three of them hopping about in our yard. I did not hear them or notice any antagonism, but I expect this will soon happen as the males start establishing their territories.

March 15th — a Sunday — dawned bright, clear and balmy. While fetching corn for the sheep I was greeted by the first meadow lark of the season, singing from the direction of my alfalfa field. As the familiar bird piped one after another of its many songs many fond recollections of those flute-like notes were awakened. How eloquently this outspoken grassland pedestrian can animate the countryside!

Before March has released its wintery grip we may hear from that optimistic minstrel of weedy fence rows, the song sparrow. How welcome, also, is the first loud, clear call announcing the return of the best known of our shore birds, the killdeer, with its winsome ways. Another March arrival is the flicker. There is nothing reticent about the flicker's announcement. That loud, snappy "wick wick wick wick" from the windbreak cannot be mistaken for the call of any other bird. Some years ago I put up a flicker nesting box. To date it has only been used by squirrels. This year I cleaned out the squirrel mess and put in some sawdust as an added inducement to the flickers, who always make a fuss over the box each spring, but never occupy it.

No March is complete without the friendly and contented warble of bluebirds. Will they be back this year? Their future is by no means certain, even with all the housing help we can give them. Our prayer should be: Let not this creature of beauty and symbol of happiness pass from our scene.

Index